VOICES
OF THE
AMERICAN PAST
DOCUMENTS IN
U.S. HISTORY

VOLUME TWO

VOICES

OF THE

AMERICAN PAST

DOCUMENTS IN
U.S. HISTORY

VOLUME TWO SINCE 1865

RAYMOND M. HYSER
J. CHRIS ARNDT

JAMES MADISON UNIVERSITY

Harcourt Brace College Publishers

Fort Worth   Philadelphia   San Diego   New York   Orlando   Austin   San Antonio
Toronto   Montreal   London   Sydney   Tokyo

Publisher	Ted Buchholz
Senior Acquisitions Editor	Drake Bush
Assistant Editor	Kristie Kelly
Project Editor	Laura J. Hanna
Associate Project Editor	Sandy J. Walton
Senior Production Manager	Ken Dunaway
Art Directors	Diana Jean Parks / Scott Baker
Picture Development Editor	Lili Weiner
Cover Designer	Edie Roberson

Cover image: "On the Avenue," Levick: Archive Photos

Photo Credits:
Unit I, Steel Works, Homestead, PA. c. 1900. Library of Congress
Unit II, Douglas Fairbanks at a liberty loan rally, April 1918, National Archives
Unit III, Women in aviation industry (Rosie the Riveter), 12/42, AP/Wide World Photos
Unit IV, Martin Luther King, "I Have a Dream" photo, UPI/Bettmann

Address for Editorial Correspondence:
Harcourt Brace College Publishers
301 Commerce Street, Suite 3700
Fort Worth, Texas 76102

Address for Orders:
Harcourt Brace & Company
6277 Sea Harbor Drive
Orlando, Florida 32887
1-800-782-4479 or 1-800-433-0001 (in Florida)

Printed in the United States of America
Library of Congress Number 94-75451

ISBN 0-15-501964-3

4567890123 066 987654321

To Pamela and Andi: Thanks for everything.

PREFACE

The way that Americans view themselves and their history has changed substantially during the last thirty years. Where the traditional view seemed to champion the progress and development of the United States, a growing number of scholars have questioned this interpretation of the past. This document reader attempts to present students with the perspectives of many different issues and events in the American past, rather than advance a particular agenda.

Like many of our colleagues, we have found document readers useful to introduce our students to some of the ideas and issues of the past. Our purpose in selecting these documents was to use readable texts that would provide a relatively balanced introduction to some of the major questions and concepts in United States history. Organized so that it can be easily used with most of the major college textbooks, we have chosen both the "great documents," as well as selections from less well-known voices to highlight these diverse issues. Each document is preceded by: 1) a brief introduction which sets the historical context, and 2) a series of questions for instructors and students to consider as they read and analyze the selection. While we have not been able to include a "point-counterpoint" on every issue, it is our hope that the documents will enable instructors and their students to begin to explore various aspects of the American past. The result has been a valuable learning experience, as it forced us to constantly rethink our views on many of the central questions in American history. We hope students and faculty will find this reader useful.

In collecting, editing, and writing this reader, many individuals too numerous to mention have been influential. A few, however, deserve special recognition and thanks. As teachers at an institution where undergraduate education is the faculty's first priority, we are grateful to our colleagues in the Department of History at James Madison University who set standards for teaching excellence that make all of us better instructors. We owe a special thanks to our colleagues Philip Riley, Sidney Bland, Clive Hallman, and Jacqueline Walker for reading early drafts and making valuable suggestions. Drake Bush, Kristie Kelly, Laura Hanna, and David Tatom of Harcourt Brace College Publishers have been especially helpful at various stages of the project. The reviewers' critical suggestions helped immeasurably to improve the quality of the reader. We would like to thank: Edward H. Beardsley of the University of South Carolina, John Belohlavek of the University of South Florida, William Benedicks, Jr., of Tallahassee Community College, Ruth Alden Doan of Hollins College, Dennis B. Downey of Millersville University, Allison B. Gilmore of the Ohio State University at Lima, David M. Katzman of the University of Kansas, Robert McMahon of the University of Florida, Randolph Roth of Ohio State University, and Janet Schmelzer of Tarleton State University. Special thanks also to Dennis Robison and Gordon Miller of James Madison University's Carrier Library for help in locating documents. Finally, we want to thank our students, past and present, who offered sharp critiques on document readability and taught us much about the American past.

TABLE OF CONTENTS

Preface   vii

I. THE TRANSFORMATION OF THE AMERICAN NATION   1

1. Reconstruction   3

1. A Northern Teacher's View of the Freedmen (1863–1865)
   Elizabeth Hyde Botume   4
2. African Americans Seek Protection (1865)
   The New York Times   6
3. Thaddeus Stevens on Reconstruction and the South (1865)   8
4. Andrew Johnson Vetoes the First Reconstruction Act (1867)   10
5. A White Southern Perspective on Reconstruction (1868)
   Howell Cobb   13
6. The Ku Klux Klan During Reconstruction (1872)   15

2. The West   19

7. The Mining Frontier (1863)
   Nathaniel P. Langford   20
8. "Report of the Commission on Indian Affairs" (1869)   22
9. A Western Newspaper Editorial on the Custer Massacre (1876)
   William N. Byer   24
10. Cultural Exchange on the Arizona Frontier (1874)
    Martha Summerhayes   26
11. A Native American Remembers the Ghost Dance (1890)
    Rising Wolf   28
12. Life on the Prairie Farms (1893)

E. V. Smalley   30

3. The Expansion of Big Business   33

13. A British Perspective on American Railroads (1865)
    Sir Samuel Morton Peto   34
14. The Impact of Mechanization (1889)
    David A. Wells   36
15. "Edison's Electric Light" (1882)
    The New York Times   38
16. The Success of Standard Oil (1899)
    John D. Rockefeller   40
17. The Gospel of Wealth (1889)
    Andrew Carnegie   43
18. Mrs. Vanderbilt's Great Fancy Dress Ball (1883)
    The New York Times   46

4. How the Other Half Lives   49

19. Child Labor in Alabama Cotton Mills (1908)
    Mother Jones   50
20. The Credit System of the South (1894)
    Charles H. Otken   51
21. The "Long Turn" in Steel (1910)
    John A. Fitch   54
22. Preamble to the Constitution of the Knights of Labor (1878)
    Terrence V. Powderly   56
23. Life in the Tenements of New York City (1890)
    Jacob A. Riis   58
24. Populist Party Platform (1892)
    Morning World-Herald (Omaha, NE)   60
25. Statement of the Strikers in Pullman (1894)   62

5. The Problems of Race and Ethnicity   67

26. Florida Jim Crow Laws (1885–1913)   68
27. "The Negro Question in the South" (1892)
    Thomas E. Watson   70
28. The Atlanta Exposition Address (1895)
    Booker T. Washington   73
29. Principles of the Niagara Movement (1905)
    The Gazette (Cleveland, OH)   75

30. The Unwanted Immigrants: The Chinese (1878)　78
31. "Statement of the Immigration Restriction League"　81
32. Description of the Padrone System (1901)　83
33. "A Hungarian Girl's Impressions of America" (1913)
　　Gertrude Barnum　85

II. DEVELOPMENT OF THE MODERN NATION　89

1. Imperialism　91

34. The Sinking of the *Maine* (1898)
　　New York Journal　92
35. An Anti-Imperialist Perspective (1899)
　　George F. Hoar　93
36. The New Manifest Destiny (1900)
　　Albert J. Beveridge　95
37. The Open Door Notes (1899)
　　John Hay　98
38. "A Colombian View of the Panama Canal Question" (1903)
　　Raúl Pérez　100
39. Roosevelt Corollary to the Monroe Doctrine (1904)
　　Theodore Roosevelt　102

2. The Progressive Movement　105

40. An Insider's View of Hull House
　　Hilda Satt Polacheck　106
41. Boss Government at Work (1903)
　　Lincoln Steffens　108
42. *The Jungle* (1906)
　　Upton Sinclair　110
43. "The Principles of Scientific Management" (1912)
　　Frederick Taylor　112
44. The New Nationalism of Theodore Roosevelt (1912)　114
45. "Why Women Should Vote" (1910)
　　Jane Addams　117

3. Making the World Safe for Democracy　121

46. Woodrow Wilson's Declaration of War Message (1917)　122
47. The Question of First Amendment Rights (1919)
　　Oliver Wendell Holmes, Jr.　124

48. A Soldier's View of the War (1918)
   Arthur P. Terry   126

49. Opposition to the League of Nations (1919)
   Henry Cabot Lodge   128

50. "What Is Behind the Negro Uprisings?" (1919)
   Herbert J. Seligmann   131

51. The Red Scare (1920)
   A. Mitchell Palmer   133

4. The Return to "Normalcy"   137

52. Farm Problems in South Dakota (1922)
   Tom Ayres   138

53. The Ku Klux Klan's Perspective (1926)
   Hiram Wesley Evans   140

54. Closing the Golden Door (1924)
   W. W. Husband   142

55. The New Woman (1927)
   Dorothy Dunbar Bromley   144

56. The Impact of the Automobile (1926)
   Lawrence Abbott   147

57. American Individualism (1928)
   Herbert Hoover   150

III. THE EMERGENCE OF THE AMERICAN COLOSSUS   153

1. FDR and the New Deal   155

58. Urban Families in the Great Depression (1931)
   Dorothy Kahn   156

59. The Great Depression in Rural America (1932)
   Oscar Ameringer   158

60. Franklin D. Roosevelt's First Inaugural Address (1933)   160

61. The "Share Our Wealth" Plan (1933)
   Huey P. Long   162

62. The "Dust Bowl" (1935)
   Literary Digest   164

63. An Editorial on the National Labor Relations Act (1935)
   William Green   166

64. Frances Perkins Endorses the Social Security Act (1935)   168

2. Isolationism and World War II   171

65. Isolation from the European War (1941)
   Charles Lindbergh   172
66. Roosevelt's Declaration of War Message (1941)
   Franklin Roosevelt   174
67. Life in a Japanese Internment Camp (1942)
   Charles Kikuchi   176
68. Women in the Homefront War Effort (1942)
   Ruth Matthews and Betty Hannah   178
69. "A Surge of Doomlike Sound" (1944)
   Ernie Pyle   180
70. Truman's Decision to Drop the Bomb (1945)   183
71. Remembering the Hiroshima Atomic Blast (1945)
   Hiroko Nakamoto   184

3. Postwar America   187

72. "Containment" (1946)
   George F. Kennan   188
73. Communists in the Government (1950)
   Joseph McCarthy   192
74. Governor Herman Talmadge's Statement on the *Brown* Decision (1954)   194
75. An African-American Newspaper Editorial on the *Brown* Decision (1954)
   Pittsburgh Courier   196
76. Suburbanization; Levittown, New York (1950)
   Time   197
77. A Reaction to Sputnik (1957)
   Life   200
78. Dwight D. Eisenhower's Farewell Address (1961)   203

IV. AMERICA IN A WORLD OF TRANSITION   207

1. The Turbulent Sixties   209

79. John F. Kennedy's Inaugural Address (1961)   210
80. "The Problem That Has No Name" (1963)

Betty Friedan   212

81. "I Have a Dream" Speech (1963)
    Martin Luther King, Jr.   215

82. America's Commitment to Southeast Asia (1965)
    Lyndon B. Johnson   217

83. American Presence in Vietnam (1964–1970)   219

84. A Report on Racial Violence in the Cities (1968)   222

85. Student Unrest on College Campuses (1969)
    Glenn S. Dumke   224

2. The National Malaise   229

86. *Roe v. Wade* (1972)
    Harry Blackmun   230

87. Soaring Energy Costs (1974)
    Newsweek   232

88. Richard Nixon's Resignation Speech (1974)   234

89. A Migration to the "Sunbelt" (1976)
    Time   237

90. The Question of Reverse Discrimination (1978)
    Chicago Tribune   239

91. A "Crisis of Confidence" (1979)
    Jimmy Carter   241

92. The Nuclear Dilemma: The Three Mile Island Accident (1979)
    The New Yorker   244

3. Our Times   247

93. The Reagan Revolution (1981)
    Ronald Reagan   248

94. The Immigration Question Renewed (1981), Select Commission on
    Immigration and Refugee Policy   250

95. Business in the 1980s: A View of Donald Trump (1985)
    Terri Thompson and Marc Frons   253

96. The Plight of the Homeless (1984)
    Mitch Snyder   255

97. A Perspective on AIDS (1987)
    David C. Jones   258

98. An Editorial on the Removal of the Berlin Wall (1989)
    The New York Times   261

99. "A New World Order" (1991)
     George Bush   262

PART I

THE TRANSFORMATION OF THE AMERICAN NATION

RECONSTRUCTION

1

After the Civil War, the nation faced the enormous task of reconstructing the republic. In particular, policymakers had to determine the status of the former Confederate states and what to do with the recently freed slaves. Devastated by the war, the South also had to cope with the influx of Northern troops, reformers, and profiteers, many of whom had their own ideas concerning the region's future. The diversity of opinions over Reconstruction deeply divided the North and occasionally brought a violent response from some Southern whites. The ensuing selections reveal how Americans of different races and regions responded to Reconstruction.

1

A NORTHERN TEACHER'S VIEW OF THE FREEDMEN (1863-1865)

Early in the Civil War, Union troops occupied the sea islands along South Carolina's coast near Beaufort. All property—plantations, cotton, and slaves—was confiscated and placed under the jurisdiction of Secretary of the Treasury Salmon P. Chase. Of particular concern was the welfare of the slaves, who at this early stage of the war were considered "contraband" if they were behind Union lines and were not returned to their owners. Sensing the opportunity to use these islands as an experiment for the future reconstruction of the South, Chase permitted benevolent organizations to send teachers, many of whom were women, to help educate the former slaves. In October 1863, the New England Freedmen's Aid Society sponsored Elizabeth Hyde Botume as a teacher in this experiment. Botume became more than a teacher in the several years she spent among the ex-slaves, as her book, *First Days Amongst the Contrabands,* revealed. Excerpted below is Botume's descriptions of the freedmen.

--

Questions to Consider: What does Botume believe are the initial problems facing the freedmen? What were the attitudes of whites toward the freedmen? How did the former slaves react to their new freedom? Were their fears justified? Why? Compare this description of the freedmen with their position in "African Americans Seek Protection" (Document 2).

--

C ontrabands were coming into the Union lines, and thence to the town, not only daily, but hourly. They came alone and in families and in gangs,—slaves who had been hiding away, and were only now able to reach safety. Different members of scattered families following after freedom, as surely and safely guided as were the Wise Men by the Star of the East.

On New Year's Day I walked around amongst these people with Major Saxton. We went to their tents and other quarters. One hundred and fifty poor refugees from Georgia had been quartered all day on the wharf. A wretched and most pitiable gang, miserable beyond description. But when we spoke to them, they invariably gave a cheerful answer. Usually to our question, "How do you do?" the response would be, "Thank God, I live!"

Sometimes they would say, "Us ain't no wusser than we been."

These people had been a long time without food, excepting a little hominy and uncooked rice and a few ground-nuts. Many were entirely naked when they started, and all were most scantily clothed and we had already had some extremely cold days, which we, who were fresh from the North, found hard to bear.

It was the same old story. These poor creatures were covered only with blan-

Elizabeth Hyde Botume, *First Days Amongst the Contrabands* (Boston, 1893), 78-79, 82-83, 117-118, 168-169, 176-177.

kets, or bits of old carpeting, or pieces of bagging, "crocus," fastened with thorns or sharp sticks. . . .

I went first to the negro quarters at the "Battery Plantation," a mile and a half away. A large number of Georgia refugees who had followed Sherman's army were quartered here. Around the old plantation house was a small army of black children, who swarmed like bees around a hive. There were six rooms in the house, occupied by thirty-one persons, big and little. In one room was a man whom I had seen before. He was very light, with straight red hair and a sandy complexion, and I mistook him for an Irishman. He had been to me at one time grieving deeply for the loss of his wife, but he had now consoled himself with a buxom girl as black as ink. His sister, a splendidly developed creature, was with them. He had also four sons. Two were as light as himself, and two were very black. These seven persons occupied this one room. A rough box bedstead, with a layer of moss and a few old rags in it, a hominy pot, two or three earthen plates, and a broken-backed chair, comprised all the furniture of the room. I had previously given one of the women a needle and some thread, and she now sat on the edge of the rough bedstead trying to sew the dress she ought, in decency, to have had on. . . .

The winter of 1864-1865 was a sad time, for so many poor creatures in our district were wretchedly ill, begging for help, and we had so little to give them. Many of the contrabands had pneumonia. Great exposure, with scanty clothing and lack of proper food, rendered them easy victims to the encroachments of any disease. I sent to Beaufort for help. The first doctor who came was exasperatingly indifferent. He might have been a brother of a "bureau officer," who was sent down especially to take care of the contrabands, and who wished all the negroes could be put upon a ship, and floated out to sea and sunk. It would be better for them and for the world. When we expressed our surprise that he could speak so of human beings, he exclaimed, "Human beings! They are only animals, and not half as valuable as cattle."

When the doctor came, I went from room to room and talked with the poor sick people, whose entire dependence was upon us. Finally I could endure his apathy and indifference no longer.

"Leave me medicines, and I will take care of these people as well as I can," I said. . . .

I could not, however, excuse the doctor, a man in government employ, drawing a good salary with no heart in his work. Beaufort was reported to be a depot for officials whom government did not know what to do with. . . .

Early in February we went to Savannah with General and Mrs. Saxton, and members of the general's staff, and other officers. How it had become known that we were to make this trip I cannot tell, but we found a crowd of our own colored people on the boat when we went aboard. To our exclamations of surprise they said with glee,—

"Oh, we're goin' too, fur us has frien's there."

We found the city crowded with contrabands who were in a most pitiable condition. Nearly all the negroes who had lived there before the war had gone away. A large number went on with the army; those left were the stragglers who had come in from the "sand hills" and low lands. The people from the plantations too had rushed into the city as soon as they knew the Union troops were in possession.

A crowd of poor whites had also congregated there. All were idle and destitute. The whites regarded the negroes as still a servile race, who must always be inferior by virtue of their black skins. The negroes felt that emancipation had lifted them out of old conditions into new relations with their fellow beings. They were no longer chattels, but independent creatures with rights and privileges like their neighbors. . . .

Nothing in the history of the world has ever equalled the magnitude and thrilling importance of the events then transpiring. Here were more than four millions of human beings just born into freedom; one day held in the most abject slavery, the next, "de Lord's free men." Free to come and to go according to the best lights given them. Every movement of their white friends was to them full of significance, and often regarded with distrust. Well might they sometimes exclaim, when groping from darkness into light, "Save me from my friend, and I will look out for my enemy."

Whilst the Union people were asking, "Those negroes! what is to be done with them?" they, in their ignorance and helplessness, were crying out in agony, "What will become of us?" They were literally saying, "I believe, O Lord! help thou mine unbelief."

They were constantly coming to us to ask what peace meant for them? Would it be peace indeed? or oppression, hostility, and servile subjugation? This was what they feared, for they knew the temper of the baffled rebels as did no others.

2

AFRICAN AMERICANS SEEK PROTECTION (1865)

The emancipation of four million slaves in the South brought significant social, political, and economic adjustment for both African Americans and white Americans. Despite obtaining freedom from their masters and the rigors of plantation life, the former slaves lost their source of shelter, food, clothing, and occupation. In short, they had little but their freedom. Realizing that they remained at the mercy of their previous owners, many African Americans gathered in conventions in cities throughout the South to discuss the best methods of protecting their fragile freedom. Some of these conventions petitioned Congress for assistance, while others turned to local officials for help. Excerpted on the next page is a petition from a convention of African Americans meeting in Alexandria, Virginia, in August 1865, that demonstrates the precarious position of the freedmen and how they proposed to protect themselves.

Questions to Consider: For what reasons are African Americans fearful of the

---

"The Late Convention of Colored Men," *The New York Times*, 13 August 1865, 3.

former Confederates? What protection does this convention request? How does this reflect the new freedom for the former slaves? Why was the convention critical of "loyalty oaths" and the Freedmen's Bureau?

———

We, the undersigned members of a convention of colored citizens of the State of Virginia, would respectfully represent that, although we have been held as slaves, and denied all recognition as a constituent of your nationality for almost the entire period of the duration of your government, and that by your permission we have been denied either home or country, and deprived of the dearest rights of human nature; yet when you and our immediate oppressors met in deadly conflict upon the field of battle—the one to destroy and the other to save your government and nationality, we, with scarce an exception, in our inmost souls espoused your cause, and watched, and prayed, and waited, and labored for your success. . . .

When the contest waxed long, and the result hung doubtfully, you appealed to us for help, and how well we answered is written in the rosters of the two hundred thousand colored troops now enrolled in your service; and as to our undying devotion to your cause, let the uniform acclamation of escaped prisoners, "Whenever we saw a black face we felt sure of a friend," answer.

Well, the war is over, the rebellion is "put down," and we are declared free! Four-fifths of our enemies are paroled or amnestied, and the other fifth are being pardoned, and the President has, in his efforts at the reconstruction of the civil government of the States, late in rebellion, left us entirely at the mercy of these subjugated but unconverted rebels, in everything save the privilege of bringing us, our wives and little ones, to the auction block. He has, so far as we can understand the tendency and bearing of his action in the case, remitted us for all our civil rights, to men, a majority of whom regard our devotions to your cause and flag as that which decided the contest against them! This we regard as destructive of all we hold dear, and in the name of God, of justice, of humanity, of good faith, of truth and righteousness, we do most solemnly and earnestly protest. Men and brethren, in the hour of your peril you called upon us, and despite all time-honored interpretation of constitutional obligations, we came at your call and you are saved; and now we beg, we pray, we entreat you not to desert us in this the hour of our peril!

We know these men—know them well—and we assure you that, with the majority of them, loyalty is only "lip deep," and that their professions of loyalty are used as a cover to the cherished design of getting restored to their former relation with the Federal Government, and then, by all sorts of "unfriendly legislation," to render the freedom you have given us more intolerable than the slavery they intended for us.

We warn you in time that our only safety is in keeping them under Governors of the military persuasion until you have so amended the Federal Constitution that it will prohibit the States from making any distinction between citizens on account of race or color. In one word, the only salvation for us besides the power of the Government, is in the possession of the ballot. Give us this, and we will protect ourselves. No class of men relatively as numerous as we were ever oppressed when armed with the ballot. But, 'tis said we are ignorant. Admit it. Yet who denies we know a traitor from a loyal man, a gentleman from a rowdy, a friend from an enemy? . . .

. . . All we ask is an equal chance with the white traitors varnished and japanned with the oath of amnesty. Can you deny us this and still keep faith with us? "But," say some, "the blacks will be overreached by the superior knowledge and cunning of the whites." Trust us for that. We will never be deceived a second time. "But," they continue, "the planters and landowners will have them in their power, and dictate the way their votes shall be cast." We did not know before that we were to be left to the tender mercies of these landed rebels for employment. Verily, we thought the Freedmen's Bureau was organized and clothed with power to protect us from this very thing, by compelling those for whom we labored to pay us, whether they liked our political opinions or not! . . .

We are "sheep in the midst of wolves," and nothing but the military arm of the Government prevents us and all the truly loyal white men from being driven from the land of our birth. Do not then, we beseech you, give to one of these "wayward sisters" the rights they abandoned and forfeited when they rebelled until you have secured our rights by the aforementioned amendment to the Constitution.

Let your action in our behalf be thus clear and emphatic, and our respected President, who, we feel confident, desires only to know your will, to act in harmony therewith, will give you his most earnest and cordial cooperation; and the Southern States, through your enlightened and just legislation, will speedily award us our rights. Thus not only will the arms of the rebellion be surrendered, but the ideas also.

3

THADDEUS STEVENS ON RECONSTRUCTION AND THE SOUTH (1865)

The debate over Reconstruction began during the Civil War and became increasingly acute as the North moved toward victory. The lines were quickly drawn between the president and Congress, though various factions within the Republican party argued vociferously for certain positions. Some of the more important issues were: How should the secessionist states be reunited with the Union? What political and social status should be conveyed to the four million freedmen? How should whites who supported the Confederacy be treated? And lastly, who should control Reconstruction? Presidential Reconstruction, begun by Abraham Lincoln in December 1863 and slightly modified when Andrew Johnson assumed the Presidency, was declared too lenient by Radical Republicans, who began advocating their own agenda. Among the leaders of the Radical Republicans was Thaddeus Stevens, a representative from Lancaster, Pennsylvania, whose quick wit, honesty, political savvy, and belief that Reconstruction offered an opportunity to establish a better country made him a powerful supporter of Congressional Reconstruction.

"Reconstruction," *Congressional Globe*, 39th Congress, 1st Session, part 1, (18 December 1865), 72-74.

Excerpted below is Stevens' speech on the status of the South and what
Congressional Reconstruction should encompass.

———

Questions to Consider: According to Stevens, what was the legal status of the
South after the war? How does he argue that Congress should supervise
Reconstruction? What does he propose for the South? What does Stevens
believe Congress should do for the freedmen? In what ways do Stevens'
proposals help shape Reconstruction policies?

———

No one doubts that the late rebel states have lost their constitutional relations
to the Union, and are incapable of representation in Congress, except by
permission of the Government. It matters but little, with this admission whether
you call them States out of the Union, and now conquered territories, or assert that
because the Constitution forbids them to do what they did do, that they are therefore only dead as to all national and political action, and will remain so until the
government shall breathe into them the breath of life anew and permit them to
occupy their former position. In other words, that they are not out of the Union,
but are only dead carcasses lying within the Union. In either case, it is very plain
that it requires the action of Congress to enable them to form a State government
and send representatives to Congress. Nobody, I believe, pretends that with their
old constitutions and frames of government they can be permitted to claim their
old rights under the Constitution. They have torn their constitutional States into
atoms, and built on their foundations fabrics of a totally different character. Dead
men cannot raise themselves. Dead States cannot restore their own existence "as it
was." Whose especial duty is it to do it? In whom does the Constitution place the
power? Not in the judicial branch of government, for it only adjudicates and does
not prescribe laws. Not in the Executive, for he only executes and cannot make
laws. Not in the Commander-in-Chief of the armies, for he can only hold them
under military rule until the sovereign legislative power of the conqueror shall give
them law. . . .

Congress alone can do it. But Congress does not mean the Senate, or the
House of Representatives, and President, all acting severally. Their joint action
constitutes Congress. . . . Congress must create States and declare when they are
entitled to be represented. Then each House must judge whether the members
presenting themselves from a recognized State possess the requisite qualifications
of age, residence, and citizenship; and whether the election and returns are according to law. The Houses, separately, can judge of nothing else. It seems amazing
that any man of legal education could give it any larger meaning.

It is obvious from all this that the first duty of Congress is to pass a law declaring the condition of these outside or defunct States, and providing proper civil
governments to them. Since the conquest they have been governed by martial law.
Military rule is necessarily despotic, and ought not to exist longer than is
absolutely necessary. As there are no symptoms that the people of these provinces
will be prepared to participate in constitutional government for some years, I know
of no arrangement so proper for them as territorial governments. There they can

learn the principles of freedom and eat the fruit of foul rebellion. Under such governments, while electing members to the Territorial Legislatures, they will necessarily mingle with those to whom Congress shall extend the right of suffrage. In Territories Congress fixes the qualifications of electors; and I know of no better place nor better occasion for the conquered rebels and the conqueror to practice justice to all men, and accustom themselves to make and obey equal laws. . . .

According to my judgment they ought never to be recognized as capable of acting in the Union, of being counted as valid States, until the Constitution shall have been so amended as to make it what its framers intended; and so as to secure perpetual ascendancy to the party of the Union; and so as to render our republican Government firm and stable forever. The first of those amendments is to change the basis of representation among the States from Federal numbers to actual voters. . . .

But this is not all that we ought to do before these inveterate rebels are invited to participate in our legislation. We have turned, or are about to turn, loose four million slaves without a hut to shelter them or a cent in their pockets. The infernal laws of slavery have prevented them from acquiring an education, understanding the commonest laws of contract, or of managing the ordinary business of life. This Congress is bound to provide for them until they can take care of themselves. If we do not furnish them with homesteads, and hedge them around protective laws; if we leave them to the legislation of their late masters, we had better have left them in bondage. Their condition would be worse than that of our prisoners at Andersonville. If we fail in this great duty now, when we have the power, we shall deserve and receive the execration of history and of all future ages.

4

ANDREW JOHNSON VETOES THE FIRST
RECONSTRUCTION ACT (1867)

Andrew Johnson became president following the assassination of Abraham Lincoln, and, despite his declared hatred for the "traitors," he pursued a mild policy of Reconstruction that his predecessor had established. Believing that the Southern states should be restored quickly, Johnson pardoned all Southern whites except Confederate leaders and plantation owners (they could receive individual pardons) and established lenient requirements for the creation of new state governments. The Southern states complied with these guidelines, but Congress—alarmed that many former Confederate leaders held positions in the new governments, that many states had enacted "Black Codes" to control the freedmen, and that African Americans were denied political rights—refused to seat the newly elected Southern officials. While many Republicans in Congress hoped to work with Johnson and modify his program, Radical Republicans called for the dissolution of the Johnson governments and the institution of Congressional Reconstruction. Early in 1867, Congress passed the First

---

"Veto Messages," *A Compilation of the Messages and Papers of the Presidents,* ed. James D. Richardson (Washington, DC, 1903), 6: 498-511.

Reconstruction Act, establishing new guidelines for the Southern states to follow. Andrew Johnson vetoed the bill and sent the following excerpted message of explanation to Congress. His comments outline Congressional Reconstruction and offer insights into the broader purpose of the act.

Questions to Consider: For what reasons does Johnson veto this bill? What does Congress require the Southern states to do before they can be readmitted? What are Johnson's views on actions affecting the African Americans? Johnson argues that the bill is politically motivated. What are the motivations?

I have examined the bill "to provide for the more efficient government of the rebel States" with the care and anxiety which its transcendent importance is calculated to awaken. I am unable to give it my assent. . . .

The bill places all the people of the ten States therein named under the absolute domination of military rulers. . . . It declared that there exists in those States no legal governments and no adequate protection for life or property, and asserts the necessity of enforcing peace and good order within their limits. Is this true as matter of fact?

It is not denied that the States in question have each of them an actual government, with all the powers—executive, judicial, and legislative—which properly belong to a free state. They are organized like the other States of the Union, and like them, they make, administer, and execute the laws which concern their domestic affairs. An existing *de facto* government, exercising such functions as these, is itself the law of the state upon all matters within its jurisdiction. To pronounce the supreme lawmaking power of an established state illegal is to say that law itself is unlawful. . . .

The bill, however, would seem to show upon its face that the establishment of peace and good order is not its real object. The fifth section declared that the preceding sections shall cease to operate in any State where certain events shall have happened. These events are, first, the selection of delegates to a State convention by an election at which negroes shall be allowed to vote; second, the formation of a State constitution by the convention so chosen; third, the insertion into the State constitution of a provision which will secure the right of voting at all elections to negroes and to such white men as may not be disfranchised for rebellion or felony; fourth, the submission of the constitution for ratification to negroes and white men not disfranchised, and its actual ratification by their vote; fifth, the submission of the State constitution to Congress for examination and approval, and the actual approval of it by that body; sixth, the adoption of a certain amendment to the Federal Constitution by a vote of the legislature elected under the new constitution; seventh, the adoption of said amendment by a sufficient number of other States to make it a part of the Constitution of the United States. All these conditions must be fulfilled before the people of any of these States can be relieved from the bondage of military domination; but when they are fulfilled, then immediately the pains and penalties of the bill are to cease, no matter whether there be peace and order or not, and without any reference to the security of life or property. . . .

The ten States named in the bill are divided into five districts. For each district an officer of the Army, not below the rank of a brigadier-general, is to be appointed to rule over the people; and he is to be supported with an efficient military force to enable him to perform his duties and enforce his authority. Those duties and that authority . . . are "to protect all persons in their rights of person and property, to suppress insurrection, disorder, and violence, and to punish or cause to be punished all disturbers of the public peace or criminals." The power thus given to the commanding officer over all the people of each district is that of an absolute monarch. His mere will is to take the place of all law. . . .

The purpose and object of the bill—the general intent which pervades it from beginning to end—is to change the entire structure and character of the State governments and to compel them by force to the adoption of organic laws and regulations which they are unwilling to accept if left to themselves. The negroes have not asked for the privilege of voting; the vast majority of them have no idea what it means. This bill not only thrusts it into their hands, but compels them, as well as the whites, to use it in a particular way. If they do not form a constitution with prescribed articles in it and afterwards elect a legislature which will act upon certain measures in a prescribed way, neither blacks nor whites can be relieved from the slavery which the bill imposes upon them. Without pausing here to consider the policy or impolicy of Africanizing the southern part of our territory, I would simply ask the attention of Congress to that manifest, well-known, and universally acknowledged rule of constitutional law which declares that the Federal Government has no jurisdiction, authority, or power to regulate such subjects for any State. To force the right of suffrage out of the hands of the white people and into the hands of the negroes is an arbitrary violation of this principle. . . .

The bill also denies the legality of the governments of ten of the States which participated in the ratification of the amendment to the Federal Constitution abolishing slavery forever within the jurisdiction of the United States and practically excludes them from the Union. If this assumption of the bill be correct, their concurrence can not be considered as having been legally given, and the important fact is made to appear that the consent of three-fourths of the States—the requisite number—has not been constitutionally obtained to the ratification of that amendment, thus leaving the question of slavery where it stood before the amendment was officially declared to have become a part of the Constitution. . . .

While we are legislating upon subjects which are of great importance to the whole people, and which must affect all parts of the country, not only during the life of the present generation, but for ages to come, we should remember that all men are entitled at least to a hearing in the councils which decide upon the destiny of themselves and their children. At present ten States are denied representation, and when the Fortieth Congress assembles on the 4th day of the present month sixteen States will be without a voice in the House of Representatives. This grave fact, with the important questions before us, should induce us to pause in a course of legislation which, looking solely to the attainment of political ends, fails to consider the rights it transgresses, the law which it violates, or the institutions which it imperils.

5

A WHITE SOUTHERN PERSPECTIVE ON RECONSTRUCTION (1868)

Congressional or Radical Reconstruction imposed a new set of requirements on the South. It divided the region into five military districts and outlined how new governments were to be created—especially granting suffrage to African Americans. Complying with these guidelines, every Southern state was readmitted into the Union by 1870. A Republican party coalition of African Americans, recently arrived Northerners (carpetbaggers), and Southern whites (scalawags) controlled nearly all these state governments. Many former supporters of the Confederacy found these Republican governments to be offensive, corrupt, and expensive (they raised taxes to pay for new services, such as public education). One of the most outspoken and uncompromising opponents of Radical Reconstruction was Howell Cobb. Born into a wealthy Georgia cotton plantation family, Cobb devoted his life to public service. He served in the House of Representatives, was elected speaker in 1849, was governor of Georgia, served as secretary of the Treasury under President James Buchanan, was a prominent secessionist, helped form the Confederate government, and was an officer in the war. Following the war, Cobb maintained a self-imposed silence on political matters, which he broke with the excerpted letter below.

·- **Questions to Consider:** Why does Howell Cobb oppose Reconstruction policies? Which policies does he particularly dispute? How did Cobb (and many white Southerners) view relations between the North and the South when the war concluded? Given the antagonism, how did white Southerners react to changes Reconstruction brought the South?

Macon [GA], 4 Jany., 1868

We of the ill-fated South realize only the mournful present whose lesson teaches us to prepare for a still gloomier future. To participate in a national festival would be a cruel mockery, for which I frankly say to you I have no heart, however much I may honor the occasion and esteem the association with which I would be thrown.

The people of the south, conquered, ruined, impoverished, and oppressed, bear up with patient fortitude under the heavy weight of their burdens. Disarmed and reduced to poverty, they are powerless to protect themselves against wrong and injustice; and can only await with broken spirits that destiny which the future has in store for them. At the bidding of their more powerful conquerors they laid down their arms, abandoned a hopeless struggle, and returned to their quiet homes under the plighted faith of a soldier's honor that they should be protected so long

Howell Cobb to J. D. Hoover, 4 January 1868, *Annual Report of the American Historical Association for the Year 1911: Vol. 2. The Correspondence of Robert Toombs, Alexander H. Stephens, and Howell Cobb,* ed. U. B. Phillips (Washington, DC, 1913), 690-694.

as they observed the obligations imposed upon them of peaceful law-abiding citizens. Despite the bitter charges and accusations brought against our people, I hesitate not to say that since that hour their bearing and conduct have been marked by a dignified and honorable submission which should command the respect of their bitterest enemy and challenge the admiration of the civilized world. Deprived of our property and ruined in our estates by the results of the war, we have accepted the situation and given the pledge of a faith never yet broken to abide it. Our conquerors seem to think we should accompany our acquiescence with some exhibition of gratitude for the ruin which they have brought upon us. We cannot see it in that light. Since the close of the war they have taken our property of various kinds, sometimes by seizure, and sometime by purchase,—and when we have asked for remuneration have been informed that the claims of rebels are never recognized by the Government. To this decision necessity compels us to submit; but our conquerors express surprise that we do not see in such ruling the evidence of their kindness and forgiving spirit. They have imposed upon us in our hour of distress and ruin a heavy and burthensome tax, peculiar and limited to our impoverished section. Against such legislation we have ventured to utter an earnest appeal, which to many of their leading spirits indicates a spirit of insubordination which calls for additional burthens. They have deprived us of the protection afforded by our state constitutions and laws, and put life, liberty and property at the disposal of absolute military power. Against this violation of plighted faith and constitutional right we have earnestly and solemnly protested, and our protests have been denounced as insolent;—and our restlessness under the wrong and oppression which have followed these acts has been construed into a rebellious spirit, demanding further and more stringent restrictions of civil and constitutional rights. They have arrested the wheels of State government, paralized the arm of industry, engendered a spirit of bitter antagonism on the part of our negro population towards the white people with whom it is the interest of both races they should maintain kind and friendly relations, and are now struggling by all the means in their power both legal and illegal, constitutional and unconstitutional, to make our former slaves *our masters,* bringing these Southern states under the power of *negro supremacy.* To these efforts we have opposed appeals, protests, and every other means of resistance in our power, and shall continue to do so until the bitter end. If the South is to be made a pandemonium and a howling wilderness the responsibility shall not rest upon our heads. Our conquerors regard these efforts on our part to save ourselves and posterity from the terrible results of their policy and conduct as a new rebellion against the constitution of our country, and profess to be amazed that in all this we have failed to see the evidence of their great magnanimity and exceeding generosity. Standing today in the midst of the gloom and suffering which meets the eye in every direction, we can but feel that we are the victims of cruel legislation and the harsh enforcement of unjust laws. . . . We regarded the close of the war as ending the relationship of enemies and the beginning of a new national brotherhood, and in the light of that conviction felt and spoke of constitutional equality. . . . We claimed that the result of the war left us a state in the Union, and therefore under the protection of the constitution, rendering in return cheerful obedience to its requirements and bearing in common with the other states of the Union the burthens of government, submitting even as we were compelled to do *to taxation without representation;* but they tell us that a successful war to keep us in the Union left us out of the Union and that the pretension we put up for constitutional protection evidences bad temper on our part and a want of appreciation of the generous spirit which declares that the constitution is not over us for the purposes of protection. . . . In such reasoning is found a justification of the policy which seeks to put the South under negro supremacy. Better, they say, to hazard the consequences of negro supremacy in the south with its sure and inevitable results upon Northern prosperity than to put faith in the people of the south who though overwhelmed and conquered have ever showed themselves a brave and generous people, true to their plighted faith in peace and in war, in adversity as in prosperity. . . .

With an Executive who manifests a resolute purpose to defend with all his power the constitution of his country from further aggression, and a Judiciary whose unspotted record has never yet been tarnished with a base subserviency to the unholy demands of passion and hatred, let us indulge the hope that the hour of the country's redemption is at hand, and that even in the wronged and ruined South there is a fair prospect for better days and happier hours when our people can unite again in celebrating the national festivals as in the olden time.

6

THE KU KLUX KLAN DURING RECONSTRUCTION
(1872)

The original Ku Klux Klan was formed in Pulaski, Tennessee, in 1866 as a social organization, but several former Confederates made the Klan a terrorist group. The Klan espoused white supremacy, the defeat of the Republican party in the South, and keeping African Americans "in their place." Incensed with the Republican party's control of state governments, especially with African Americans voting and holding public office, and intrigued with the secrecy, unusual names, and disguises of the Klan, thousands joined the organization in the late 1860s. The Klan embarked on a terrorist campaign with intimidation, whippings, beatings, property destruction, shootings, or simply riding disguised in the countryside as its hallmarks. Most often, blacks who affirmed their rights were Klan targets, but white Republicans were also singled out. Much of the South was spared Klan activity, but locations where both races or political parties were almost equally balanced often witnessed Klan terrorism, especially near election time. In 1871, a congressional committee traveled in the South investigating Klan activities and taking statements from many of its victims. Excerpted next is Edward "Ned" Crosby's testimony on Klan intimidation in Mississippi.

⌐ **Questions to Consider:** How did the Klan intimidate "Ned" Crosby in

U.S. Congress, *Testimony Taken by the Joint Select Committee to Inquire into the Condition of Affairs in the Late Insurrectionary States* (Washington, DC, 1872), 12: 1133-1134.

particular and African Americans in general? What were the reasons for this intimidation? How were elections conducted that allowed for influencing African-American votes? How were African Americans coerced into voting for the Democratic party?

———

Columbus, Mississippi, November 17, 1871

EDWARD CROSBY (colored) sworn and examined.
By the Chairman:

Question. Where do you live?

Answer. Right near Aberdeen—ten miles east of Aberdeen.

Question. State whether you were ever visited by the Ku-Klux; and, if so, under what circumstances.

Answer. I have been visited by them. They came to my house, and came into my house. . . . It looked like there were thirty-odd of them, and I didn't know but what they might interfere with me, and I just stepped aside, out in the yard to the smokehouse. They came up there and three of them got down and came in the house and called for me, and she told them I had gone over to Mr. Crosby's. . . . She didn't know but they might want something to do to me and interfere with me and they knocked around a while and off they went.

Question. Was this in the night-time?

Answer. Yes, sir.

Question. Were they disguised?

Answer. Yes, sir.

Question. Had you been attempting to get up a free-school in your neighborhood?

Answer. Yes, sir.

Question. Colored school?

Answer. Yes, sir.

Question. Do you know whether their visit to you had reference to this effort?

Answer. No, sir; I don't know only this: I had spoken for a school, and I had heard a little chat of that, and I didn't know but what they heard it, and that was the thing they were after.

Question. Were their horses disguised?

Answer. Yes. Sir. . . .

Question. Did you know any of the men?

Answer. No, sir; I didn't get close enough to know them. I could have known them, I expect, if I was close up, but I was afraid to venture.

Question. Did they ever come back?

Answer. No, sir.

Question. What do you know as to the whipping of Green T. Roberts?

Answer. Only from hearsay. He told me himself. They didn't whip him. They took him out and punched him and knocked him about right smart, but didn't whip him.

Question. Was he a colored man?

Answer. He was a white man—a neighbor of mine.

Question. Who took him out?

Answer. The Ku-Klux. . . .

Question. What if anything do you know of any colored men being afraid to vote the republican ticket and voting the democratic ticket at the election this month, in order to save their property, and to save themselves from being outraged?

Answer. Well sir, the day of the election there was, I reckon, thirty or forty; I didn't count them, but between that amount; they spoke of voting the radical ticket. It was my intention to go for the purpose. I had went around and saw several colored friends on that business. . . . I knew some of the party would come in and maybe they would prevent us from voting as we wanted to. I called for the republican tickets and they said there was none on the ground. I knocked around amongst them, and I called a fellow named Mr. Dowdell and asked if there would be any there; he said he didn't know; he asked me how I was going to vote; I told him my opinion, but I was cramped for fear. They said if we didn't act as they wanted they would drop us at once. There is only a few of us, living amongst them like lost sheep where we can do the best; and they were voting and they stood back and got the colored population and pushed them in front and let them vote first, and told them there was no republican tickets on the ground. I didn't see but three after I voted. Shortly after I voted, Mr. James Wilson came with some, and a portion of the colored people had done voting. I met Mr. Henderson; I was going on to the other box at the Baptist church. He asked if there were any colored voters there; I told him there was thirty or forty, and there was no republican tickets there. Mr. Wilson had some in his pocket, but I didn't see them. I saw that I was beat at my own game, and I had got on my horse and dropped out.

Question. Who told you that unless the colored people voted the democratic ticket it would be worse for them?

Answer. Several in the neighborhood. Mr. Crosby said as long as I voted as he voted I could stay where I was, but he says, "Whenever Ned votes my rights away from me, I cast him down."

Question. Was he a democrat?

Answer. A dead-out democrat.

Question. Did you hear any other white men make the same declaration?

Answer. Not particular; I only heard them talking through each other about the colored population. I heard Mr. Jerome Lamb—he lived nigh Athens—tell a fellow named Aleck that lived on his place, he spoke to him and asked him if he was going to vote as he did; Aleck told him he was—he did this in fear, mind you—and Aleck went and voted, and after he voted he said, "Aleck, come to me;" says he, "Now, Aleck, you have voted?" Aleck says, "Yes sir;" he said, "Well, now, Aleck, you built some very nice houses. Now, I want you to wind your business up right carefully. I am done with you; off of my land."

Question. Had Aleck voted the republican ticket?

Answer. Yes, sir.

Question. Did all the colored men except these three vote the democratic ticket that day?

Answer. Up at Grub Springs all voted the democratic ticket. There was no republican ticket given to the colored people at all.

Question. Did they vote the democratic ticket from fear that they would be thrown out of employment or injured?

Answer. That was their intention. You see pretty nigh every one of them was the same way I was, but there was none there; and them they were all living on white people's land, and were pretty fearful. The Ku-Klux had been ranging around through them, and they were all a little fearful.

Question. Do you think they were all radical in sentiment, and would have been glad to have voted the radical ticket if uninfluenced?

Answer. They would. They had a little distinction up amongst themselves—the white and colored people. One of them said. "Ned, put in a republican ticket." Well, there was none on the ground, and I remarked, "If there is any radical tickets on the ground I will take one of them, and I will not take a democratic ticket, and I will fold them up and drop that in the box, and they will never tell the difference," and it got out that I had voted the radical ticket, and some were very harsh about it.

Question. Would the colored people of your county vote the radical ticket if left alone?

Answer. Well, sir, I suppose they would have done it.

_ . _

THE WEST

2

Following the Civil War, many Americans expressed a renewed interest in the Trans-Mississippi West. With the war concluded, construction proceeded on the Trans-Mississippi railroad; great fortunes were being made in Western mines, and people began migrating to the Great Plains region. For many, especially those displaced by the war, the West offered a new beginning. The individuals who began to flood the West in the last third of the 19th century included Chinese and Irish laborers, African-American cowboys, white American farmers, and European immigrant miners, to name but a few. The land they entered was not an empty one, but one long inhabited by Native Americans and Mexicans. The meeting of these different groups triggered conflict over the region's future. The following documents describe the interactions of these groups in the Western environment.

7

THE MINING FRONTIER (1863)

The lure of finding wealth in gold or silver drew thousands into the Western mountains as the Civil War raged in the East. This mining migration was twofold; many Easterners moved west, while disappointed prospectors in California and Nevada relocated to the East. Most Western territories witnessed some form of mining "rush," but the largest and most prolonged occurred in Idaho, Montana, and Colorado. Virtually overnight ramshackle communities—initially tents or brush shelters ("wakiups")—sprang up when gold or silver was discovered; some became permanent settlements, but many were abandoned when the metal "played out." Seeking his own fortune, Nathaniel P. Langford arrived in southwest Montana in 1863, one year after gold was discovered. He observed the Montana gold rush, was instrumental in organizing vigilantes to suppress local lawlessness, and played a role in creating Yellowstone National Park (serving as its first superintendent). Langford also became an amateur historian and wrote *Vigilante Days and Ways* (1890), an account of life in the Montana gold fields. Excerpted below is his description of a mining frontier community.

―――

·⌐ **Questions to Consider:** How does Langford describe the development of Alder Gulch? Who was attracted to the gold fields besides miners? Why did the lawlessness exist in the gold fields? What happened on Sundays? What changed to allow law and order to eventually prevail in Alder Gulch?

―――

In May, 1863, a company of miners, while returning from an unsuccessful exploring expedition, discovered the remarkable placer afterwards known as Alder Gulch. . . . Hundreds started at once to the new placer, each striving to outstrip the other, in order to secure a claim. . . . In less than a week from the date of the first arrival, hundreds of tents, brush wakiups, and rude log cabins, extemporized for immediate occupancy, were scattered at random over the spot, now for the first time trodden by white men. For a distance of twelve miles from the mouth of the gulch to its source in Bald Mountain, claims were staked and occupied by the men fortunate enough first to assert an ownership. . . .

Of the settlements in Alder Gulch, Virginia City was the principal, though Nevada [a nearby town], two miles below, at one time was of nearly equal size and population. A stranger from the Eastern States entering the gulch for the first time, two or three months after its discovery, would be inspired by the scene and its associations with reflections of the most strange and novel character. This human hive, numbering at least ten thousand people, was the product of ninety days. Into it were crowded all the elements of a rough and active civilization. Thousands of cabins and tents and brush wakiups, thrown together in the roughest form, and scattered at random along the banks, and in the nooks of the hills, were seen on

―――

Nathaniel P. Langford, *Vigilante Days and Ways: The Pioneers of the Rockies* (New York, 1890), 206-207, 222-224.

every hand. Every foot of the gulch, under the active manipulations of the miners, was undergoing displacement, and it was already disfigured by huge heaps of gravel, which had been passed through the sluices, and rifled of their glittering contents. In the gulch itself all was activity. Some were removing the superincumbent earth to reach the pay-dirt, others who had accomplished that were gathering up the clay and gravel upon the surface of the bed-rock, while by others still it was thrown into the sluice boxes. This exhibition of mining industry was twelve miles long. Gold was abundant, and every possible device was employed by the gamblers, the traders, the vile men and women that had come with the miners to the locality, to obtain it. Nearly every third cabin in the towns was a saloon where vile whiskey was peddled out for fifty cents a drink in gold dust. Many of these places were filled with gambling tables and gamblers, and the miner who was bold enough to enter one of them with his day's earnings in his pocket, seldom left until thoroughly fleeced. Hurdy-gurdy dance-houses were numerous, and there were plenty of camp beauties to patronize them. There too, the successful miner, lured by siren smiles, after an evening spent in dancing and carousing at his expense, steeped with liquor, would empty his purse into the lap of his charmer for an hour of license in her arms. Not a day or night passed which did not yield its full fruition of fights, quarrels, wounds, or murders. The crack of the revolver was often heard above the merry notes of the violin. Street fights were frequent, and as no one knew when or where they would occur, every one was on his guard against a random shot.

Sunday was always a gala day. The miners then left their work and gathered about the public places in the towns. The stores were all open, the auctioneers specially eloquent on every corner in praise of their wares. Thousands of people crowded the thoroughfares, ready to rush in any direction of promised excitement. Horse-racing was among the most favored amusements. Prize fights were formed, and brawny men engaged at fisticuffs until their sight was lost and their bodies pommelled to a jelly, while hundreds of on-lookers cheered the victor. Hacks rattled to and fro between the several towns, freighted with drunken and rowdy humanity of both sexes. Citizens of acknowledged respectability often walked, more often perhaps rode side by side on horseback, with noted courtesans in open day through the crowded streets, and seemingly suffered no harm in reputation. Pistols flashed, bowieknives flourished, and braggart oaths filled the air, as often as men's passions triumphed over their reason. This was indeed the reign of unbridled license, and men who at first regarded it with disgust and terror, by constant exposure soon learned to become part of it, and forget that they had ever been taught else. All classes of society were represented at this general exhibition. Judges, lawyers, doctors, even clergymen, could not claim exemption. Culture and religion afforded feeble protection, where allurement and indulgence ruled the hour.

Underneath this exterior of recklessness, there was in the minds and hearts of the miners and business men of this society, a strong and abiding sense of justice,—and that saved the Territory. . . .

8

"REPORT OF THE COMMISSION ON INDIAN AFFAIRS" (1869)

Increased white migration through the Great Plains threatened the Native American way of life, often jeopardizing earlier treaty agreements and frequently leading to open hostilities. Sensitive to this growing problem, President U. S. Grant appointed Ely S. Parker, a Seneca sachem (chief) and lifelong champion of his people, to the position of commissioner of Indian Affairs in 1869. In an attempt to provide justice to Native Americans, Grant also selected a commission to examine the conduct of Indian affairs, government policies, and Indian relations. The commission traveled to reservations, speaking to Indian agents and Native Americans before submitting its report to Parker. Excerpted below is the commission's findings, which Parker included in his first annual "Report."

————

Questions to Consider: To many Americans, the Native American was a "savage," less than human. Does this report reinforce this concept? Explain. Whom does the commission blame for the injustices against the Native Americans? What solutions does the commission present? Are they feasible?

————

While it cannot be denied that the government of the United States, in the general terms and temper of its legislation, has evinced a desire to deal generously with the Indians, it must be admitted that the actual treatment they have received has been unjust and iniquitous beyond the power of words to express.

Taught by the government that they had rights entitled to respect; when those rights have been assailed by the rapacity of the white man, the arm which should have been raised to protect them has been ever ready to sustain the aggressor.

The history of the government connections with the Indians is a shameful record of broken treaties and unfulfilled promises.

The history of the border white man's connection with the Indians is a sickening record of murder, outrage, robbery, and wrongs committed by the former as the rule, and occasional savage outbreaks and unspeakably barbarous deeds of retaliation by the latter as the exception. . . .

The testimony of some of the highest military officers of the United States is on record to the effect that in our Indian wars, almost without exception, the first aggressions have been made by the white man, and the assertion is supported by every civilian of reputation who has studied the subject. In addition to the class of robbers and outlaws who find impunity in their nefarious pursuits upon the frontiers, there is a large class of professedly reputable men who use every means in their power to bring on Indian wars, for the sake of the profit to be realized from the presence of troops and the expenditure of government funds in their midst.

United States, Department of the Interior, Bureau of Indian Affairs, "Report of the Commission on Indian Affairs," 41st Congress, 2nd Session, House Executive Documents, 3: 487-493.

They proclaim death to the Indians at all times, in words and publications, making no distinction between the innocent and the guilty. They incite the lowest class of men to the perpetration of the darkest deeds against their victims, and, as judges and jurymen, shield them from the justice due to their crimes. Every crime committed by a white man against an Indian is concealed or palliated; every offense committed by one Indian against a white man is borne on the wings of the post or the telegraph to the remotest corner of the land, clothed with all the horrors which the reality or imagination can throw around it. . . . Against the inhuman idea that the Indian is only fit to be exterminated, and the influence of the men who propagate it, the military arm of the government cannot be too strongly guarded. It is hardly to be wondered at that inexperienced officers, ambitions for distinction, when surrounded by such influences, have been incited to attack Indian bands without adequate cause, and involve the nation in an unjust war. It should, at least, be understood that in the future such blunders should cost the officer his commission, and that such destruction is infamy.

Paradoxical as it may seem, the white man has been the chief obstacle in the way of Indian civilization. The benevolent measures attempted by the government for their advancement have been almost uniformly thwarted by the agencies employed to carry them out. The soldiers, sent for their protection, too often carried demoralization and disease into their midst. The agent, appointed to be their friend and counsellor, business manager, and the almoner of the government bounties, frequently went among them only to enrich himself in the shortest possible time, at the cost of the Indians, and spend the largest available sum of the government money with the least ostensible beneficial result. . . . If in spite of these obstacles a tribe made some progress in agriculture, or their lands became valuable from any cause, the process of civilization was summarily ended by driving them away from their homes with fire and sword, to undergo similar experiences in some new locality. . . .

To assert that "the Indian will not work" is as true as it would be to say that the white man will not work. . . . Why should the Indian be expected to plant corn, fence lands, build houses, or do anything but get food from day to day, when experience has taught him that the product of his labor will be seized by the white man tomorrow! . . .

The policy of collecting the Indian tribes upon small reservations contiguous to each other, and within the limits of a large reservation, eventually to become a State of the Union, and of which the small reservations will probably be the counties, seems to be the best that can be devised. . . .

The treaty system should be abandoned, as soon as any just method can be devised to accomplish it, existing treaties should be abrogated.

The legal status of the uncivilized Indians should be that of wards of the government; the duty of the latter being to protect them, to educate them in industry, the arts of civilization, and the principles of Christianity; elevate them to the rights of citizenship, and to sustain and clothe them until they can support themselves.

The payment of money annuities to the Indians should be abandoned, for the reason that such payments encourage idleness and vice, to the injury of those whom it is intended to benefit. Schools should be established, and teachers employed by the government to introduce the English language in every tribe. It is believed that many of the difficulties with Indians occur from misunderstandings as to the meaning and intention of either party. The teachers employed should be nominated by some religious body having a mission nearest to the location of the school. The establishment of Christian missions should be encouraged, and their schools fostered. The pupils should at least receive the rations and clothing they would get if remaining with their families. The religion of our blessed Saviour is believed to be the most effective agent for the civilization of any people.

9

A WESTERN NEWSPAPER EDITORIAL ON THE CUSTER MASSACRE (1876)

The country was still euphoric over the celebration of the Centennial when word of Colonel George A. Custer's massacre spread throughout the nation. Custer was part of a military operation to drive portions of the disgruntled Sioux (Lakota) tribe back to their reservation when he ordered an attack on the Native American encampment along the Little Big Horn River in present-day southeastern Montana. Custer and 264 of his men were killed in what became known as "Custer's Last Stand." William N. Byer, author of the editorial excerpted below, was considered a Western "pioneer," having traveled and lived throughout the West. In 1859, he established the *Rocky Mountain News*, the first newspaper in the Colorado territory, and continued to edit and publish the paper for over 19 years. Besides his newspaper, Byer took an active role in pushing Colorado statehood and was closely identified with promoting the growth and development of Denver. His editorial reveals much about Western attitudes of the time toward Native Americans and Easterners.

Questions to Consider: Whom does William N. Byer blame for Custer's massacre? Was it valid? Why does Byer fear the massacre will harm the "new west"? What is Byer's solution to the "Indian problem"?

The wish was father to the thought when yesterday we hazarded the assertion that the report of the annihilation of Custer's command bore the appearance of exaggeration, if not of entire fabrication. The details published in this morning's dispatches, although many of them emanate from not particularly trustworthy newspaper correspondents, forbid further incredulity, and we . . . accept the terrible truth in all its enormity, that some of the bravest officers in the service and a large fraction of one of the finest cavalry regiments, have fallen victim to the picayune policy that domineers in all matters appertaining to Indian affairs. The blood must boil in the veins of the most fishlike, at reading the horrible story of the massacre of three hundred United States soldiers at the hands of ten times that

---

"Extermination the Only Remedy," *Rocky Mountain News* (Denver, CO), 8 July 1876, 2

number of savages, when it is remembered that all this is the fruit of the do-nothing system of the Indian department. Custer and his men have been murdered, not by Indians, who were only the instruments of their death, but by the sleek, smooth talking, Quaker advocates of the peace policy, who have always insisted that the Indian was a man and a brother, and an elder brother, at that, with all the rights of primogeniture. Had the Indian problem been treated properly, long years since it would have been solved, and Custer would not now be a mangled corpse, from their being either no Indians alive to kill him, or the remnants of the race so restrained within bounds that it would not be possible for them to perpetrate the deed that they have. The Indian bureau has all along realized Dicken's conception of the Circumlocution Office. How not to do it has ever been its aim, and the success with which it has carried out its design is a blot on the entire fabric of government. What a spectacle, indeed, is it for foreign nations to sneer at, when the great republic of the west, for all its population of forty-four millions of people, allows its soldiers to be overcome by odds of ten to one, although its antagonist numbers but a few paltry thousand of savages. The entire system pursued towards the Indians, crowned as it is with this terrible disaster, is unworthy of the government and a disgrace to the country.

While the entire nation has come to mourn the blot on its escutcheon caused by the catastrophe to Custer, we of the new west have a right to feel outraged, not for the sake of the honor that Falstaff dubbed but a word, but for the wrong that is done as is preventing the increase of our population and capital, by permitting the impression to gain ground abroad that our settlements are liable to hostile inroads. The states people have vague ideas of distance, and the [location] in which Custer and those with him met their death is liable to be located anywhere between Long and Pike's Peaks, while very likely is the extreme east, the Platte is supposed to be the river from Gen. Reno at last got water, after suffering from a thirty-six hours' thirst. The prosperity of the entire country from the Missouri river to the Rocky Mountains is injured for years to come, more than it will easily be believed, by the destruction of the Seventh cavalry. The shot that killed Custer was heard around the world and everywhere that it aroused the echoes, it frightened possible population and certain capital from the new west. The injury done this entire region, indeed, will be almost irreparable, unless the Sioux are at once exterminated. This is the only alternate. Do what we will, it will be impossible to make it known in the states that Denver is as secure from Indian attack as New York, and that Custer fell half a thousand miles from the northern boundary of Colorado. Distance leads exaggeration to danger. No coward so great as capital, and even the consumptive, flying from the deadly east winds of the coast will think twice before he exposes himself to what he believes to be the scalping knives of the Sioux.

In the name, then, of the people of the new west, we demand that instant measures be taken to, at once and forever, prevent the possibility of the recent defeat of the troops being repeated. Let the story of Custer's death be lost in the terrible vengeance taken for it. Let real war be in order for once. Custer would never have met with his disaster had he been properly supported. In place of a few scattered companies of cavalry, at least three thousand frontiersmen, together with half that number of regular soldiers should scour the enemy's country, and no quarter should be given, as it certainly has not been taken. The extermination of the Sioux and the destruction of all that is theirs, is necessary for the future prosperity of the entire new west. For years we have had population and capital frightened away from us by fears of the Indians, and we call upon the government for redress at the eleventh hour. And by redress we mean the extermination of the hostile tribes.

10

CULTURAL EXCHANGE ON THE ARIZONA FRONTIER (1874)

As Americans migrated to the West, they did not enter a vacant land, particularly in the Southwest, where various Native American tribes had lived for several centuries. The Spanish explored the region as early as the 1540s and established trading posts and missions (Santa Fe was made the capital in 1619). As a far-flung northern province of Mexico, a distinct Spanish-Native American culture evolved. The first Anglos (white traders and settlers) came to Arizona prior to the Civil War, but they remained a minority until the early 20th century. The influx of whites brought conflict with the Native Americans, and as outrages on both sides escalated, the U. S. Army was sent to maintain order. In 1874, Captain Jack Summerhayes' unit was detached to Arizona. Accompanying Summerhayes was his recent bride, Martha, a well-educated New England woman who kept an account of life in frontier Arizona, which she later published. The Summerhayeses spent four years on various outposts in Arizona, but one of their initial stops was Ehrenberg, a Colorado River town. In the selection below, Martha Summerhayes observes local (Mexican) customs.

Questions to Consider: Why does Martha Summerhayes regret the American way of life in Arizona? Why does she not change? What Mexican customs, especially the activities of the women, fascinated Summerhayes? Why?

So work was begun immediately on the kitchen. My first stipulation was, that the new rooms were to have wooden *floors;* for, although the Cocopah Charley kept the adobe floors in perfect condition, by sprinkling them down and sweeping them out every morning, they were quite impossible, especially where it concerned white dresses and children, and the little sharp rocks in them seemed to be so tiring to the feet.

Life as we Americans live it was difficult in Ehrenberg. I often said: "Oh! if we could only live as the Mexicans live, how easy it would be!" For they had their fire built between some stones piled up in their yard, a piece of sheet iron laid over the

Martha Summerhayes, *Vanished Arizona: Recollections of the Army Life of a New England Woman,* 2nd edition (Salem, MA, 1911), 144-148.

top: this was the cooking-stove. A pot of coffee was made in the morning early, and the family sat on the low porch and drank it, and ate a biscuit. Then a kettle of *frijoles* was put over to boil. These were boiled slowly for some hours, then lard and salt were added, and they simmered down until they were deliciously fit to eat, and had a thick red gravy.

Then the young matron, or daughter of the house, would mix the peculiar paste of flour and salt and water, for *tortillas,* a species of unleavened bread. These *tortillas* were patted out until they were as large as a dinner plate, and very thin; then thrown onto the hot sheet-iron, where they baked. Each one of the family then got a *tortilla,* the spoonful of beans was laid upon it, and so they managed without the paraphernalia of silver and china and napery.

How I envied them the simplicity of their lives! Besides, the *tortillas* were delicious to eat, and as for the *frijoles,* they were beyond anything I had ever eaten in the shape of beans. I took lessons in the making of *tortillas.* A woman was paid to come and teach me; but I never mastered the art. It is in the blood of the Mexican, and a girl begins at a very early age to make the *tortilla.* It is the most graceful thing to see a pretty Mexican toss the wafer-like disc over her bare arm, and pat it out until transparent.

This was their supper; for, like nearly all people in the tropics, they ate only twice a day. Their fare was varied sometimes by a little *carni seca,* pounded up and stewed with *chile verde* or *chile colorado.*

Now if you could hear the soft, exquisite, affectionate drawl with which the Mexican woman says *chile verde* you could perhaps come to realize what an important part the delicious green pepper plays in the cookery of these countries. They do not use it in its raw state, but generally roast it whole, stripping off the thin skin and throwing away the seeds, leaving only the pulp, which acquires a fine flavor by having been roasted or toasted over the hot coals.

The women were scrupulously clean and modest, and always wore, when in their *casa,* a low-necked and short-sleeved white linen *camisa,* fitting neatly, with bands around neck and arms. Over this they wore a calico skirt; always white stockings and black slippers. When they ventured out, the younger women put on muslin gowns, and carried parasols. The older women wore a linen towel thrown over their heads, or, in cool weather, the black *riboso.* I often cried: "Oh! if I could only dress as the Mexicans do! Their necks and arms do look so cool and clean."

I have always been sorry I did not adopt their fashion of house apparel. Instead of that, I yielded to the prejudices of my conservative partner, and sweltered during the day in high-necked and long-sleeved white dresses, kept up the table in American fashion, ate American food in so far as we could get it, and all at the expense of strength. . . .

There was no market, but occasionally a Mexican killed a steer, and we bought enough for one meal; but having no ice, and no place away from the terrific heat, the meat was hung out under the *ramada* with a piece of netting over it, until the first heat had passed out of it, and then it was cooked.

The Mexican, after selling what meat he could, cut the rest into thin strips and hung it up on ropes to dry in the sun. It dried hard and brittle, in its natural state, so pure is the air on that wonderful river bank. They called this *carni seca,* and the

Americans called it "jerked beef."

Patrocina often prepared me a dish of this, when I was unable to taste the fresh meat. She would pound it fine with a heavy pestle, and then put it to simmer, seasoning it with the green or red pepper. It was most savory. There was no butter at all during the hot months, but our hens laid a few eggs, and the Quartermaster was allowed to keep a small lot of commissary stores, from which we drew our supplies of flour, ham, and canned things. We were often without milk for weeks at a time, for the cows crossed the river to graze, and sometimes could not get back until the river fell again, and they could pick their way back across the shifting sand bars.

The Indian brought the water every morning in buckets from the river. It looked like melted chocolate. He filled the barrels, and when it had settled clear, the *ollas* were filled, and thus the drinking water was a trifle cooler than the air. One day it seemed unusually cool, so I said: "Let us see by the thermometer how cool the water really is." We found the temperature of the water to be 86 degrees; but that, with the air at 122 in the shade, seemed quite refreshing to drink.

11

A NATIVE AMERICAN REMEMBERS THE GHOST DANCE (1890)

By 1890, the Great Plains Indian tribes had experienced severe hardships. Whites had invaded their traditional lands, the American bison (buffalo) was nearly exterminated, new diseases ravaged some tribes, often with fatal results, and the Native Americans were placed on reservations with unfilled promises of government assistance. Disenchanted and witnessing the collapse of their culture, many Plains Indians embraced the preachings of a Paiute messiah named Wovoka (also known as Jack Wilson), who led a revival of the Ghost Dance on a Nevada reservation. A religious movement soon spread throughout the West. Wovoka taught the Ghost Dance ceremony and instructed the Native Americans to live peacefully with one another and with the whites. Many tribes sent delegations to meet with Wovoka to learn the Ghost Dance, so that the promised return of the old ways could be achieved. Among those who consulted Wovoka was Rising Wolf, who retold his Ghost Dance participation to novelist Hamlin Garland. Rising Wolf was interviewed while Garland toured the West to gather materials for future writing projects. Rising Wolf's account, excerpted below, was published in the popular *McClure's Magazine*.

Questions to Consider: What did Wovoka and the Ghost Dance promise? Why were the Native Americans so captivated with the Ghost Dance? What were the reactions of whites to the Ghost Dance? Many argue that the Ghost Dance marked the tragic conclusion of Native American life. What happened as a result of the Ghost Dance?

Hamlin Garland, "Rising Wolf - Ghost Dancer," *McClure's Magazine* 12 (January 1899): 241-248.

One night there came into our midst a Snake messenger with a big tale. "Away in the west," he said to us in sign talk, "a wonderful man has come. He speaks all languages and he is the friend of all red men. He is white, but not like other white men. He has been nailed to a tree by the whites. I saw the holes in his hands. He teaches a new dance, and that is to gather all the Indians together in council. He wants a few head men of all tribes to meet him where the big mountains are, in the place where the lake is surrounded by pictured rocks. There he will teach us how to make mighty magic and drive away the white man and bring back the buffalo."

All that he told us we pondered long, and I said: "It is well, I will go to see this man. I will learn his dance." . . .

A day passed, and he did not come; but one night when we sat in council over his teachings, he suddenly stepped inside the circle. He was a dark man, but not so dark as we were. He had long hair on his chin, and long, brown head-hair, parted in the middle. I looked for the wounds on his wrists; I could not see any. He moved like a big chief, tall and swift. He could speak all tongues. He spoke Dakota, and many understood. I could understand the language of the Cut-throat people, and this is what he said: My people, before the white man came you were happy. You had many buffalo to eat and tall grass for your ponies. You could come and go like the wind. When it was cold, you could go into the valleys to the south, where the healing springs are; and when it grew warm, you could return to the mountains in the north. The white man came. He dug the bones of our mother, the earth. He tore her bosom with steel. He built big trails and put iron horses on them. He fought you and beat you, and put you in barren places where a horned toad would die. He said you must stay there; you must not hunt in the mountains.

Then he breathed his poison upon the buffalo, and they disappeared. They vanished into the earth. One day they covered the hills, the next nothing but their bones remained. Would you remove the white man? Would you have the buffalo come back? Listen, and I will tell you how to make great magic. I will teach you a mystic dance, and then let everybody go home and dance. When the grass is green, the change will come. Let everybody dance four days in succession, and on the fourth day the white man will disappear and the buffalo come back; our dead will return with the buffalo. . . .

You have forgotten the ways of the fathers; therefore great distress is upon you. You must throw away all that the white man has brought you. Return to the dress of the fathers. You must use the sacred colors, red and white, and the sacred grass, and in the spring, when the willows are green, the change will come. . . .

Then he taught us the song and the dance which white people call the ghost dance, and we danced all together, and while we danced near him he sat with bowed head. No one dared to speak to him. The firelight shone on him. Suddenly he disappeared. No one saw him go. Then we were sorrowful, for we wished him to remain with us. . . .

At last we reached home, and I called a big dance, and at the dance I told the people what I had seen, and they were very glad. "Teach us the dance," they cried to me. . . .

Then they did as I bid, and when the moon was round as a shield, we beat the drum and called the people to dance. . . .

The agent came to see us dance, but we did not care. He was a good man, and we felt sorry for him, for he must also vanish with the other white people. He listened to our crying, and looked long, and his interpreter told him we prayed to the great Spirits to destroy the white man and bring back the buffalo. Then he called me with his hand, and because he was a good man I went to him. He asked me what the dance meant, and I told him, and he said, "It must stop." "I cannot stop it," I said. "The Great Spirits have said it. It must go on." . . .

On the fourth night, while we danced, soldiers came riding down the hills, and their chiefs, in shining white hats, came to watch us. All night we prayed and danced. We prayed in our songs.

But the agent smiled, and the soldiers of the white chiefs sat not far off, their guns in their hands, and the moon passed by, and the east grew light, and we were very weary, and my heart was heavy. I looked to see the red come in the east. "When the sun looks over the hills, then it will be," I said to my friends. "The white man will become as smoke. The wind will sweep him away."

As the sun came near we all danced hard. My voice was almost gone. My feet were numb, my legs were weak, but my heart was big. . . .

But the sun came up, the soldiers fired a big gun, and the soldier chiefs laughed. Then the agent called to me, "Your Great Spirit can do nothing. Your Messiah lied." . . .

All day I lay there with my head covered. I did not want to see the light of the sun. I heard the drum stop and the singing die away. Night came, and then on the hills I heard the wailing of my people. Their hearts were gone. Their bones were weary.

When I rose, it was morning. I flung off my blankets, and looked down on the valley where the tepees of the white soldiers stood. I heard their drums and their music. I had made up my mind. The white man's trail was wide and dusty by reason of many feet passing thereon, but it was long. The trail of my people was ended.

12

LIFE ON THE PRAIRIE FARMS (1893)

The Homestead Act of 1862 and its promise of 160 acres of free land if it were improved for five consecutive years enticed people to settle the Great Plains. This vast grassland, once considered "desert" and uninhabitable, was passed over by earlier westward migrants. But new agricultural techniques (dry farming, the chilled iron plow, drought- and disease-resistant wheat) helped transform the region into America's breadbasket. Despite these changes, many settlers found that economic survival was difficult; their homesteads did not contain enough land to grow wheat or corn profitably as overproduction drove prices down. Responses to the plight of the farmer were frequently politically or economically motivated, but journalist E. V. Smalley, author of the following excerpt, focused

E. V. Smalley, "The Isolation of Life on Prairie Farms," *Atlantic Monthly* 72 (September 1893): 378-382.

on the social aspect of agriculture. His depiction of life on prairie farms gave readers of the respected *Atlantic Monthly* a sense of the solitude facing families on the Great Plains.

――――

Questions to Consider: According to E. V. Smalley, what helped establish the farm isolation on the Great Plains? Explain the living conditions on family farms. What perpetuates the lack of social events on the Great Plains? Why does Smalley believe the solitude will eventually end?

――――

E very homesteader must live upon his claim for five years to perfect his title and get his patent; so that if there were not the universal American custom of isolated farm life to stand in the way, no farm villages would be possible in the first occupancy of a new region in the West without a change in our land laws. If the country were so thickly settled that every quarter section of land (160 acres) had a family upon it, each family would be half a mile from any neighbor, supposing the houses to stand in the center of the farms; and in any case the average distance between them could not be less. But many settlers own 320 acres, and a few have a square mile of land, 640 acres.

Then there are school sections, belonging to the state, and not occupied at all; and everywhere you find vacant tracts owned by Eastern speculators or by mortgage companies, to which former settlers have abandoned their claims, going to newer regions and leaving their debts and their land behind. Thus the average space separating the farmsteads is, in fact, always more than a half a mile, and many settlers must go a mile or two to reach a neighbor's house. This condition obtains not on the frontiers alone but in fairly well-peopled agricultural districts.

If there be any region in the world where the natural gregarious instinct of mankind should assert itself, that region is our Northwestern prairies, where a short, hot summer is followed by a long, cold winter and where there is little in the aspect of nature to furnish food for thought. On every hand the treeless plain stretches away to the horizon line. In summer, it is checkered with grain fields or carpeted with grass and flowers, and it is inspiring in its color and vastness; but one mile of it is almost exactly like another, save where some watercourse nurtures a fringe of willows and cottonwoods. When the snow covers the ground, the prospect is bleak and dispiriting. No brooks babble under icy armor. There is no bird life after the wild geese and ducks have passed on their way south. The silence of death rests on the vast landscape, save when it is swept by cruel winds that search out every chink and cranny of the buildings and drive through each unguarded aperture the dry powdery snow.

In such a region, you would expect the dwellings to be of substantial construction, but they are not. The new settler is too poor to build of brick or stone. He hauls a few loads of lumber from the nearest railway station and puts up a frail little house of two, three, or four rooms that looks as though the prairie winds would blow it away. Were it not for the invention of tarred building paper, the flimsy walls would not keep out the wind and snow. With this paper the walls are sheathed under the weatherboards. The barn is often a nondescript affair of sod walls and straw roof. Lumber is much too dear to be used for dooryard fences, and there is no enclosure about the house. . . .

In this cramped abode, from the windows of which there is nothing more cheerful in sight than the distant houses of other settlers, just as ugly and lonely, and stacks of straw and unthreshed grain, the farmer's family must live. In the summer there is a school for the children, one, two, or three miles away; but in winter the distances across the snow-covered plains are too great for them to travel in severe weather; the schoolhouse is closed, and there is nothing for them to do but to house themselves and long for spring. Each family must live mainly to itself, and life, shut up in the little wooden farmhouses, cannot well be very cheerful.

A drive to the nearest town is almost the only diversion. There the farmers and their wives gather in the stores and manage to enjoy a little sociability. The big coal stove gives out a grateful warmth, and there is a pleasant odor of dried codfish, groceries, and ready-made clothing. The women look at the display of thick cloths and garments and wish the crop had been better so that they could buy some of the things of which they are badly in need. The men smoke corncob pipes and talk politics. It is a cold drive home across the windswept prairies, but at least they have had a glimpse of a little broader and more comfortable life than that of the isolated farm.

There are few social events in the life of these prairie farmers to enliven the monotony of the long winter evenings; no singing schools, spelling schools, debating clubs, or church gatherings. Neighborly calls are infrequent because of the long distances which separate the farmhouses and because, too, of the lack of homogeneity of the people. They have no common past to talk about. They were strangers to one another when they arrived in this new land, and their work and ways have not thrown them much together.

Often the strangeness is intensified by differences of national orign. There are Swedes, Norwegians, Germans, French Canadians, and perhaps even such peculiar people as Finns and Icelanders, among the settlers, and the Americans come from many different states. It is hard to establish any social bond in such a mixed population, yet one and all need social intercourse, as the thing most essential to pleasant living, after food, shelter, and clothing. . . .

The plains of the West extend from the Gulf of Mexico to the valley of the Saskatchewan in the British territory. A belt about 300 miles wide on the eastern side of this vast region receives sufficient rainfall for farming. This belt is the granary of the continent, and even with its present sparse settlement it produces an enormous yearly surplus of wheat and corn. Its cultivators have thus far been engaged in a hard struggle to establish themselves on the soil, procure the necessaries of existence, and pay off their mortgages. They are getting ahead year by year; and in the older settled districts good houses are taking the places of the pioneer shanties, and the towns show thrift and progress. Before long these prairie people will begin to grapple with the problems of a higher civilization. . . .

THE EXPANSION OF
BIG BUSINESS

3

The market revolution that transformed America before the Civil War brought about even greater changes after the war. This postwar industrial revolution included the spread of many prewar economic developments as well as the emergence of new technologies, which expanded economic production. In particular, the railroads helped create a national market for American goods with inexpensive transportation costs; mass production of items through increased mechanization and commercial applications of inventions such as electricity, the telephone, and steel production helped fuel the economic growth. The economic transformation of the late 19th century occurred in an environment where government policy was "laissez faire" and business followed the creed of "survival of the fittest." The ensuing selections describe some of the new technologies and chronicle the attitudes of those who benefited from the new economic realities.

13

A BRITISH PERSPECTIVE ON AMERICAN RAILROADS (1865)

By 1860, the United States was the world's leader in railroad construction, having built more miles of track than any other country. Yet the United States still needed additional tracks, particularly in the West, and British investors were eager to help finance the expansion. British railroad entrepreneur Samuel Morton Peto toured the country in 1865 to examine the existing railroad "system" and assess future investment opportunities in American railroads. Peto took an active role in railroad construction in Great Britain, Canada, Australia, France, and Germany, so his evaluation was both authoritative and influential. His book, *The Resources and Prospects of America,* published after his tour and excerpted below, is an excellent commentary on the strengths and weaknesses of American railroads.

Questions to Consider: According to Peto, who invests in the railroads and for what purpose? What does Peto believe are the problems with American railroads? What is his overall assessment of American railroads for potential British investors?

The system . . . on which railroads have been permitted to be constructed in America has been one of great simplicity. . . . In America . . . every one in the country has, felt from the first . . . that the construction of a railroad through his property, or to the city, town, or village he inhabited, was a source of prosperity and wealth, not only to the district in which he resided, but to himself personally. . . .

As a rule, nothing has been easier than to obtain from the legislative authority of a State in America a concession, or as it is there styled, a "charter," to lay down a road. The land in many cases, especially where it belonged to the public, has been freely given the line; in other cases, where landed proprietors were affected, comparatively small compensation have sufficed to satisfy their claims. The citizens residing in the towns and populous places of the different districts, have hailed the approach of a railroad as a blessing. Under certain regulations, lines have been permitted to be laid down in the main streets and thoroughfares of the cities, so that the trains may traverse them at prescribed speeds, and so that goods may be put upon trucks at the very doors of the warehouses and shops.

The influence of railroads on the value of real estates along their lines, and in the cities in which they terminate, is so well understood in America, as to have afforded important financial facilities to their construction. It is not the public who are invited in America to take railway shares; they are subscribed for in a wholly different manner. In order to promote the construction of a line, not only does the State which it traverses frequently afford it facilities with respect to land, but pecu-

---

Sir Samuel Morton Peto, *Resources and Prospects of America* (New York, 1869), 255-265.

niary facilities are often given by the cities and towns giving securities for certain amounts on their Municipal Bonds. The cities in which it is to have its termini also agree to subscribe for portions of its share capital, and so do the inhabitants of the towns and villages through which it is to pass. This is a very important feature of the American railway system, inasmuch as it gives the inhabitants of each district which a railway traverses, a direct local and individual interest in the promotion and well-working of the line. Every one, in fact, is interested in contributing to his own railway.

Not only the whole cost of maintaining the roads, but a very considerable proportion of the cost of their construction, has, in the case of the majority of the lines in America, been thrown upon revenue. I am afraid that the consequence of this has been injurious to public confidence in the American railways as commercial securities. Where lines are imperfectly constructed in the first instance—where they have to bear all the effects of climate and of wear and tear, whilst in indifferent condition, it is quite obvious that the cost of reparations, even in the very early stages of their working, must be a serious burden. And where all this is thrown, at once, on revenue, adequate dividends cannot be expected. . . .

Most of the American lines were originally made in short lengths, as lines of communication between different towns in the same State; and without regard to any general system of communication for the nation. It follows, that even in the cases of lines which are now united and brought under a single management, much diversity of construction, and a great want of unity of system is observable. One of the great deficiencies of the American railroad system is, in fact, the absence of a general policy of management. Scarcely any attempts are made to render the working of lines convenient to travellers, by working the trains of one company in conjunction with another; and this gives rise to complaints on the part of the public, which may, some day or other, be made to afford a ground of excuse for governmental interference. Nothing can be more desirable for the success of American railroad enterprises than well-considered general arrangements for the working and interchange of traffic.

Remarkable as has been the rapidity with which the American railroads have been constructed, and great as is the total mileage already made, the railroad accommodation of the United States is not to be regarded as by any means meeting the requirements of the country. The rapid growth of the system has only been co-equal with the rapid growth of the population: the extent of mileage is attributable to the vast extent of territory settled, and the great distances between the seats of population.

In many parts of the States, indeed, the existing railways are quite insufficient. In the South, the system is very imperfectly developed. Whilst slaves existed, there was a determined hostility in the Southern States to the expansion of any general railway system, arising from the apprehension that it would be used for the escape of slaves. . . .

From West to East, also, the present railways are quite insufficient for the growing traffic. The lines of communication from the West by canal, &c., which existed previously to railways, have not been affected by their construction. The produce of the Western States has, in fact, increased faster than the means of transport, and additional facilities for the conveyance of goods are urgently required. It is of the utmost importance to the development of the West that no time should be lost in making this additional provision.

_·_ _·_

14

THE IMPACT OF MECHANIZATION (1889)

The rapid adaptation of machinery for mass production created significant transformations in the American economy in the post-Civil War period. The author of the excerpt below, David A. Wells, realized the consequences of the machine age for both the business community and society. His background as an inventor, publisher of scientific information, political activist, and an economist, who advised Presidents Lincoln, Garfield, and Grant on business and currency matters, gave Wells a unique perspective to observe the technological changes taking place and analyze their implications. In his book *Recent Economic Changes,* Wells offered a commentary on the growing size of businesses and how that affected the nature of enterprise. Wells was also among the first economists to recognize that machines displaced workers—creating "technological unemployment"—and that business was changing American society. His observations indicate that both business and society were adjusting to the technological progress of the time.

Questions to Consider: What does David A. Wells consider as important changes in business after the Civil War? How had the role of employees changed? What did Wells consider to be the most revolutionary aspect of modern business? Why? Compare Wells' description of work conditions with those presented in "Child Labor in Alabama Cotton Mills" (Document 19).

Machinery is now recognized as essential to cheap production. Nobody can produce effectively and economically without it, and what was formerly known as domestic manufacture is now almost obsolete. But machinery is one of the most expensive of all products, and its extensive purchase and use require an amount of capital far beyond the capacity of the ordinary individual to furnish. There are very few men in the world possessed of an amount of wealth sufficient to individually construct and own an extensive line of railway or telegraph, a first-class steamship, or a great factory. It is also to be remembered that, for carrying on production by the most modern and effective methods, large capital is needed, not only for machinery but also for the purchasing and carrying of extensive stocks of crude material and finished products. . . .

. . . Hence, from such conditions have grown up great corporations or stock companies, which are only forms of associated capital organized for effective use

---

David A. Wells, *Recent Economic Changes* (New York, 1889), 91–94, 98, 109, 111.

and protection. They are regarded to some extent as evils; but they are necessary, as there is apparently no other way in which the work of production and distribution, in accordance with the requirements of the age, can be prosecuted. The rapidity, however, with which such combinations of capital are organizing for the purpose of promoting industrial and commercial undertakings on a scale heretofore wholly unprecedented, and the tendency they have to crystalize into something far more complex than what has been familiar to the public as corporations, with the impressive names of syndicates, trusts, etc., also constitute one of the remarkable features of modern business methods. It must also be admitted that the whole tendency of recent economic development is in the direction of limiting the area within which the influence of competition is effective.

And when once a great association of capital has been effected, it becomes necessary to have a mastermind to manage it—a man who is competent to use and direct other men, who is fertile in expedient and quick to note and profit by any improvements in methods of production and variations in prices. Such a man is a general of industry, and corresponds in position and functions to the general of an army.

What, as a consequence, has happened to the employees? Coincident with and as a result of this change in the methods of production, the modern manufacturing system has been brought into a condition analogous to that of a military organization, in which the individual no longer works as independently as formerly, but as a private in the ranks, obeying orders, keeping step, as it were, to the tap of the drum, and having nothing to say as to the plan of his work, of its final completion, or of its ultimate use and distribution. In short, the people who work in the modern factory are, as a rule, taught to do one thing—to perform one, and generally a simple, operation; and when there is no more of that kind of work to do, they are in a measure helpless. The result has been that the individualism or independence of the producer in manufacturing has been in a great degree destroyed, and with it has also in a great degree been destroyed the pride which the workman formerly took in his work—that fertility of resource which formerly was a special characteristic of American workmen, and that element of skill that comes from long and varied practice and reflection and responsibility. Not many years ago every shoemaker was or could be his own employer. The boots and shoes passed directly from an individual producer to the consumer. Now this condition of things has passed away. Boots and shoes are made in large factories; and machinery has been so utilized, and the division of labor in connection with it has been carried to such an extent, that the process of making a shoe is said to be divided into sixty-four parts, or the shoemaker of to-day is only the sixty-fourth part of what a shoemaker once was. . . .

Another exceedingly interesting and developing feature of the new situation is that, as machinery has destroyed the handicrafts and associated capital has placed individual capital at a disadvantage, so machinery and associated capital in turn, guided by the same common influences, now war upon machinery and other associated capital. Thus the now well-ascertained and accepted fact, based on long experience, that power is most economically applied when applied on the largest possible scale, is rapidly and inevitably leading to the concentration of manufacturing in the largest establishments and the gradual extinction of those which are small. . . .

In the great beef slaughtering and packing establishments at Chicago, which slaughter 1,000 head of cattle and upward in a day, economies are effected which are not possible when this industry is carried on, as usual, upon a very small scale. Every part of the animal—hide, horns, hoofs, bones, blood and hair—which in the hands of the ordinary butcher are of little value or a dead loss, are turned to a profit by the Chicago packers in the manufacture of glue, bone dust, fertilizers, etc.; and accordingly the great packers can afford to and do pay more for cattle than would otherwise be possible—an advance estimated by the best authorities at $2 a head. Nor does this increased price which Western stock-growers receive come out of the consumer of beef. It is made possible only by converting the portions of an ox that would otherwise be sheer waste into products of value. . . .

The same influences have also to a great degree revolutionized the nature of retail trade. . . . Experience has shown that, under a good organization of clerks, shopmen, porters, and distributors, it costs much less proportionally to sell a large amount of goods than a small amount; and that the buyer of large quantities can, without sacrifice of satisfactory profit, afford to offer to his retail customers such advantages in respect to prices and range of selection as almost to preclude competition on the part of dealers operating on a smaller scale, no matter how otherwise capable, honest, and diligent they may be. The various retail trades in the cities and larger towns of all civilized countries are accordingly being rapidly superseded by vast and skillfully organized establishments . . . which can sell at little over wholesale prices a great variety of merchandise, dry goods, manufactures of leather, books, stationery, furs, ready-made clothing, hats and caps, and sometimes groceries and hardware, and at the same time give their customers far greater conveniences than can be offered by the ordinary shopkeeper or tradesman. . . .

From these specimen experiences it is clear that an almost total revolution has taken place, and is yet in progress, in every branch and in every relation of the world's industrial and commercial system. Some of these changes have been eminently destructive, and all of them have inevitably occasioned, and for a long time yet will continue to occasion, great disturbances in old methods and entail losses of capital and changes of occupation on the part of individuals. . . .

—————

15

"EDISON'S ELECTRIC LIGHT" (1882)

The development of new technologies and inventions that were applicable to business activities spurred the post-Civil War Industrial Revolution. The Bessemer process in steel, the telephone, and the refining of petroleum are just

—————

"Edison's Electric Light," *The New York Times*, 5 September 1882, 8.

some examples of this inventiveness. The business of invention, then, played a significant role in the industrial expansion. Chief among all inventors was Thomas A. Edison, who was widely recognized at the time for his "genius" (he holds 1,093 patents). Born in Ohio in 1847 and educated by his mother, his early inventions were labor-saving devices for telegraphs, but his greatest contribution was in electrical lighting. In 1879, he perfected the incandescent bulb and made it commercially practical. Edison also developed the complex system needed to generate electrical power and distribute it to each bulb. He introduced his lighting system to lower Manhattan in 1882; the Pearl Street Station generated electricity, and most of the financial district (including the Stock Exchange, the home of J. Pierpont Morgan, and two newspapers) was wired for lights. Excerpted below is *The New York Times* report of the light bulb and its first day in commercial use.

·— **Questions to Consider:** According to *The New York Times* article, why would Edison's light replace gas fixtures? Has electric lighting changed since Edison's initial installation? How did the electric light revolutionize business and people's lives at home?

E dison's central station, at No. 257 Pearl Street, was yesterday one of the busiest places down town, and Mr. Edison was by far the busiest man in the station. The giant dynamos were started up at 3 o'clock in the afternoon, and, according to Mr. Edison, they will go on forever unless stopped by an earthquake. One-third of the lower district was lighted up, the territory being within the boundaries of Nassau and Pearl streets and Spruce and Wall streets. During the past few weeks the Edison Electric Illuminating Company has been engaged in completing the installations in the presence of its customers by the insertion of meters and lamps. . . .

Yesterday for the first time *The Times* Building was illuminated by electricity. Mr. Edison had at last perfected his incandescent light, had put his machinery in order, and had started up his engines, and last evening his company lighted up about one-third of the lower City district in which *The Times* building stands. The light came on in sections. First there came a series of holes in the floors and walls, then several miles of protected wires, then a transparent little egg-shaped glass globe, and, last of all, the fixtures and ground glass shades that made everything complete. They were temporary fixtures to give the light a trial, and so were put in with as little tearing and cutting as possible. To each of the gas fixtures in the establishment a bronze arm was attached, and the electric lamps were suspended from the ends of these arms. The lamp is simplicity itself. At the top is a brass circle, from which are suspended the shade and the lamp proper. The latter is a glass globe about four inches long, and the shape of a dropping tear, broad at the bottom, narrow in the neck, in which is inclosed the carbon horseshoe that gives the light. The globe is air-tight, and the air has been exhausted, leaving the carbon horseshoe in a perfect vacuum. When the thumbscrew is turned, and the connection with the electric wires is thus formed, the electric current makes the carbon so brilliant that it would be unpleasant to look at. It is not intended to be looked at, however, being entirely hidden by the ground glass shade. The whole lamp looks so much like a gas-burner surmounted by a shade that nine people out of ten would not have known the rooms were lighted by electricity, except that this light was more brilliant than gas and a hundred times steadier. To turn on the light nothing is required but to turn the thumbscrew; no matches are needed, no patent appliances. As soon as it is dark enough to need artificial light, you turn the thumbscrew and the light is there, with no nauseous smell, no flicker and no glare.

It was about five o'clock yesterday afternoon when the lights were put in operation. It was then broad daylight, and the light looked dim. It was not until about 7 o'clock, when it began to grow dark, that the electric light really made itself known and showed how bright and steady it is. Then the 27 electric lamps in the editorial rooms and the 25 lamps in the counting-rooms made those departments as bright as day, but without any unpleasant glare. It was a light that a man could sit down under for hours without the consciousness of having any artificial light about him. There was a very slight amount of heat from each lamp, but not nearly as much as from a gas-burner—one-fifteenth as much as from gas, the inventor says. The light was soft, mellow and grateful to the eye, and it seemed almost like writing by daylight to have a light without a particle of flicker and with scarcely any heat to make the head ache. The electric lamps in The Times Building were as thoroughly tested last evening, and tested by men who have battered their eyes sufficiently by years of night work to know the good and bad points of the lamp, and the decision was unanimously in favor of the Edison electric lamp as against gas. One night is a brief period in which to judge of the merits or demerits of a new system of lighting, but so far as it has been tested in The Times office the Edison electric light has proved in every way satisfactory. When the composing-rooms, the press-rooms, and the other parts of The Times Building are provided with these lamps there will be from 300 to 400 of them in operation in the building—enough to make every corner of it as bright as day.

16

THE SUCCESS OF STANDARD OIL (1899)

The early petroleum industry was filled with chaotic inefficiency and fierce competition between numerous refiners. John D. Rockefeller and his associates transformed this business into a stable and orderly enterprise, with their company, Standard Oil, dominating the industry. Forming the Standard Oil Trust (the first of its kind) in 1882 to permit legal ownership of companies in several states and

U.S. Congress, Industrial Commission, "John D. Rockefeller, Answers to Interrogatories," *Reports of the Industrial Commission: Vol. 2. Hearings before the Industrial Commission* (Washington, DC, 1900), 794-797.

to allow continued consolidation of his enterprise, Rockefeller came to control about 90 percent of the petroleum industry. In 1900, its net profit was $55.5 million. Naturally, the success of the Standard Oil Trust led other businessmen to use the trust to create monopolies within certain industries (sugar and tobacco, for example), and the term "trust" became synonymous with monopoly. Alarmed at the growth and economic influence of trusts, Congress formed the Industrial Commission in 1898 to investigate. While many businessmen testified before this body, Rockefeller's business tactics and Standard Oil were particularly scrutinized. Excerpted below is part of Rockefeller's response to questions about Standard Oil's success.

·⁓ **Questions to Consider:** How did the rebate policy of the railroads help Standard Oil? According to John D. Rockefeller, how did Standard Oil become successful? Why does Rockefeller believe "combinations" are a necessity for American business prosperity?

3. Q. Did the Standard Oil Company or other affiliated interests at any time before 1887 receive from the railroads rebates on freight shipped, or other special advantages?—A. The Standard Oil Company of Ohio, of which I was president, did receive rebates from the railroads prior to 1880, but received no special advantages for which it did not give full compensation. The reason for rebates was that such was the railroad's method of business. A public rate was made and collected by the railway companies, but so far as my knowledge extends, was never really retained in full, a portion of it was repaid to the shippers as a rebate. By this method the real rate of freight which any shipper paid was not known by his competitors nor by the other railway companies, the amount being in all cases a matter of bargain with the carrying company. Each shipper made the best bargain he could, but whether he was doing better than his competitor was only a matter of conjecture. Much depended upon whether the shipper had the advantage of competition of carriers. The Standard Oil Company of Ohio, being situated at Cleveland, had the advantage of different carrying lines, as well as water transportation in the summer, and taking advantage of those facilities made the best bargains possible for its freights. All other companies did the same, their success depending largely upon whether they had the choice of more than one route. The Standard sought also to offer advantages to the railways of the purpose of lessening rates of freight. It offered freights in large quantity carloads and trainloads. It furnished loading facilities and discharging facilities. It exempted railways from liability for fire. For these services it obtained contracts for special allowances on freights. These never exceeded, to the best of my present recollections, 10 per cent. But in almost every instance it was discovered subsequently that our competitors had been obtaining as good, and, in some instances, better rates of freight than ourselves. . . .

9. Q. To what advantages, or favors, or methods of management do you ascribe chiefly the success of the Standard Oil Company?—A. I ascribe the suc-

cess of the Standard to its consistent policy to make the volume of its business large through the merits and cheapness of its products. It has spared no expense in finding, securing, and utilizing the best and cheapest methods of manufacture. It has sought for the best superintendents and workmen and paid the best wages. It has not hesitated to sacrifice old machinery and old plants for new and better ones. It has placed its manufactories at the points where they could supply markets at the least expense. It has not only sought markets for its principal products, but for all possible by-products, sparing no expense in introducing them to the public. It has not hesitated to invest millions of dollars in methods for cheapening the gathering and distribution of oils by pipe lines, special cars, tank steamers, and tank wagons. It has erected tank stations at every important railroad station to cheapen the storage and delivery of its products. It has spared no expense in forcing its products into the markets of the world among people civilized and uncivilized. It has had faith in American oil, and has brought together millions of money for the purpose of making it what it is, and holding its market against the competition of Russia and all the many countries which are producers of oil and competitors against American oil. . . .

It is too late to argue about advantages of industrial combinations. They are a necessity. And if Americans are to have the privilege of extending their business in all the States of the Union, and into foreign countries as well, they are a necessity on a large scale, and require the agency of more than one corporation. . . .

I speak from my experience in the business with which I have been intimately connected for about 40 years. Our first combination was a partnership and afterwards a corporation in Ohio. That was sufficient for a local refining business. But dependent solely upon local business we should have failed long ago. We were forced to extend our markets and to seek for export trade. This latter made the seaboard cities a necessary place of business, and we soon discovered that manufacturing for export could be more economically carried on at the seaboard, hence refineries at Brooklyn, at Bayonne, at Philadelphia, and necessary corporations in New York, New Jersey, and Pennsylvania.

We soon discovered as the business grew that the primary method of transporting oil in barrels could not last. The package often cost more than the contents, and the forests of the country were not sufficient to supply the necessary material for an extended length of time, hence we devoted attention to other methods of transportation, adopted the pipe-line system, and found capital for pipe-line construction equal to the necessities of the business.

To operate pipe-lines required franchises from the States in which they were located and consequently corporations in those States, just as railroads running through different States are forced to operate under separate State charters. To perfect the pipe-line system of transportation required in the neighborhood of fifty millions of capital. This could not be obtained or maintained without industrial combination. The entire oil business is dependent upon this pipe-line system. Without it every well would shut down and every foreign market would be closed to us. . . .

I have given a picture rather than a detail of the growth of one industrial combination. It is a pioneer, and its work has been of incalculable value. There are other American products besides oil for which the markets of the world can be opened, and legislators will be blind to our best industrial interests if they unduly hinder by legislation the combination of persons and capital requisite for the attainment of so desirable an end.

11. Q. What are the chief disadvantages or dangers to the public arising from them?—A. The dangers are that the power conferred by combination may be abused; that combinations may be formed for speculation in stocks rather than for conducting business, and that for this purpose prices may be temporarily raised instead of being lowered. These abuses are possible to a greater or less extent in all combinations, large or small, but this fact is no more of an argument against combinations than the fact that steam may explode is an argument against steam. Steam is necessary and can be used comparatively safe. Combination is necessary and its abuses can be minimized; otherwise our legislators must acknowledge their incapacity to deal with the most important instrument of industry. Hitherto most legislative attempts have been an effort not to control but to destroy; hence their futility.

17

THE GOSPEL OF WEALTH (1889)

A new intellectual tenet—social Darwinism—helped justify the position of wealthy businessmen while simultaneously explaining poverty, misery, and unemployment. Social Darwinists, led by Englishman Herbert Spencer, who coined the term "survival of the fittest," broadened the theory of evolution to include all phenomena, especially society. Spencer argued that industrial leaders were products of natural selection; the best prospered while the unfit fell by the wayside. Any attempt to criticize or limit these survivors was contrary to natural law, and those less fortunate were the price modern society had to pay for progress. Andrew Carnegie, who amassed a fortune from the steel industry and was one of the few immigrant "rags to riches" examples of the era, understood that social Darwinism could weaken democratic ideals. He published "Wealth," excerpted next, in the prominent journal *North American Review* in an effort to encourage businessmen to properly administer their wealth. Carnegie set the example and followed his "Gospel of Wealth" until the day he died.

·⁀ **Questions to Consider:** How does Andrew Carnegie justify the contrast between the wealthy and the working poor? What does Carnegie believe is the "proper administration of wealth"? Why does he believe it is the best? Is it the best way to administer wealth? Is Carnegie a social Darwinist?

Andrew Carnegie, "Wealth," *North American Review* 148 (1889): 653-64.

The problem of our age is the proper administration of wealth, so that the ties of brotherhood may still bind together the rich and poor in harmonious relationship. The conditions of human life have not only been changed, but revolutionized, within the past few hundred years. . . . The contrast between the palace of the millionaire and the cottage of the laborer with us to-day measures the change which has come with civilization. . . .

This change, however, is not to be deplored, but welcomed as highly beneficial. It is well, nay, essential for the progress of the race, that the houses of some should be homes for all that is highest and best in literature and the arts, and for all the refinements of civilization, rather than that none should be so. Much better this great irregularity than universal squalor. . . .

The price which society pays for the law of competition, like the price it pays for cheap comforts and luxuries, is also great; but the advantages of this law are also greater still, for it is to this law that we owe our wonderful material development, which brings improved conditions in its train. But . . . [while] the law may be sometimes hard for the individual, it is best for the race, because it insures the survival of the fittest in every department. We accept and welcome, therefore, as conditions to which we must accommodate ourselves, great inequality of environment, the concentration of business, industrial and commercial, in the hands of a few, and the law of competition between these, as being not only beneficial, but essential for the future progress of the race. . . .

We start, then, with a condition of affairs under which the best interests of the race are promoted, but which inevitably gives wealth to the few. Thus far, accepting conditions as they exist, the situations can be surveyed and pronounced good. The question then arises, . . . What is the proper mode of administering wealth after the laws upon which civilization is founded have thrown it into the hands of the few? . . .

There are but three modes in which surplus wealth can be disposed of. It can be left to the families of the decedents; or it can be bequeathed for public purposes; or, finally, it can be administered during their lives by its possessors. Under the first and second modes most of the wealth of the world that has reached the few has hitherto been applied. Let us in turn consider each of these modes. The first is the most injudicious. In monarchical countries, the estates and the greatest portion of the wealth are left to the first son, that the vanity of the parent may be gratified by the thought that his name and title are to descend to succeeding generations unimpaired. The condition of this class in Europe to-day teaches the futility of such hopes or ambitions. The successors have become impoverished through their follies or from the fall in the value of land. . . .

As to the second mode, that of leaving wealth at death for public uses, it may be said that this is only a means for the disposal of wealth, provided a man is content to wait until he is dead before it becomes of much good in the world. Knowledge of the results of legacies bequeathed is not calculated to inspire the brightest hopes of much posthumous good being accomplished. The cases are not few in which the real object sought by the testator is attained, nor are they few in which his real wishes are thwarted. In many cases the bequests are so used as to become only monuments of his folly. . . .

There remains, then, only one mode of using great fortunes; but in this we have the true antidote for the temporary unequal distribution of wealth, the reconciliation of the rich and the poor—a reign of harmony—another ideal, differing, indeed, from that of the communist in requiring only the further evolution of existing conditions, not the total overthrow of our civilization. It is founded upon the present most intense individualism, and the race is prepared to put it in practice by degrees whenever it pleases. Under its sway we shall have an ideal state, in which the surplus wealth of the few will become, in the best sense, the property of the many, because administered for the common good, and this wealth, passing through the hands of a few, can be made a much more potent force for the elevation of our race than if it had been distributed in small sums to the people themselves. . . .

This, then, is held to be the duty of the man of Wealth: First, to set an example of modest, unostentatious living, shunning display or extravagance; to provide moderately for the legitimate wants of those dependent upon him; and after doing so to consider all surplus revenues which come to him simply as trust funds, which he is called upon to administer, and strictly bound as a matter of duty to administer in the manner which, in his judgment, is best calculated to produce the most beneficial results for the community—the man of wealth thus becoming the mere agent and trustee for his poorer brethren, bringing to their service his superior wisdom, experience, and ability to administer, doing for them better than they would or could do for themselves. . . .

In bestowing charity, the main consideration should be to help those who will help themselves; to provide part of the means by which those who desire to improve may do so; to give those who desire to rise the aids by which they may rise; to assist, but rarely or never to do all. Neither the individual nor the race is improved by alms-giving. . . . He is the only true reformer who is as careful and as anxious not to aid the unworthy as he is to aid the worthy, and, perhaps, even more so, for in alms-giving more injury is probably done by rewarding vice than by relieving virtue. . . .

Thus is the problem of Rich and Poor to be solved. The laws of accumulation will be left free; the laws of distribution free. Individualism will continue, but the millionaire will be but a trustee for the poor; intrusted for a season with a great part of the increased wealth of the community, but administering it for the community far better than it could or would have done for itself. The best minds will thus have reached a stage in the development of the race in which it is clearly seen that there is no mode of disposing of surplus wealth creditable to thoughtful and earnest men into whose hands it flows save by using it year by year for the general good. This day already dawns. . . yet the man who dies leaving behind him millions of available wealth, which was his to administer during life, will pass away "unwept, unhonored, and unsung," no matter to what uses he leaves the dross which he cannot take with him. Of such as these the public verdict will then be: "The man who dies thus rich dies disgraced."

Such, in my opinion, is the true gospel concerning Wealth, obedience to which is destined some day to solve the problem of the Rich and the Poor, and to bring "Peace on earth, among men Good-Will."

18

MRS. VANDERBILT'S GREAT FANCY DRESS BALL
(1883)

The prosperous businessmen of the Gilded Age acquired unprecedented wealth. While the American people denounced these "Robber Barons" because of their seemingly ruthless and manipulative control over others, there was also widespread fascination with their lives, a certain awe of their abilities and wealth. These businessmen and their families became the American nobility: watched, envied, idolized, loathed from below. Although they made financial commitments to philanthropic efforts (schools, libraries, museums), these elites flaunted their opulence with ostentatious displays—such as extravagantly decorated mansions, lavish summer homes, rare art collections, and large wine cellars—in an effort to outclass other wealthy families. But it was the great social gatherings that attracted the most attention, as some wealthy families competed to host the most spectacular reception in their home. One of the most grandiose social functions of the era was the costume ball of Mr. and Mrs. William K. Vanderbilt, held in 1883 in their French chateau on New York's Fifth Avenue at a cost of $75,000. Excerpted below is *The New York Times'* front-page story of this event.

———

·͢ **Questions to Consider:** Was the tone of this article sarcastic or in awe? Why does the author provide detailed descriptions of the Vanderbilt home and certain costumes? Are there similar events in "our time"?

———

The Vanderbilt Ball has agitated New York society more than any social event that has occurred here in many years. Since the announcement that it would take place, which was made about a week before the beginning of Lent, scarcely anything else has been talked about. It has been on every tongue and a fixed idea in every head. It has disturbed the sleep and occupied the waking hours of social butterflies, both male and female, for over six weeks. . . . Invitations have, of course, been in great demand, and in all about 1,200 were issued. . . .

The scene outside the brilliantly lighted mansion, as the guests began to arrive, was novel and interesting. Early in the evening a squad of police officers arrived to keep the expected crowd of sightseers in order and to direct the movements of drivers and cabmen. Before 10 o'clock men and women were wandering about the streets outside of the house and glancing at the windows, or peering under the double canopies which led up to the door. . . . At 11 o'clock the maskers began to arrive in numbers, and the eager on-lookers in the street were able to catch glimpses through the windows of flashing sword-hilts, gay costumes, beautiful flowers, and excited faces. Handsome women and dignified men were assisted from the carriage in their fanciful costumes over which were thrown shawls, ulsters, and other light wraps. Pretty and excited girls and young men who made

———

"All Society in Costume," *The New York Times*, 27 March 1883, 1.

desperate efforts to appear blase, were seen to descend and run up the steps into the brilliantly lighted hall. . . . At 11:30 o'clock the throng of carriages before the mansion and waiting at the corners was so great that the utmost efforts of the Police were necessary to keep the line in order, and many gentlemen left their carriages in adjacent streets and walked up to the canopy which was the entrance to the fairyland. Most of the gentlemen gave orders to their coachmen to call for them at 3 o'clock. Others made the hour as late as 4, and some of the more seasoned and wiser party-goers ordered their carriages as early as 1 or 2 o'clock. The guests had all arrived, save a few stragglers, at midnight, and the crowd began to disperse. . . .

The guests on arriving found themselves in a grand hall about 65 feet long, 16 feet in height, and 20 feet in width. Under foot was a floor of polished and luminous Echallion stone, and above them a ceiling richly paneled in oak. Over a high wainscoting of Caen stone, richly carved, are antique Italian tapestries, beautifully worked by hand. Out of this hall to the right rises the grand stairway, which is not only the finest piece of work of its kind in this country, but one of the finest in the world. The stairway occupies a space 30 feet square, the whole structure of the stairway being of the finest Caen stone, carved with wonderful delicacy and vigor. It climbs by ample easy stages to a height of 50 feet, ending in a pendentive dome. . . .

Winding through the motley crowd of princes, monks, cavaliers, highlanders, queens, kings, dairy-maids, bull-fighters, knights, brigands, and nobles, the procession passed down the grand stairway and through the hall into a noble room on the front of the house in the style of Francois Prethier, 25 feet in width by 40 in length, wainscoted richly and heavily in carved French walnut and hung in dark red plush. Vast carved cabinets and an immense, deep fire-place give an air of antique grandeur to this room, from which the procession passed into a bright and charming salon of the style of Louis XV, 30 feet in width by 35 in length, wainscoted in oak and enriched with carved work and gilding. The whole wainscoting of this beautiful apartment was brought from a chateau in France. On the walls hang three French Gobelin tapestries a century old, but in the brilliance and freshness of their coloring seemingly the work of yesterday. . . . Thence the procession swept on into the grand dining-hall, converted last night into a ball-room, and the dancing began. . . .

Among the hundreds of striking and unique costumes but a few can possibly be noted. These, however, will convey some idea of the scene as it presented itself at midnight, when the hall, the grand stairway, and the spacious apartments were all thronged with animated groups enjoying the double pleasure of seeing and being seen.

Mrs. Vanderbilt's irreproachable taste was seen to perfection in her costume as a Venetian Princess. . . . The waist was of blue satin covered with gold embroidery—the dress was cut square in the neck, and the flowing sleeves were of transparent gold tissue. She wore a Venetian cap, covered with magnificent jewels, the most noticeable of these being a superb peacock in many colored gems.

Mr. W. K. Vanderbilt appeared as the Duke de Guise, wearing yellow silk tights, yellow and black trunks, a yellow doublet and a black velvet cloak embroidered with gold. . . . Mr. Cornelius Vanderbilt appeared as Louis XVI, in a *habit de cour* and breeches of fawn-colored brocade, . . . trimmed with real silver lace. . . . He wore a jabot and ruffles of lace and a diamond-hilted sword.

Mrs. Cornelius Vanderbilt appeared as the "Electric Light," in white satin trimmed with diamonds, and with a magnificent diamond head-dress. . . .

HOW THE OTHER
HALF LIVES

4

The same economic forces that created unprecedented fortunes had another side. The new, more capital-intensive industries prevented many from taking advantage of the emerging opportunities. With businesses determined to secure a profit and a government that refused to intervene, large numbers of Americans had increasingly less control over their lives, working longer hours in more dangerous jobs for low wages. The response of American workers varied, though many sought to change the system through collective action such as labor unions and political parties. The following documents provide a glimpse of some of the conditions these workers faced and also their responses.

19

CHILD LABOR IN ALABAMA COTTON MILLS (1908)

Women and children were an essential part of the labor force in the cotton textile mills of the South, even though they were blatantly exploited. Perhaps the best known champion of all workers was Mary Harris Jones, known as "Mother Jones." She devoted her entire life to improving labor conditions, but especially toiled to abolish child labor and to help women workers. The diminutive, white-haired woman was a brilliant public speaker, able to hold a crowd spellbound, then rouse them into a frenzy using humor that ranged from irony to sarcastic ridicule. She traveled the country to give speeches on behalf of workers, organized protest marches of women and children, pushed the unionization of coal miners, and always seemed to appear wherever labor troubles developed. Jones posed as a textile millworker in Alabama and several other states in the 1890s to investigate work conditions for women and children. In 1908, the *St. Louis Labor* asked Mother Jones to write an article describing changes in the Alabama cotton mills after her most recent trip to the state. Her article is excerpted below.

Questions to Consider: Is Mother Jones' label of "slaves" for the millworkers accurate? According to Mother Jones, what changes had taken place in the mills since her first visit? Why were women and children the labor force in Southern textile mills? Why would they continue to work in such conditions? How does Mother Jones' description of millwork compare to that presented in "The Impact of Mechanization" (Document 14)?

It had been thirteen years since I bid farewell to the workers in Alabama and went forth to other fields to fight their battles. I returned again in 1908 to see what they were doing for the welfare of their children. Governor Comer, being the chief star of the state, I went out to Avondale, on the outskirts of Birmingham, to take a glance at his slave pen. I found there somewhere between five and six hundred slaves. . . . Of all the God-cursed conditions that surround any gathering of slaves, or slave pen, Comer's mill district beats them all. As you look at them you immediately conclude they have been lashed too far, but they still have some spirit of revolt in them. They work all of thirteen hours a day. They are supposed to go in at 6 in the morning, but the machinery starts up soon after 5, and they have to be there. They are supposed to get 45 minutes for dinner, but the machinery starts up again after they are out for 20 minutes and they have to be at their post. When I was in Alabama, 13 years ago, they had no child labor law. Since then they passed a very lame one, so-called. They evade the law in this way: A child who has passed his or her twelfth year can take in his younger brothers or sisters from 6 years on and get them to work with him. They are not on the pay roll, but the pay for these little ones goes into the elder one's pay. So that when you look at the pay

---

Mother Jones, "Governor Comer's Alabama Cotton Mills," *St. Louis Labor,* 24 October 1908, 3.

roll you think this one child makes quite a good bit, when perhaps there is two or three younger than him under the lash. . . . One woman told me her mother had gone into that mill and worked and took her four children in with her. She said: "I have been in the mill since I was 4 years old. I am now 34." She looked to me as if she were 60. She had a kindly nature if treated right, but her whole life and spirit were crushed out beneath the iron wheels of Comer's greed. When you think of the little ones that this mother brings forth you can see that society is cursed with an abnormal human being. She knew nothing but the whiz of the machinery in the factory. . . . When in Alabama, 13 years ago, these women ran from four to five looms; today I find them running some 24 looms; and when you think of the high tension, when you think of the cruelty to their nerves, the glory of their lives are gone. The days when their labor was not a burden perhaps is over; now it is all a hot rush and worry and incessant sweat, as they scratch their bits of corn out of these hard days. Think of the picture of these young girls and children on their feet guiding that machinery for twelve or thirteen hours a day; running that machinery hour by hour. . . . It is hell, worse than hell. Think of these children standing in the midst of these spindles, every thread of which must be incessantly watched so that it may be instantly pieced together, in a hot room amid its roaring machinery, so loud that one can not hear another, no matter how close they are at hand. Amid the whizzing wheels and bands and switch racks that would snatch off a limb for one second's carelessness; all this in hot air so that in summer a great thirst scorches their throat, the weavers are encircled by 24 terrific looms in a steamed atmosphere which is even worse than hell. The method of communication used is as if they were dumb animals, because at any moment a rebellious shuttle may shoot forth and knock an eye out. A loose shirt may be seized by a wheel or a strap and then the horrors of the accident can be better imagined than told. Their mentality is dwarfed, and if they say a word the cruel boss, who is a scab, goes after them. They tell me that when they get thirsty they can not get enough water to drink. They are all victims of some ailment. They are never free from headache. Owing to the necessity of cleaning machinery, they do not eat at noon hour. The unpleasant odor coming from the oil and grease, the rumbling of shafts and drums, the squeaking of wheels and spindles make them sick and languorous. They rise at 4 o'clock in the morning to prepare to enter that slave pen at 5:30. They are all pale, dyspeptic, hollow-chested, and it seems as if life has no charms for them. They can not go and seek other employment because the energy has been all used up from childhood in their particular line of industry.

20

THE CREDIT SYSTEM OF THE SOUTH (1894)

The Civil War destroyed the slave-based, plantation system of the South and brought revolutionary economic adjustments for both white and black Americans. Many of the former slaves refused to work on the plantations as wage laborers (preferring to farm land independently), but the plantation owners retained possession of the land. A new labor arrangement emerged to serve both parties—

sharecropping. Many plantation owners broke up their estates into small tracts and permitted former slaves and poor whites to farm these lands in return for a "share" of the crop grown on the land. Since most sharecroppers were poor, they had to borrow seed, tools, food, clothing, and other necessities on credit from a local merchant, often using the pending fall harvest as a lien on the debt. This system of credit pervaded the South and became a standard for doing business. In the following selection, Charles H. Otken, a Mississippi Baptist minister and concerned observer of the South's economic plight, describes this credit system and its problems in his book *The Ills of the South.*

Questions to Consider: What does Charles H. Otken consider to be the problems with sharecropping in the South? How did this system of credit develop? Why is Otken so pessimistic about the economic future of the South? Are his reasons valid? Does this credit system help or hinder the sharecropper?

The business system prevailing with such hurtful and dangerous tendencies in the Southern States, is enslaving the people, and, by its insidious operations, concentrating productive wealth in the hands of the few. It reduces a large body of people to a state of beggary, fosters a discontented spirit, checks consumption, produces recklessness on the part of the consumer, places a discount on honesty, and converts commerce into a vast pawning shop where farmers pledge their lands for hominy and bacon upon ruinous terms in harmony with the pawning system. . . .

(1) This system is responsible for an indefiniteness as it respects the debtor, which amounts to tyranny. When A borrows a hundred dollars from B, he knows definitely the rate of interest he has agreed to pay B. The rate of interest is determined before the money is taken. By this method there is no such understanding. All the satisfaction the debtor can get is, he must pay certain prices. If the merchant has agreed to furnish him, it is sufficient for the farmer to know that he must pay these prices. Whether the prices are moderate, reasonable, unreasonable, exorbitant, or ruinous, does not concern the purchaser. It is a financial transaction which is clear as the noonday sun to one party, the creditor, and as dark as a starless night to the other party, the debtor. Would that this statement were fiction instead of a hard, ugly fact! The purchaser is enveloped in mists. He travels in the dark twelve months in the year. He does not know whether he pays forty or a hundred per cent. profit. This is a secret not to be divulged. . . .

(2) The debtor is bound to the creditor when once he has commenced to make a purchase. If he has incurred a debt with one merchant, he can not readily get credit from another merchant. The reason is obvious. The risk under the system is great. No merchant cares to take a customer who is already in debt to another. . . . The debt chains the farmer to the firm with whom he is trading. He can not buy where it suits him. . . .

Charles H. Otken, *The Ills of the South* (New York, 1894), 12, 15–25.

(3) Those who buy supplies under this system can not tell how much they have bought during the year until the cotton crop is delivered. It is believed to be true of 75 per cent. The only check to the making of purchases is upon the class of poor farmers whose property is small, and whose crop consists in a half-dozen bales of cotton. The limit is fixed at $50, $75, or $100. When merchandise to the amount agreed upon has been bought, a halt to further advances is called. The merchant may not be blamed for refusing to extend the credit beyond the value of the expectant crop. No such limit is fixed for the man whose real estate is large, and whose personal property in the form of horses, mules, and cattle is ample. . . . He kept no account of his purchases. In a vast number of cases, the bill, as it is commonly known, is called for in November and December of the year. The wail of merchants in January is generally, "We have large balances to carry over for next year." The size of the crop, the price of cotton, and the purchases made, determine the size and the number of balances. Few are the years that from 50 per cent. to 75 per cent. of the farmers who thus bought supplies did not come out in debt to their merchants at the close of the year. . . .

(4) The mode of doing business is the wicked foster-mother of much careless-ness is not the basis of prosperity. It may be business to some people, but it has a greedy heart. "I haven't had a settlement," said a farmer of ordinary intelligence, "in six years." "Do you ask your merchant to make out your account at the end of the year?" "No! I sometimes ask him how we stand; and when he says, 'You are all right,' I'm satisfied. I have done business with him for twenty years, and have never asked him for a bill." . . .

(5) When all the cotton made during the year has been delivered and sold, and the farmer comes out in debt on the 31st of December, that farmer has taken the first step toward bankruptcy. . . . Thus, or nearly thus, this system operates in thousands of cases. Each year the plunge into debt is deeper; each year the burden is heavier. The struggle is woe-begone. Cares are many, smiles are few, and the comforts of life are scantier. This is the bitter fruit of a method of doing business which comes to the farmer in the guise of friendship, but rules him with despotic power. . . .

(6) "A bad crop year, Mr. Tafton." "Mighty bad, mighty bad," replies Mr. Goff. "We are ruined. I reckon our merchants won't furnish us another year unless we give a mortgage on our land." . . . On some dreary cold day in Decem-ber, when nothing can well be done on the farm, these men ride to town, each to execute that hard instrument called a mortgage, which in so many cases means ruin to themselves and their families. These ugly handcuffs are hard to get off. . . .

(7) Thus it is that not a few farmers in the South who held a fee-simple title to their property, lost all in ten years. . . . There is a cause. It sleeps within the womb of this business arrangement. There must be an enormous abuse lurking some-where in these operations; it involves well-meaning and innocent men who keep no accounts, and, as a rule, apply no business principles to their farm work or their expenses, in hopeless poverty. Neither the merchants alone, as a class, nor the farmers alone, as a class, are to blame for this state of things; but the commercial contract, under whose articles they formed a joint copartnership to do business, deserves full and signal justice. . . .

These are some of the ugly features of this business method. It has done much to debauch public sentiment. It has enslaved thousands of good people. It has brought about a state of dependence that reduces the great body of agricultural people to a condition of serfs, the name excepted. It deserves serious consideration. The situation is alarming to free men. It is no small matter that 3,000,000 farmers should be dependent upon 10,000 men.

21

THE "LONG TURN" IN STEEL (1910)

The steel industry was an integral part of the Industrial Revolution in the United States, as it supplied essential materials to the railroads and later the auto industry. The techniques of steel production, however, changed little since the introduction of the Bessemer process and the open-hearth method in the 1860s. Steel mills relied almost exclusively on an unskilled male work force because the hours were long and the work physically demanding under the most severe conditions. Steelworkers were often recent immigrants to America and received relatively little pay. There was frequent turnover in the work force. Starting in 1907, several individuals conducted the "Pittsburgh Survey," an investigation that focused on the life and labor of steelworkers in and around Pittsburgh, Pennsylvania, the premier steel city in America. John A. Fitch was a part of this survey and wrote *The Steel Workers* based on his research of work in the mills. The selection below is his interview with a longtime steel worker and a description of the "long turn," a labor practice common throughout the industry.

———

- **Questions to Consider:** What happened to the work force in the mills? Why did this take place? What were the purposes of the Sunday "long turn"? Why did the steel industry maintain the seven-day work week?

———

John Griswold is a Scotch-Irish furnace boss who came to America and got a laborer's position at a Pittsburgh blast furnace when the common labor force was largely Irish. Those were the days before the advent of the "furriners." I sat in Griswold's sitting room in his four-room cottage one evening and he told me about the men who work at the furnaces, and about the "long turn."

"Mighty few men have stood what I have, I can tell you. I've been twenty years at the furnaces and been workin' a twelve-hour day all that time, seven days a week. We go to work at seven in the mornin' and we get through at night at six. We work that way for two weeks and then we get the long turn and change to the night shift of thirteen hours. The long turn is when we go on at seven Sunday mornin' and work up through the whole twenty-four hours up to Monday mornin'. That puts us onto the night turn for the next two weeks, and the other

John A. Fitch, *The Steel Workers* (New York, 1910), 11-12, 174-176.

crew onto the day. The next time they get the long turn and we get twenty-four hours off, but it don't do us much good. I get home at about half past seven Sunday mornin' and go to bed as soon as I've had breakfast. I get up at noon so as to get a bit o' Sunday to enjoy, but I'm tired and sleeps all the afternoon. Now, if we had eight hours it would be different. I'd start work, say, at six and I'd be done at two and I'd come home, and after dinner me and the missus could go to the park if we wanted to, or I could take the children to the country where there ain't any saloons. That's the danger,—the children runnin' on the streets and me with no time to take them any place else. That's what's driven the Irish out of the industry. It ain't the Hunkies,—they couldn't do it,—but the Irish don't have to work this way. There was fifty of them here with me sixteen years ago and now where are they? I meet 'em sometimes around the city, ridin' in carriages and all of them wearin' white shirts, and here I am with these Hunkies. They don't seem like men to me hardly. They can't talk United States. You tell them something and they just look at you and say 'Me no fustay, me no fustay,' that's all you can get out of 'em. And I'm here with them all the time, twelve hours a day and every day and I'm all alone,—not a mother's son of 'em that I can talk to. Everybody says I'm a fool to stay here,—I dunno, mebbe I am. It don't make so much difference though. I'm gettin' along, but I don't want the kids ever to work this way. I'm goin' to educate them so they won't have to work twelve hours." . . .

For other departments it was harder to make estimates, but the situation as regards Sunday work is by no means set forth when we have discussed blast furnaces and open-hearth plants. The heating furnaces are never allowed to grow cold. Whether the suspension be the ordinary one, from Saturday night to Sunday night, or whether it be a shut-down for many weeks, the fires are not allowed to go out, and men are on duty tending gas, changing the flame from one side of the furnace to the other. In the open-hearth department the second helpers take turns tending gas on Saturday nights. In the soaking-pits and the re-heating furnaces, either the heater or some of his assistants remain with the furnaces all through the period of suspension. Sometimes this involves a twenty-four-hour shift, and sometimes that is avoided, but Sunday work is inevitable. In 1907-8 Sunday was the repair day. Repairs were made through the week, but everything that could possibly wait was left until Sunday, so that no time might be lost in the mills, and so that the repair men might work without being endangered or impeded by moving machinery. The practice was not defended by some of the men in authority, but the efforts made to stop it were without practical result. In a normal year the steel mills are crowded with work. Sunday was, the year of my inquiry, a day for clearing up, for tardy departments to get even with swifter ones. Often the mills rolled out the finished product faster than the shears or the transportation department could take care of it. Then there was great activity of traveling cranes and narrow-gauge or dinkey engines, and when the rolling mills began again on Sunday evening everything was cleared away, and all departments were ready for another week. Whenever there was construction work of any sort it was customary for it to go on without interruption until it was finished. Loading cars and unloading them frequently continued on Sunday, and for all this work many laborers, crane men, engineers, firemen, millwrights and machinists, besides the regular mill watchmen, were on duty seven nights in the week. . . .

Added to and intensifying the evils of Sunday work is the "long turn" of twenty-four hours that comes every second week to 60 per cent of the blast furnace workers and to many others. This is involved in the variations referred to on a previous page. The men average seven working days a week by working six days one week and the next week eight. Every Sunday the shifts change about. The men on the night shift give place on Sunday morning to the men on the day shift, and these work through until Monday morning, a full twenty-four hours, so as to change to the night shift for the week succeeding, while the old night shift changes to the day. The men who get through Sunday morning have a twenty-four hour interval. Theoretically they have a day of rest, but they must choose between trying to take advantage of it without resting from a twelve hour night of work, or going to bed and waking, later, to find most of the precious day of freedom gone. . . .

22

PREAMBLE TO THE CONSTITUTION OF THE KNIGHTS OF LABOR (1878)

Faced with the growing size and complexity of business, small groups of skilled workers began to form labor organizations or societies to protect their jobs and gain a share of the wealth that business generated. Many of the early societies were secretive to protect against employer retaliation. Often these organizations were small, confined to certain industries, and usually they failed to achieve their goals. Among the earliest labor organizations that created a national following was the Knights of Labor. Begun as a secret trade union of tailors in Philadelphia in 1869, the Knights grew slowly until Terrence V. Powderly assumed the leadership in 1879. Powderly advocated including all workers—regardless of trade—and women and African Americans (though in separate locals) into the Knights. He also believed in arbitration of disputes and the use of boycotts, but opposed the use or threat of a strike when confronting business. Powderly, who served three terms as mayor of Scranton, Pennsylvania, while leading the Knights, assisted in writing the preamble to the constitution of the Knights of Labor, which is excerpted below.

Questions to Consider: The demands of the Knights of Labor reveal much about conditions for many laborers. What were some of the obstacles facing workers during this time period? What appear to be the key issues the Knights want addressed? How were these demands to be realized? Were these demands realized?

The recent alarming development and aggression of aggregated wealth, which, unless checked, will invariably lead to the pauperization and hopeless degradation of the toiling masses, render it imperative, if we desire to enjoy the blessings

---

Terrence V. Powderly, *Thirty Years of Labor* (Columbus, OH, 1889), 243-245.

of life, that a check should be placed upon its power and upon unjust accumulation, and a system adopted which will secure to the laborer the fruits of his toil; and as this much-desired object can only be accomplished by the thorough unification of labor, and the united efforts of those who obey the divine injunction that "In the sweat of thy brow shalt thou eat bread," we have formed the ★ ★ ★ ★ ★ with a view of securing the organization and direction, by co-operative effort, of the power of the industrial classes; and we submit to the world the object sought to be accomplished by our organization, calling upon all who believe in securing "the greatest good to the greatest number" to aid and assist us:

I. To bring within the folds of organization every department of productive industry, making knowledge a standpoint for action, and industrial and moral worth, not wealth, the true standard of individual and national greatness.

II. To secure to the toilers a proper share of the wealth that they create; more of the leisure that rightfully belongs to them; more societary advantages; more of the benefits, privileges, and emoluments of the world; in a word, all those rights and privileges necessary to make them capable of enjoying, appreciating, defending, and perpetuating the blessings of good government.

III. To arrive at the true condition of the producing masses in their educational, moral, and financial condition, by demanding from the various governments the establishment of bureaus of Labor Statistics.

IV. The establishment of co-operative institutions, productive and distributive.

V. The reserving of the public lands—the heritage of the people—for the actual settler;—not another acre for railroads or speculators.

VI. The abrogation of all laws that do not bear equally upon capital and labor, the removal of unjust technicalities, delays, and discriminations in the administration of justice, and the adopting of measures providing for the health and safety of those engaged in mining, manufacturing, or building pursuits.

VII. The enactment of laws to compel chartered corporations to pay their employes weekly, in full, for labor performed during the preceding week, in the lawful money of the country.

VIII. The enactment of laws giving mechanics and laborers a first lien on their work for their full wages.

IX. The abolishment of the contract system of national, State, and municipal work.

X. The substitution of arbitration for strikes, whenever and wherever employers and employes are willing to meet on equitable grounds.

XI. The prohibition of the employment of children in workshops, mines, and factories before attaining their fourteenth year.

XII. To abolish the system of letting out by contract the labor of convicts in our prisons and reformatory institutions.

XIII. To secure for both sexes equal pay for equal work.

XIV. The reduction of the hours of labor to eight per day, so that the laborers may have more time for social enjoyment and intellectual improvement, and be enabled to reap the advantages conferred by the labor saving machinery which their brains have created.

XV. To prevail upon governments to establish a purely national circulating medium based upon the faith and resources of the nation, and issued directly to the people, without the intervention of any system of banking corporations, which money shall be a legal tender in payment of all debts, public or private.

--- --- --- --- --- --- --- --- --- --- --- --- --- --- --- --- --- --- --- ---

23

LIFE IN THE TENEMENTS OF NEW YORK CITY
(1890)

In the post-Civil War period, cities swelled in population as a twin migration of immigrants and rural Americans flocked to the glittering urban environment hoping for a better life. For many, especially those lacking urban work skills, the city offered a difficult life amid squalid living conditions. While poor districts have always existed in urban areas, never had poverty affected so many people in America. Danish-born newspaper reporter Jacob Riis made millions aware of the urban slums. As a New York City police reporter, Riis frequently entered the tenement districts to gather evidence for his stories, but the wretched life of the people shocked him into writing vivid articles and later books about life in the tenement slums. Riis hoped that the depictions would result in urban housing reform. His first book, *How the Other Half Lives,* which is excerpted below, was widely read and gave many Americans their first description of life in the tenement slums of New York City.

Questions to Consider: According to Jacob Riis, what are some of the problems of tenement life in New York City? How did these conditions develop, and why did they persist? Could a reporter find similar conditions in American cities in the 1990s?

Be a little careful, please! The hall is dark and you might stumble over the children pitching pennies back there. Not that it would hurt them; kicks and cuffs are their daily diet. They have little else. Here where the hall turns and dives into utter darkness is a step, and another, another. A flight of stairs. You can feel your way, if you cannot see it. Close? Yes! What would you have? All the fresh air that ever enters these stairs comes from the hall-door that is forever slamming, and from the windows of dark bedrooms that in turn receive from the stairs their sole supply of the elements God meant to be free, but man deals out with such niggardly hand. That was a woman filling her pail by the hydrant you just bumped against. The sinks are in the hallway, that all the tenants may have access—and all be poisoned alike by their summer stenches. Hear the pump sweak! It is the lullaby of tenement-house babes. In summer, when a thousand thirsty throats pant for a cooling drink in this block, it is worked in vain. But the saloon, whose open door

---

Jacob A. Riis, *How the Other Half Lives* (New York, 1890), 33-34, 121-122, 124.

you passed in the hall, is always there. The smell of it has followed you up. Here is a door. Listen! That short hacking cough, that tiny, helpless wail—what do they mean? They mean that the soiled bow of white you saw on the door downstairs will have another story to tell—Oh! a sadly familiar story—before the day is at an end. The child is dying with measles. With half a chance it might have lived; but it had none. The dark bedroom killed it. . . .

In the dull content of life bred on the tenement-house dead level there is little to redeem it, or to calm apprehension for a society that has nothing better to offer its toilers; while the patient efforts of the lives finally attuned to it to render the situation tolerable, and the very success of these efforts, serve only to bring out in stronger contrast the general gloom of the picture by showing how much farther they might have gone with half a chance. Go into any of the "respectable" tenement neighborhoods—the fact that there are not more than two saloons on the corner, nor over three or four in the block will serve as a fair guide—where live the great body of hard-working Irish and German immigrants and their descendants, who accept naturally the conditions of tenement life, because for them there is nothing else in New York; be with the menagerie view that, if fed, they have no cause of complaint, you shall come away agreeing with me that, humanly speaking, life there does not seem worth the living. Take at random one of these uptown tenement blocks, not of the worst nor yet of the most prosperous kind, within hail of what the newspapers would call a "fine residential section." These houses were built since the last cholera scare made people willing to listen to reason. The block is not like the one over on the East Side in which I actually lost my way once. There were thirty or forty rear houses in the heart of it, three or four on every lot, set at all sorts of angles, with odd, winding passages, or no passage at all, only "runaways" for the thieves and toughs of the neighborhood. These yards are clear. There is air there, and it is about all there is. The view between brick walls outside is that of a stony street; inside, of rows of unpainted board fences, a bewildering maze of clothes-posts and lines; underfoot, a desert of brown, hard-baked soil from which every blade of grass, every stray weed, every speck of green, has been trodden out, as must inevitable be every gently thought and aspiration above the mere wants of the body in those whose moral natures such home surroundings are to nourish. In self-defense, you know, all life eventually accommodates itself to its environment, and human life is no exception. Within the house there is nothing to supply the want thus left unsatisfied. Tenement-houses have no aesthetic resources. If any are to be brought to bear on them, they must come from the outside. There is the common hall with doors opening softly on every landing as the strange step is heard on the stairs, the air-shaft that seem always so busy letting out foul stenches from below that it has no time to earn its name by bringing down fresh air, the squeaking pumps that hold no water, and the rent that is never less than one week's wages out of the four, quite as often half of the family earnings.

Why complete the sketch? It is drearily familiar already. Such as it is, it is the frame in which are set days, weeks, months, and years of unceasing toil, just able to fill the mouth and clothe the back. Such as it is, it is the world, and all of it, to which these weary workers return nightly to feed heart and brain after wearing out the body at the bench, or in the shop. . . .

With the first hot nights in June police despatches, that record the killing of men and women by rolling off roofs and window-sills while asleep, announce that the time of greatest suffering among the poor is at hand. It is in hot weather, when life indoors is well-nigh unbearable with cooking, sleeping, and working, all crowded into the small rooms together, that the tenement expands, reckless of all restraint. Then a strange and picturesque life moves upon the flat roofs. In the day and early evening mothers air their babies there, the boys fly their kites from the house-tops, undismayed by police regulations, and the young men and girls court and pass the growler. In the stifling July nights, when the big barracks are like fiery furnaces, their very walls giving out absorbed heat, men and women lie in restless, sweltering rows, panting for air and sleep. . . .

24

POPULIST PARTY PLATFORM (1892)

In the late 1880s, the American farmer increased agricultural production, yet plummeting prices and "middle-men" costs removed much of the anticipated profit; some farmers went bankrupt and were forced off their land. In response to these circumstances and disillusioned with both traditional parties, the People's party (Populist) was formed in 1892 to represent small producers—particularly farmers—against large corporations, the railroads, and banks. Labeling itself a party of reform, the People's party was a fusion of several agricultural groups, especially the Farmer's Alliance, which advocated a program to rectify agricultural problems while representing the interests of the common man. Adapting the earlier plan of the Farmer's Alliance, Ignatius Donnelly, a rabid Populist, drafted the Omaha Platform, which the People's party national convention, meeting in Omaha, Nebraska, accepted on July 4, 1892. The platform expressed Populist frustrations with the influence of big business while offering some remedies to correct the situation.

———

·⁓ **Questions to Consider:** How would the platform resolve agricultural problems and also provide for more democracy? What aspects of the platform are designed to attract votes from non-farmers? The Populist platform was considered radical in the 1890s. What are some of its more radical reforms? What happens to most of these reforms?

———

W hile our sympathies as a party of reform are naturally upon the side of every proposition which will tend to make men intelligent, virtuous, and temperate, we nevertheless regard these questions, important as they are, as secondary to the great issues now pressing for solution, and upon which not only our individual prosperity but the very existence of free institutions depend; and we ask all men to

---

"People's Party Platform," Omaha *Morning World-Herald*, 5 July 1892, 6.

first help us determine whether we are to have a republic to administer before we differ as to the conditions upon which it is to be administered, believing that the forces of reform this day organized will never cease to move forward until every wrong is remedied and equal rights and equal privileges securely established for all the men and women of this country.

We declare, therefore—

First—That the union of the labor forces of the United States this day consummated shall be permanent and perpetual; may its spirit enter into all hearts for the salvation of the Republic and the uplifting of mankind.

Second—Wealth belongs to him who creates it, and every dollar taken from industry without an equivalent is robbery. "If any will not work neither shall he eat." The interests of rural and civil labor are the same; their enemies are identical.

Third—We believe that the time has come when the railroad corporations will either own the people or the people must own the railroads; and should the government enter upon the work of owning and managing any and all railroads, we should favor an amendment to the constitution by which all persons engaged in the government service shall be placed under a civil service regulation of the most rigid character, so as to prevent the increase of power of the national administration by the use of such additional government employes.

We demand that national currency, safe, sound, and flexible, issued by the general government only, a full legal tender for all debts, public and private, and that without the use of banking corporations, a just, equitable, and efficient means of distribution direct to the people, at a tax not to exceed 2 per cent per annum, be provided, as set forth in the sub-treasury plan of the farmers' alliance, or some better system; also by payments in discharge of its obligations for public improvements.

We demand free and unlimited coinage of silver and gold at the present legal ratio of 16 to 1.

We demand that the amount of the circulating medium be speedily increased to not less than $50 per capita.

We demand a graduated income tax.

We believe that the money of the country should be kept as much as possible in the hands of the people, and hence we demand that all state and national revenues shall be limited to the necessary expenses of the government, economically and honestly administered.

We demand that postal savings banks be established by the government for the safe deposit of the earnings of the people and to facilitate exchange.

Transportation being a means of exchange and a public necessity, the government should own and operate the railroads in the interest of the people.

The telegraph and telephone, like the post office system, being a necessity for the transmission of news, should be owned and operated by the government in the interest of the people.

The land, including all the natural sources of wealth, is the heritage of the people, and should not be monopolized for speculative purposes, and alien ownership of land should be prohibited. All land now held by railroads and other corporations in excess of their actual needs, and all lands now owned by aliens should be reclaimed by the government and held for actual settlers only. . . .

Whereas, other questions have been presented for our consideration, we hereby submit the following, not as a part of the platform of the people's party, but as resolutions expressive of the sentiment of this convention.

First—Resolved, That we demand a free ballot and a fair count in all elections, and pledge ourselves to secure it to every legal voter without federal intervention, through the adoption by the states of the unperverted Australian or secret ballot system.

Second—Resolved, That the revenue derived from a graduated income tax should be applied to the reduction of the burden of taxation now levied upon the domestic industries of this country.

Third—Resolved, That we pledge our support to fair and liberal pensions to ex-union soldiers and sailors.

Fourth—Resolved, That we condemn the fallacy of protecting American labor under the present system, which opens our ports to the pauper and criminal classes of the world and crowds out our wage earners; and we denounce the present ineffective laws against contract labor, and demand the further restriction of undesirable emigration.

Fifth—Resolved, That we cordially sympathize with the efforts of organized workingmen to shorten the hours of labor, and demand a rigid enforcement of existing eight-hour law on government work, and ask that a penalty clause be added to the said law.

Sixth—Resolved, That we regard the maintenance of a large standing army of mercenaries, known as the Pinkerton system, as a menace to our liberties, and we demand its abolition; and we condemn the recent invasion of the territory of Wyoming by the hired assassins of plutocracy, assisted by federal officers.

Resolved, That we commend to the favorable consideration of the people, and the reform press the legislative system known as the initiative and referendum.

Resolved, That we favor a constitutional provision limiting the office of president and vice-president to one term, and providing for the election of senators of the United States by a direct vote of the people.

Resolved, That we oppose any subsidy or national aid to any private corporation for any purpose.

25

STATEMENT OF THE STRIKERS IN PULLMAN (1894)

George Pullman created a "model" industrial community—Pullman—outside Chicago to produce passenger cars for the railroads. When the Panic of 1893 struck and a depression followed, orders for the Pullman Palace Car dropped

U.S. Congress, Strike Commission, "Statement from the Pullman Strikers," *Report on the Chicago Strike of June-July, 1894* (Washington, DC, 1895), 87-91.

abruptly: Pullman began laying off workers and cutting wages for those who remained, while maintaining rent and public utility costs the workers paid to the company. In protest many workers joined the American Railway Union, which demanded that wages be restored to previous levels. But the company refused (saying the decline of business could not support it), and workers of a grievance committee were fired after meeting with company officials. Pullman workers went out on strike, then presented the following statement to the convention of the American Railway Union to help justify their action and seek the union's support. The union ordered a nationwide sympathy boycott of Pullman cars, leading the country into the most significant labor dispute of the era. When violence erupted and the mail was not delivered, the federal government intervened and used court injunctions based on the Sherman Antitrust Act to order union leaders to stop the strike. When they refused, they were arrested and the strike collapsed.

———

·⌐ **Questions to Consider:** Why did the Pullman workers go on strike? What are the workers' views of George Pullman? According to the strikers, how was Pullman able to make large profits despite the Panic of 1893? Why was this strike so significant to labor relations at the time?

———

Mr. President and brothers of the American Railway Union: We struck at Pullman because we were without hope. We joined the American Railway Union because it gave us a glimmer of hope. Twenty thousand souls, men, women, and little ones, have their eyes turned toward this convention today, straining eagerly through dark despondency for a glimmer of the heaven-sent message you alone can give us on this earth.

In stating to this body our grievance, it is hard to tell where to begin. You all must know that the proximate cause of our strike was the discharge of two members of our Grievance Committe the day after George M. Pullman, himself, and Thomas H. Wickes, his second vice president, had guaranteed them absolute immunity. The more remote causes are still imminent. Five reductions in wages, in work, and in conditions of employment swept through the shops at Pullman between May and December 1893. The last was the most severe, amounting to nearly 30 percent, and our rents had not fallen. We owed Pullman $70,000 when we struck May 11. We owe him twice as much today. He does not evict us for two reasons: one, the force of popular sentiment and public opinion; the other because he hopes to starve us out, to break through in the back of the American Railway Union, and to deduct from our miserable wages when we are forced to return to him the last dollar we owe him for the occupancy of his houses.

Rents all over the city in every quarter of its vast extent have fallen, in some cases to one-half. Residences, compared with which ours are hovels, can be had a few miles away at the prices we have been contributing to make a millionaire a billionaire. What we pay $15 for in Pullman is leased for $8 in Roseland; and remember that just as no man or woman of 4,000 toilers has ever felt the friendly pressure of George M. Pullman's hand, so no man or woman of us all has ever owned or can ever hope to own one inch of George M. Pullman's land. Why, even the very streets are his. His ground has never been platted of record, and today he may debar any man who has acquiring rights as his tenant from walking in his highways. And those streets; do you know what he has named them? He says after the four great inventors in methods of transportation. And do you know what their names are? Why, Fulton, Stephenson, Watt, and Pullman.

Water which Pullman buys from the city at 8 cents a gallon he retails to us at 500 percent advance and claims he is losing $400 a month on it. Gas which sells at 75 cents per thousand feet in Hyde Park, just north of us, he sells for $2.25. When we want to tell him our grievances, he said we were all his "children."

Pullman, both the man and the town, is an ulcer on the body politic. He owns the houses, the schoolhouses, and churches of God in a town he gave his once humble name. The revenue he derives from these, the wages he pays out with one hand—the Pullman Palace Car Company—he takes back with the other—the Pullman Land Association. He is able by this to bid under any contract car shop in this country. His competitors in business, to meet this, must reduce the wages of their men. This gives him the excuse to reduce ours to conform to the market. His business rivals must in turn scale down; so must he. And thus the merry war—the dance of skeletons bathed in human tears—goes on; and it will go on, brothers, forever unless you, the American Railway Union, stop it; end it; crush it out.

Our town is beautiful. In all these thirteen years no word of scandal has arisen against one of our women, young or old. What city of 20,000 persons can show the like? Since our strike, the arrests, which used to average four or five a day, had dwindled down to less than once a week. We are peaceable; we are orderly; and but for the kindly beneficience of kindly hearted people in and about Chicago we would be starving. We are not begging for bread. But George M. Pullman, who ran away from the public opinion that has arisen against him like the genii from the bottle in the *Arabian Nights,* is not feeding us. He is patiently seated behind his millions waiting for what? To see us starve.

We have grown better acquainted with the American Railway Union these conventional days, and as we have heard sentiments of the noblest philanthropy fall from the lips of our general officers—your officers and ours—we have learned that there is a balm for all our troubles, and that the box containing it is in your hands today, only awaiting opening to disseminate its sweet savor of hope.

George M. Pullman, you know, has cut our wages from 30 to 70 percent. George M. Pullman has caused to be paid in the last year the regular quarterly divident of 2 percent on his stock and a extra slice of 1 1/2 percent, making 9 1/2 percent on $30 million of capital. George M. Pullman, you know, took three contracts on which he lost less than $5,000. Because he loved us? No. Because it was cheaper to lose a little money in his freight car and his coach shops than to let his workingmen go, but that petty loss, more than made up by us from money we needed to clothe our wives and little ones, was his excuse for effecting a gigantic reduction of wages in every department of his great works, of cutting men and boys with equal zeal, including everyone in the repair shops of the Pullman Palace cars on which such preposterous profits have been made.

George M. Pullman will tell you, if you could go to him today, that he was paying better wages than any other car shops in the land. George M. Pullman might better save his breath. We have worked too often beside graduates from other establishments not to know that, work for work and skill for skill, no one can compete with us at wages paid for work well done. If his wage list showed a little trifle higher, our efficiency still left us heavily the loser. He does not figure on our brain and muscle. He makes his paltry computation in dollars and cents. . . .

THE PROBLEMS OF
RACE AND ETHNICITY

5

The extraordinary growth of the American economy after the Civil War attracted millions of immigrants. The influx of these newcomers compounded problems of race and ethnicity, which had plagued the nation throughout its history. By the 1880s, the emergence of "scientific racism" combined with more traditional forms of ethnocentrism, racial hatred, and religious bigotry to sanction efforts to preserve white, Anglo-Saxon supremacy. Recent immigrants joined African Americans in experiencing this new, more virulent form of discrimination and exploitation. The subsequent documents indicate some of these responses as well as reveal how those who suffered various forms of discrimination responded to their status.

26

FLORIDA JIM CROW LAWS (1885-1913)

Race relations in the post-Civil War South were varied, but overall there was a sense of moderation. Even though discrimination and segregation existed in some places, a strict "color line" was seldom drawn. Many African Americans voted, some held government office (elective and appointive), and there was a reluctant social acceptance, with racial mixing occurring in public places. This moderate situation changed quickly as it became apparent that Northern Republicans in Congress would no longer protect the rights of African Americans in the South. Southern states began to disfranchise African-American voters and pass "Jim Crow" laws as early as the 1880s. Named for a character in minstrel shows of the 1830s, the term Jim Crow became associated with laws permitting racial segregation in public facilities. The Supreme Court upheld these laws in its *Plessy v. Ferguson* (1896) decision, which permitted segregated facilities as long as they were "separate but equal." Listed below are some Jim Crow laws the Florida Legislature passed from 1881 to 1913.

―――

Questions to Consider: In what instances of racial contact did Florida's Jim Crow laws apply? Were there exceptions? Why? How did the excerpted Florida Jim Crow laws change over time? How could government officials justify the legal separation of the races? Were these Florida laws typical for Southern states?

―――

1881

The People of the State of Florida, represented in Senate and Assembly, do enact as follows: Section 1. Any colored man and white woman, who are not married to each other, who shall habitually live in and occupy in the night the same room, no other person over fifteen years of age being present, shall be deemed guilty of a misdemeanor. . . .

1881

The People of the State of Florida, represented in Senate and Assembly, do enact as follows:

Section 1. That if any white man shall intermarry with a negro, mulatto or any person who has one-eighth of negro blood in her, or if any white woman shall intermarry with a negro, mulatto or any person who has one-eighth negro blood in him, such persons who so intermarry shall be fined not more than one thousand dollars nor less than fifty dollars, or imprisoned in the State Prison not more than ten years nor less than six months. . . .

―――――――――――

The Acts and Resolutions Adopted by the Legislature of Florida, Florida State Archives, Tallahassee, FL.

1887

Be it enacted by the Legislature of the State of Florida:

Section 1. That all railroad companies doing business in this State shall sell to all respectable persons of color first-class tickets, on application, at the same rates that white persons are charged: and shall furnish and set apart for the use of persons of color who purchased such first-class tickets a car or cars in each passenger train as may be necessary to convey passengers equally as good, and provided with the same facilities for comfort, as shall or may be provided with the same facilities for white persons using and travelling as passengers on first-class tickets.

Section 2. That no conductor or person in charge of any passenger train on any railroad in this State shall suffer or permit any white person to ride, sit or travel, or to do any act or thing, to insult or annoy any person of color, while sitting, riding and traveling in said car so set apart for the use of colored persons, as mentioned in section one of this act, nor shall he or they, while so in charge of such train, suffer or permit any person of color, nor shall such person attempt to ride, sit or travel in the car or cars set aside for the use of white persons travelling as first-class passengers; Provided, That nothing in this act shall be construed to prevent female colored nurses having the care of children or sick persons from riding or traveling in such car.

1895

Be it enacted by the Legislature of the State of Florida.

Section 1. It shall be a penal offense for any individual, body of individuals, corporation or association to conduct within this State any school of any grade, public, private or parochial wherein white persons and negroes shall be instructed or boarded within the same building, or taught in the same class, or at the same time by the same teachers.

1905

Section 1. That it shall be unlawful for any sheriff, constable, bailiff, guard or other officer having prisoners in their custody, to chain, handcuff, or in any manner fasten white female or male prisoners to colored persons in their charge.

1907

Section 1. That all persons, association of persons, firms or corporations operating urban and suburban (or either) electric cars as common carriers of passengers in this State, shall furnish equal but separate accommodations for white and negro passengers on all cars so operated.

Section 2. That the separate accommodations for white and negro passengers directed in Section one of this act shall be by separate cars, fixed divisions, movable screens, or other method of division in the cars. . . .

Section 6. That any passenger belonging to one race who wilfully occupies or attempts to occupy a car or division provided for passengers of the other race, or who occupying such car or division, refuses to leave the same when requested to do so by the conductor or other person in charge of such car, shall be deemed guilty of a misdemeanor. . . .

Section 7. That on the car or division provided for white passengers shall be marked in plain letters in a conspicuous place, "For White," and on the car or division provided for negro passengers shall be marked in plain letters in a conspicuous place, "For Colored."

1907

Section 1. That all railroad companies and terminal companies in this State are required, within six months after the passage of this act, to provide separate waiting rooms and ticket windows of equal accommodation for white and colored passengers at all depots along lines of railway owned, controlled or operated by them, and at terminal passenger stations controlled and operated by them.

1909

Section 1. The County Commissioners of the respective counties of this State are hereby required, within twelve months from the passage of this Act, to so arrange the jails of their respective counties that it shall be unnecessary to confine in said jails in the same room, cell or apartment white and negro prisoners, or male and female prisoners.

Section 2. . . . It shall be unlawful for white and negro prisoners to be confined in the county jails of this State in the same cell, room or apartment, or be so confined as to be permitted to commingle together; . . . and it shall be the duty of the Sheriffs of this State to confine and separate all prisoners in their custody or charge in accordance with this Act.

1913

Section 1. From and after the passage of this Act it shall be unlawful in this State, for white teachers to teach negroes in negro schools, and for negro teachers to teach in white schools.

27

"THE NEGRO QUESTION IN THE SOUTH" (1892)

The People's party (Populist) faced the problem of all new political organizations: convincing voters to abandon the traditional political parties and join their cause. In the South this task was especially difficult because race relations had to be considered. The Democratic party had established white solidarity in the state governments as the radical Reconstruction governments collapsed, while the Republican party, comprising mostly blacks and some disaffected whites, was disintegrating. Some Populists sought the African-American vote to remove the Democrats from office and establish a new political power in the South. Among the more fervent supporters of this approach was Tom Watson of Georgia. Known for his combative nature and charismatic speeches, Watson served one

Thomas E. Watson, "The Negro Question in the South," *Arena* 6 (October 1892): 540–550.

term in Congress before joining the Populist party. In 1892, he explained the reasons for creating a fusion party of black and white voters in the South to readers of the national magazine, *Arena*. Watson's article is excerpted below.

·- **Questions to Consider:** What will be the foundation of the proposed fusion party? What perpetuates the "Negro Question"? How do the Populists propose to resolve the race issue? What happens to this proposal? Does Tom Watson's description of Southern agriculture compare with that depicted in "The Credit System of the South" (Document 20)?

The Negro Question in the South has been for nearly thirty years a source of danger, discord, and bloodshed. It is an ever-present irritant and menace. . . .

Now consider: here were two distinct races dwelling together, with political equality established between them by law. They lived in the same section; won their livelihood by the same pursuits; cultivated adjoining fields on the same terms; enjoyed together the bounties of a generous climate; suffered together the rigors of cruelly unjust laws; spoke the same language; bought and sold in the same markets; classified themselves into churches under the same denominational teachings; neither race antagonizing the other in any branch of industry; each absolutely dependent on the other in all the avenues of labor and employment; and yet, instead of being allies, as every dictate of reason and prudence and self-interest and justice said they should be, they were kept apart, in dangerous hostility, that the sordid aims of partisan politics might be served!

So completely has this scheme succeeded that the Southern black man almost instinctively supports any measure the Southern white man condemns, while the latter almost universally antagonizes any proposition suggested by a Northern Republican. We have, then, a solid South as opposed to a solid North; and in the South itself, a solid black vote against the solid white.

That such a condition is most ominous to both sections and both races is apparent to all. . . .

Having given this subject much anxious thought, my opinion is that the future happiness of the two races will never be assured until the political motives which drive them asunder, into two distinct and hostile factions, can be removed. There must be a new policy inaugurated, whose purpose is to allay the passions and prejudices of race conflict, and which makes its appeal to the sober sense and honest judgment of the citizen regardless of his color.

To the success of this policy two things are indispensable—a common necessity acting upon both races, and a common benefit assured to both—without injury or humiliation to either.

. . . The two races can never act together permanently, harmoniously, beneficially, till each race demonstrates to the other a readiness to leave old party affiliations and to form new ones, based upon the profound conviction that, in acting together, both races are seeking new laws which will benefit both. On no other basis under heaven can the "Negro Question" be solved.

Now, suppose that the colored man were educated upon these questions just as the whites have been; suppose he were shown that his poverty and distress came from the same sources as ours; suppose we should convince him that our platform principles assure him an escape from the ills he now suffers, and guarantee him the fair measure of prosperity his labor entitles him to receive,—would he not act just as the white Democrat who joined us did? . . .

The People's Party will settle the race question. First, by enacting the Australian [secret] ballot system. Second, by offering to white and black a rallying point which is free from the odium of former discords and strifes. Third, by presenting a platform immensely beneficial to both races and injurious to neither. Fourth, by making it to the interest of both races to act together for the success of the platform. Fifth, by making it to the interest of the colored man to have the same patriotic zeal for the welfare of the South that the whites possess.

The white tenant lives adjoining the colored tenant. Their houses are almost equally destitute of comforts. Their living is confined to bare necessities. They are equally burdened with heavy taxes. They pay the same high rent for gullied and impoverished land. . . .

Now the People's Party says to these two men, "You are kept apart that you may be separately fleeced of your earnings. You are made to hate each other because upon that hatred is rested the keystone of the arch of financial despotism which enslaves you both. You are deceived and blinded that you may not see how this race antagonism perpetuates a monetary system which beggars both."

This is so obviously true it is no wonder both these unhappy laborers stop to listen. No wonder they begin to realize that no change of law can benefit the white tenant which does not benefit the black one likewise; that no system which now does injustice to one of them can fail to injure both. Their every material interest is identical. The moment this becomes a conviction, mere selfishness, the mere desire to better their conditions, escape onerous taxes, avoid usurious charges, lighten their rents, or change their precarious tenements into smiling happy homes, will drive these two men together, just as their mutually inflamed prejudices now drive them apart.

Concede that in the final event, a colored man will vote where his material interests dictate that he should vote; concede that in the South the accident of color can make no possible difference in the interests of farmers, croppers, and laborers; concede that under full and fair discussion the people can be depended upon to ascertain where their interests lie—and we reach the conclusion that the Southern race question can be solved by the People's Party on the simple proposition that each race will be led by self-interest to support which benefits it, when so presented that neither is hindered by the bitter party antagonisms of the past. . . .

The question of social equality does not enter into the calculation at all. That is a thing each citizen decides for himself. No statute ever yet drew the latch of the humblest home—or ever will. Each citizen regulates his own visiting list—and always will.

The conclusion, then, seems to me to be this: The crushing burdens which now oppress both races in the South will cause each to make an effort to cast them off. They will see a similarity of cause and similarity of remedy. They will recognize that each should help the other in the work of repealing bad laws and enacting good ones. They will become political allies, and neither can injure the other without weakening both. It will be to the interest of both that each should have justice. And on these broad lines of mutual interest, mutual forbearance, and mutual support the present will be made the stepping-stone to future peace and prosperity.

28

THE ATLANTA EXPOSITION ADDRESS (1895)

Booker T. Washington became a prominent spokesman for the African-American community after his Atlanta Exposition Address (1895), which is excerpted below. Born into slavery in Virginia, he attended the Hampton Institute for three years (1872-1875) as a result of a Northern friend's patronage. In 1881, Washington was selected to begin a vocational education school for African Americans in Alabama, which became Tuskegee Institute. A persuasive and forceful public speaker, Washington was remarkably successful in obtaining funding for the institute from Northern businessmen and Southern politicians by stressing that students work hard, acquire a lifelong education, and learn to cooperate with both races. In 1895, Atlanta, Georgia, business leaders held the Cotton States Exposition to emphasize the potential industrial growth for the South and to address the issue of race relations; the organizers invited Booker T. Washington to speak to the mostly white audience. His epochal speech defined his life's work and was aimed at both whites and blacks. The moderate message and emphasis on accommodation pleased whites while also serving as motivation for many blacks, even though some intellectuals opposed his views because Washington ignored political rights. The address catapulted Washington into national fame.

Questions to Consider: Why was Booker T. Washington critical of African-American actions in the first 30 years of freedom? How does his message appeal simultaneously to Southern whites and African Americans? Why does Washington believe business should locate in the South? How does "The Atlanta Exposition Address" compare with the ideas expressed in the "Principles of the Niagara Movement" (Document 29)?

M r. President and Gentlemen of the Board of Directors and Citizens. One-third of the population of the South is of the Negro race. No enterprise seeking the material, civil, or moral welfare of this section can disregard this element of our population and reach the highest success. I but convey to you, Mr. President and Directors, the sentiment of the masses of my race when I say that in

---

Booker T. Washington, *Up from Slavery: The Autobiography of Booker T. Washington* (New York, 1901), 218-225.

no way have the value and manhood of the American Negro been more fittingly and generously recognized than by the managers of this magnificent Exposition at every stage of its progress. It is a recognition that will do more to cement the friendship of the two races than any occurrence since the dawn of our freedom.

Not only this, but the opportunity here afforded will awaken among us a new era of industrial progress. Ignorant and inexperienced, it is not strange that in the first years of our new life we began at the top instead of at the bottom; that a seat in Congress or the state legislature was more sought than real estate or industrial skill; that the political convention of stump speaking had more attractions than starting a dairy farm or truck garden.

. . . To those of my race who depend on bettering their condition in a foreign land or who underestimate the importance of cultivating friendly relations with the Southern white man, who is their next-door neighbor, I would say: "Cast down your bucket where you are"—cast it down in making friends in every manly way of the people of all races by whom we are surrounded.

Cast it down in agriculture, mechanics, in commerce, in domestic service, and in the professions. And in this connection it is well to bear in mind that whatever other sins the South may be called to bear, when it comes to business, pure and simple, it is in the South that the Negro is given a man's chance in the commercial world, and in nothing is this exposition more eloquent than in emphasizing this chance. Our greatest danger is that in the great leap from slavery to freedom we may overlook the fact that the masses of us are to live by the productions of our hands, and fail to keep in mind that we shall prosper in proportion as we learn to dignify and glorify common labor and put brains and skill into the common occupations of life; shall prosper in proportion as we learn to draw the line between the superficial and the substantial, the ornamental gewgaws of life and the useful. No race can prosper till it learns that there is as much dignity in tilling a field as in writing a poem. It is at the bottom of life we must begin, and not at the top. Nor should we permit our grievances to overshadow our opportunities.

To those of the white race who look to the incoming of those of foreign birth and strange tongue and habits for the prosperity of the South, were I permitted I would repeat what I say to my own race, "Cast down your bucket where you are." Cast it down among the eight millions of Negroes whose habits you know, whose fidelity and love you have tested in days when to have proved treacherous meant the ruin of your firesides. Cast down your bucket among these people who have, without strikes and labor wars, tilled your fields, cleared your forests, builded your railroads and cities, and brought forth treasures from the bowels of the earth, and helped make possible this magnificent representation of the progress of the South. Casting down your bucket among my people, helping and encouraging them as you are doing on these grounds, and to education of head, hand and heart, you will find that they will buy your surplus land, make blossom the waste places in your fields, and run your factories. While doing this, you can be sure in the future, as in the past, that you and your families will be surrounded by the most patient, faithful, law-abiding, and unresentful people that the world has seen. . . . In all things that are purely social we can be as separate as the fingers, yet one as the hand in all things essential to mutual progress. . . .

The wisest among my race understand that the agitation of questions of social equality is the extremist folly, and that progress in the enjoyment of all the privileges that will come to us must be the result of severe and constant struggle rather than of artificial forcing. No race that has anything to contribute to the markets of the world is long in any degree ostracized. It is important and right that all privileges of the law be ours, but it is vastly more important that we be prepared for the exercises of these privileges. The opportunity to earn a dollar in a factory just now is worth infinitely more than the opportunity to spend a dollar in an opera-house.

In conclusion, may I repeat that nothing in thirty years has given us more hope and encouragement, and drawn us so near to you of the white race, as this opportunity offered by the exposition; and here bending, as it were, over the altar that represents the results of the struggles of your race and mine, both starting practically empty-handed three decades ago, I pledge that in your effort to work out the great and intricate problem which God has laid at the doors of the South, you shall have at all times the patient, sympathetic help of my race; only let this be constantly in mind, that, while from representations in these buildings of the product of field, of forest, of mine, of factory, letters, and art, much good will come, yet far above and beyond material benefits will be that higher good, that, let us pray God, will come, in a blotting out of sectional differences and racial animosities and suspicions, in a determination to administer absolute justice, in a willing obedience among all classes to the mandates of law. This, coupled with our material prosperity, will bring into our beloved South a new heaven and a new earth.

29

PRINCIPLES OF THE NIAGARA MOVEMENT (1905)

Among a group of African-American intellectuals who opposed the views of Booker T. Washington was W. E. B. Du Bois. The first African American to earn a doctorate from Harvard, Du Bois taught at several universities, committed his life to ending segregation and discrimination, and helped shape the modern African-American identity. Du Bois believed that only by confronting whites—revealing the inequity of discrimination and segregation—and pushing for political rights could the overall condition for African Americans improve. In 1905, Du Bois organized a meeting of selected African-American leaders at Niagara Falls, New York, but no American hotel would permit them to register, so the group met on the Canadian side. Their meeting and the goals they established were called the Niagara Movement. They adopted a set of principles, which are excerpted next, that would be distributed to the entire country. The Niagara Movement did not sway public opinion or change laws, but it is often considered the forerunner of the National Association for the Advancement of Colored People (NAACP), founded in 1909-1910 by white and black intellectuals to end discrimination. Du Bois became the NAACP director of publicity and editor of its journal, *The Crisis*.

"Like Niagara," *The Gazette* (Cleveland, OH), 22 July 1905, 1.

'– **Questions to Consider:** What problems does the Niagara Movement want
addressed? What solutions do they propose? How would both whites and
blacks react to the stated "Principles"? How do the "Principles" compare to
"The Atlanta Exposition Address" (Document 28)? How is the tone different?

The members of the conference, known as the Niagara Movement, . . . con-
gratulate the Negro Americans on certain undoubted evidences of progress
in the last decade, particularly the increase of intelligence, the buying of property,
the checking of crime, the uplift in homelife, the advance in literature and art, and
the demonstration of constructive and executive ability in the conduct of great religious, economic, and educational institutions.

At the same time, we believe that this class of American citizens should protest
emphatically and continually against the curtailment of their political rights. We
believe in manhood suffrage; we believe that no man is so good, intelligent, or
wealthy as to be entrusted wholly with the welfare of his neighbor.

We believe also in protest against the curtailment of our civil rights. All American citizens have the right to equal treatment in places of public entertainment
according to their behavior and desires.

We especially complain against the denial of equal opportunities to us in economic life; in the rural districts of the south this amounts to peonage and virtual
slavery; all over the south it tends to crush labor and small business enterprises;
and everywhere American prejudice, helped often by iniquitous laws, is making it
more difficult for Negro-Americans to earn a decent living.

Common school education should be free to all American children and compulsory. High school training should be adequately provided for all, and college
training should be the monopoly of no class or race in any section of our common
country. We believe that in defense of its own institutions, the United States
should aid common school education, particularly in the south, and we especially
recommend concerted agitation to this end. We urge an increase in public high
school facilities in the south, where the Negro-Americans are almost wholly without such provisions. We favor well-equipped trade and technical schools for the
training of artisans, and the need of adequate and liberal endowment for a few
institutions of higher education must be patient to sincere well-wishers of the race.

We demand upright judges in courts, juries selected without discrimination on
account of color, and the same measure of punishment and the same efforts at
reformation for black as for white offenders. We need orphanages and farm
schools for dependent children, juvenile reformatories for delinquents, and the
abolition of the dehumanizing convict-lease system.

We note with alarm the evident retrogression in this land of sound public
opinion on the subject of manhood rights, republican government, and human
brotherhood; and we pray God that this nation will not degenerate into a mob of
boasters and oppressors, but rather will return to the faith of the fathers, that all
men were created free and equal, with certain unalienable rights.

We plead for health—for an opportunity to live in decent houses and localities, for a chance to rear our children in physical and moral cleanliness.

We hold up for public execration the conduct of two opposite classes of men: the practice among employers of importing ignorant Negro-American laborers in emergencies, and then affording them neither protection nor permanent employment; and the practice of labor unions of proscribing and boycotting and oppressing thousands of their fellow toilers simply because they are black. These methods have accentuated and will accentuate the war of labor and capital, and they are disgraceful to both sides.

We refuse to allow the impression to remain that the Negro-American assents to inferiority, is submissive under oppression, and apologetic before insults. Through helplessness we may submit, but the voice of protest of 10 million Americans must never cease to assail the ears of their fellows so long as America is injust.

Any discrimination based simply on race or color is barbarous, we care not how hallowed it be by custom, expediency, or prejudice. Differences made on account of ignorance, immorality, poverty, or disease may be legitimate methods of reform, and against them we have no word of protest; but discriminations based simply and solely on physical peculiarities, place of birth, color or skin, are relics of that unreasoning human savagery of which the world is and ought to be thoroughly ashamed.

We protest against the "Jim Crow" car, since its effect is and must be to make us pay first-class fare for third-class accommodations, render us open to insults and discomfort, and to crucify wantonly our manhood, womanhood, and self-respect.

We regret that this nation has never seen fit adequately to reward the black soldiers who, in its five wars, have defended their country with their blood and yet have been systematically denied the promotions which their abilities deserve. And we regard as unjust the exclusion of black boys from the military and Navy training schools.

We urge upon congress the enactment of appropriate legislation for securing the proper enforcement of those articles of freedom, the thirteenth, fourteenth, and fifteenth amendments of the constitution of the United States.

We repudiate the monstrous doctrine that the oppressor should be the sole authority as to the rights of the oppressed.

The Negro race in America stolen, ravished and degraded, struggling up through difficulties and oppression, needs sympathy and receives criticism; needs help and is given hindrance, needs protection and is given mob-violence, needs justice and is given charity, needs leadership and is given cowardice and apology, needs bread and is given a stone. This nation will never stand justified before God until these things are changed.

Especially are we surprised and astonished at the recent attitude of the church of Christ—on the increase of a desire to bow to racial prejudice, to narrow the bounds of human brotherhood, and to segregate black men in some outer sanctuary. This is wrong, unchristian and disgraceful to the twentieth century civilization.

Of the above grievances we do not hesitate to complain, and to complain loudly and insistently. To ignore, overlook, or apologize for these wrongs is to prove ourselves unworthy of freedom. Persistent, manly agitation is the way to liberty, and toward this goal the Niagara Movement has started and asks the cooperation of all men of all races.

At the same time we want to acknowledge with deep thankfulness the help of our fellowmen from the abolitionist down to those who today still stand for equal opportunity and who have given and still give of their wealth and of their poverty for our advancement.

And while we are demanding, and ought to demand, and will continue to demand the rights enumerated above, God forbid that we should ever forget to urge corresponding duties upon our people:

The duty to vote.
The duty to respect the rights of others.
The duty to work.
The duty to obey the laws.
The duty to be clean and orderly.
The duty to send our children to school.
The duty to respect ourselves, even as we respect others.

This statement, complaint, and prayer we submit to the American people, and to Almighty God.

30

THE UNWANTED IMMIGRANTS: THE CHINESE (1878)

Fleeing political and economic hardships, Chinese immigrants came to the West Coast and settled first in California. Initially it was the California gold rush that attracted Chinese immigrants, but the Western railroad companies actively recruited large number of Chinese immigrants to construct their tracks. Known for their willingness to work long hours for little pay, these "coolies," as whites called them, filled many manual labor jobs when railroad construction declined. White workers came to resent the industrious Chinese and their different customs and life-style, and they began pressuring state governments for action. Even though the Chinese composed 1 percent of California's population in 1878 (and only .002 percent of the nation's), the California Legislature investigated the nature and impact of Chinese immigration. The committee's report, excerpted next, warned the nation about the "evils" of the Chinese and reflected the racism that had developed; four years later Congress passed the Chinese Exclusion Act (1882), which suspended Chinese immigration for ten years.

California, Senate, Special Committee on Chinese Immigration, "An Address to the American People of the United States upon the Evils of Chinese Immigration," *Report of the Special Committee on Chinese Immigration to the California State Senate, 1878*, 8-9, 25, 35, 46-47.

·⌐ **Questions to Consider:** Why do the Californians so oppose the Chinese immigrants? Why have the Chinese been singled out? Were they a threat? To what? How do the living conditions described in this document compare with those portrayed in "Life in the Tenements of New York City" (Document 23)?

The Chinese have now lived among us, in considerable numbers, for a quarter of a century, and yet they remain separate, distinct from, and antagonistic to our people in thinking, mode of life, in tastes and principles, and are as far from assimilation as when they first arrived.

They fail to comprehend our system of government; they perform no duties of citizenship; they are not available as jurymen; cannot be called upon as a *posse comitatus* to preserve order, nor be relied upon as soldiers.

They do not comprehend or appreciate our social ideas, and they contribute but little to the support of any of our institutions, public or private.

They bring no children with them, and there is, therefore, no possibility of influencing them by our ordinary educational appliances.

There is, indeed, no point of contact between the Chinese and our people through which we can Americanize them. The rigidity which characterizes these people forbids the hope of any essential change in their relations to our own people or our government.

We respectfully submit the admitted proposition that no nation, much less a republic, can safely permit the presence of a large and increasing element among its people which cannot be assimilated or made to comprehend the responsibilities of citizenship.

The great mass of the Chinese residents of California are not amenable to our laws. It is almost impossible to procure the conviction of Chinese criminals, and we are never sure that a conviction, even when obtained, is in accordance with justice.

This difficulty arises out of our ignorance of the Chinese language and the fact that their moral ideas are wholly distinct from our own. They do not recognize the sanctity of an oath, and utterly fail to comprehend the crime of perjury. Bribery, intimidation, and other methods of baffling judicial action, are considered by them as perfectly legitimate. It is an established fact that the administration of justice among the Chinese is almost impossible, and we are, therefore, unable to protect them against the persecutions of their own countrymen, or punish them for offenses against our own people. This anomalous condition, in which the authority of law is so generally vacated, imperils the existence of our republican institutions to a degree hitherto unknown among us. . . .

We now come to an aspect of the question more revolting still. We would shrink from the disgusting details did not a sense of duty demand that they be presented. Their lewd women induce, by the cheapness of their offers, thousands of boys and young men to enter their dens, very many of whom are inoculated with venereal diseases of the worst type. Boys of eight and ten years of age have been found with this disease, and some of our physicians treat a half dozen cases daily.

The fact that these diseases have their origin chiefly among the Chinese is well established. . . .

But we desire to call your attention to the sanitary aspect of the subject. The Chinese herd together in one spot, whether in city or village, until they transform the vicinage into a perfect hive—there they live packed together, a hundred living in a space that would be insufficient for an average American family.

Their place of domicile is filthy in the extreme, and to a degree that cleansing is impossible except by the absolute destruction of the dwellings they occupy. But for the healthfulness of our climate, our city populations would have long since been decimated by pestilence from these causes. And we do not know how long this natural protection will suffice us.

In almost every house is found a room devoted to opium smoking, and these places are visited by white boys and women, so that the deadly opium habit is being introduced among our people. . . .

We now call attention to an aspect of the subject of such huge proportions, and such practical and pressing importance, that we almost dread to enter upon its consideration, namely, the effect of Chinese labor upon our industrial classes. We admit that the Chinese were, in the earlier history of the State, when white labor was not attainable, very useful in the development of our peculiar industries; that they were of great service in railroad building, in mining, gardening, general agriculture, and as domestic servants.

We admit that the Chinese are exceedingly expert in all kinds of labor and manufacturing; that they are easily and inexpensively handled in large numbers.

We recognize the right of all men to better their condition when they can, and deeply sympathize with the overcrowded population of China. . . .

Our laborers cannot be induced to live like vermin, as the Chinese and these habits of individual and family life have ever been encouraged by our statesmen as essential to good morals.

Our laborers require meat and bread, which have been considered by us as necessary to that mental and bodily strength which is thought to be important in the citizens of a Republic which depends upon the strength of its people, while the Chinese require only rice, dried fish, tea, and a few simple vegetables. The cost of sustenance to the whites is four-fold greater than that of the Chinese, and the wages of the whites must of necessity be greater than the wages required by the Chinese. The Chinese are, therefore, able to underbid the whites in every kind of labor. They can be hired in masses; they can be managed and controlled like unthinking slaves. But our laborer has an individual life, cannot be controlled as a slave by brutal masters, and this individuality has been required of him by the genius of our institutions, and upon these elements of character the State depends for defense and growth. . . .

As a natural consequence the white laborer is out of employment, and misery and want are fast taking the places of comfort and plenty.

Now, to consider and weigh the benefits returned to us by the Chinese for these privileges and for these wrongs to our laboring classes. They buy little or nothing from our own people, but import both their food and clothing from

China; they send their wages home; they have not introduced a single industry peculiar to their own country; they contribute nothing to the support of our institutions; can never be relied upon as defenders of the State; they have no intention of becoming citizens; they acquire no homes, and are a constant tax upon the public treasury. . . .

31

"STATEMENT OF THE IMMIGRATION RESTRICTION LEAGUE"

Until roughly 1890, the majority of immigrants who came to America were from northern and western European countries—the so-called "old" immigration. But in the 25 years after 1890, a dramatic shift took place: 18 million immigrants flooded into the country, with 80 percent coming from southern and eastern European countries. This wave of humanity is often called the "new" immigration. In this period, three million Italians came across the Atlantic, as did two million Jews (mostly from Russia) and one million Poles. These new immigrants were different than previous ones: they tended to be uneducated, encountered language barriers, possessed unusual customs and habits, and often had difficulty "Americanizing." Alarmed at the large number of immigrants arriving in America (1907 was the peak year with 1,285,349 arrivals), a group of Boston professors, lawyers, and philanthropists (including Henry Cabot Lodge) founded the Immigration Restriction League in 1894 to advocate limiting immigration. League members did not want to stop immigration completely, but chose to filter out the undesirables. Their proposal, which is excerpted below, had considerable appeal; on several occasions Congress passed a required literacy test for immigrants, but presidential vetoes prevented them from becoming law.

Questions to Consider: How does the Immigration Restriction League propose to filter out undesirable immigrants? Who are the undesirable immigrants? Why? What are the League's reasons for limiting immigration? What are the similarities between the California report on the Chinese (Document 30) and the league's position?

The league believes that the present laws are inadequate and that further selection of immigration is necessary and desirable from (a) the social and moral standpoint, (b) the economic standpoint, (c) the eugenic standpoint.

U.S. Congress, Immigration Commission, "Statement of the Immigration Restriction League," *Reports of the Immigration Commission: Vol. 41. Statements and Recommendations Submitted by Societies and Organizations Interested in the Subject of Immigration* (Washington, DC, 1911), 103-107.

The league recommends that—

1. A reading test for aliens of 15 years or over in any language or dialect the alien may choose.

2. An increase of the present head tax to at least $10.

3. Requiring immigrants to be in possession of money for their support while securing employment; say, $50 for single immigrant and heads of families and $25 additional for a wife and each minor child.

4. Abolishing the existing provision for admitting immigrants on bond.

5. Increasing the fines on steamship companies to $500 and extending the system of fines to all cases where the ineligibility of the alien could have been detected at embarkation by careful inspection.

6. Providing for the deportation of aliens without time limit, for causes, other than due to accident, whether arising prior to or subsequent to landing. . . .

The league believes that, great as is the burden of aliens who fall into the definite classes known as the defectives and delinquents, there is an even greater burden upon and danger to the community from the immigration of large numbers of aliens of low intelligence, poor physique, deficient in energy, ability, and thrift. Many of these have to be supported by public or private charity, are a menace to the average of our population. The league believes that a considerable portion of this class would be excluded by the legislation it proposes, as experience shows that poverty, ignorance, and incapacity in general go together. . . .

. . . The league would call attention to the following: (1) That the true wealth of a country consists in the character of its institutions and of its people and not in the number of miles of its railways or the rapid exhaustion of its resources. (2) That what demand there is for free immigration has always come from employers who want to force wages down regardless of the effect upon the community. (3) That the immigration of cheap labor has just this effect, forcing the workman already here to lower his standard of living and often to lose his job. (4) That just so far as immigration of cheap labor injures the status of the native workingmen it prevents the immigration of efficient and desirable foreign workingmen who will not come here to compete with cheap labor. Labor economically cheap is moreover never socially cheap. . . .

We should see to it that the breeding of the human race in this country receives the attention which it so surely deserves. We should see to it that we are protected, not merely from the burden of supporting alien dependents, delinquents, and defectives, but from what George William Curtis called "that watering of the nation's lifeblood," which results from their breeding after admission.

A considerable proportion of immigrants now coming are from races and countries, or parts of countries, which have not progressed, but have been backward, downtrodden, and relatively useless for centuries. If these immigrants "have not had opportunities," it is because their races have not made the opportunities: for they have had all the time that any other races have had; in fact, often come from older civilizations. There is no reason to suppose that a change of location will result in a change of inborn tendencies.

32

DESCRIPTION OF THE PADRONE SYSTEM (1901)

Many immigrants faced exploitation and discrimination when they arrived in America. The unfamiliarity with American customs, the language barrier, and the lack of applicable job skills helped create a dependence on fellow countrymen who were acquainted with America. Italian immigrants, however, encountered exploitation from fellow Italians who operated the padrone system. Initially, the *padroni* promoted immigration by training children (often from orphanages) as street musicians or acrobats to earn a living in America. The practice was declared illegal and it died out. But the padrone system continued in a modified form: working with Italian shipping lines, bankers, and labor bureaus, *padroni* recruited and contracted unskilled workers on a commission basis for American businesses. Some *padroni* preyed on recently arrived Italians by offering employment and housing for a fee. Many Italians became indebted to the padrone system; approximately two-thirds of the Italian workers in New York owed the *padroni* for their living. The selection below is a description of the padrone system that was presented to the U.S. Industrial Commission in 1901.

Questions to Consider: What services do the *padroni* provide their fellow countrymen? Why was Italian immigration mostly male? How did this help the *padroni?* What was the role of the Italian banker? How is the system exploitive? Why did the padrone system cease to exist?

A s a result of this demand for laborers and the activities of the padroni, the Italian immigrants have been largely males, and until recent years have not come by families, as have the other nationalities, notably the German and Scandinavian people. . . .

Under these changed conditions it is probable that the padrone has very little to do with bringing Italians into the country, since it is no longer necessary to have a contract to bring them in, and because it is even unsafe according to Federal statutes. The padrone is now nothing more than an employment agent, and exists only because of the immigrants and their illiteracy and ignorance of American institutions. He procures his subjects at the port, upon their landing, by promising them steady work at high wages. If the immigrant does not get under the control of the padrone by this means, the immigrant need only go to the colony of his race in any of the large cities, where he will readily be picked up by one of the padroni and promised employment. By this means the newcomers are attached to the padrone, who is able to fulfill his promises, because he "stands in" with the contractors, he knows officials and bosses of the railroads, and he is thus in a way to furnish

---

U.S. Congress, Industrial Commission, "The Padrone System," *Reports of the U.S. Industrial Commission: Vol. 15. Immigration* (Washington, DC, 1901): 432-434.

employment for his fellow countrymen who can not speak English and have no other way of finding employment. . . .

But the padrone does not employ the men alone and upon his own responsibility. He works together with the Italian banker, who is a somewhat more respectable party than the padrone; at least the men have more faith in him, because it is through him that they send money back to Italy, and with whom they keep their small savings. It is through the banker that the call is made for the number of men who are wanted, and it is in his office where the arrangements with the men are made. He may advance the money for transportation, and even the commission if the men do not have the money. The padrone takes charge of the men in the capacity of a boss, takes them to the place of work, runs the boarding house or shanty store at the place of work, and acts as interpreter for the contractor. . . .

For furnishing employment he receives a commission from the laborer. This commission depends upon the (1) length of the period of employment, (2) the wages to be received, and (3) whether they board themselves. If they board themselves, the commission is higher and varies from $1 to $10 a head. For a job of 5 or 6 months the commission may even rise to $10. In some cases the wages are paid to the padrone, but this is only when the contractor is dishonest and receives a share from the padrone. But if the contractor is honest, he knows that the people are generally cheated, and so he pays the men direct, deducting, however, the board and other charges as shown by the padrone. . . .

The padrone has a further hold upon these people as a result of irregular employment. During the winter there is almost no employment at all. This means that during the greater part of 5 months these people are without work. When work is plentiful, the laborer who boards with his boss is said to be fortunate if he can save more than one-half of his earnings. Some of these earnings are sent to Italy or frequently squandered, so that the laborer often finds himself in winter without resources of his own. In such cases he finds it convenient to go to the boarding house of the boss or banker, where he remains until spring, when it is understood that he shall enter the employ of the boss. In New York there are large tenements owned by Italian bankers which serve as winter quarters for these laborers. Here the men are crowded together, a dozen or more in one room, under the worst sanitary conditions. It is frequently said that the padrone encourages the men in extravagance in order to have a firmer hold on their future earnings. The employment is even made irregular by the padrone, who furnishes employment for several weeks at a time and then keeps them idle, claiming that the work is not regular. . . .

The padrone provides transportation for the men. But in the rates he overcharges the men, charging for first-class transportation or regular ticket rates, and securing greatly reduced rates because of the large number. If the work is some distance from the city, the padrone often boards the men, and usually buys the privilege from the contractor at a fixed rate per head per month. In some cases the privilege is given by the contractor free, because the padrone saves him trouble in employing men, and is convenient to have around in managing the men. But lodging and wearing apparel, the cost of which is generally deducted from their wages. In consideration of the many advantages which the padroni have in this transaction, they generally have to pay pretty high prices for the privilege, which naturally comes out of the pockets of the immigrants. If the men board themselves, their food must be bought at the shanty store, which is operated by the padrone. Notices are posted to this effect, and fines are imposed for disobedience. Even dismissal is often the penalty. Occasionally a fixed daily amount of purchases is required by the padrone, but usually the men are allowed to spend at their pleasure, but only at the padrone store. For example, in 1894 Italian laborers were shipped from New York to Brunswick, Ga., for work on a sewerage contract. Each man paid the padrone $1 for finding the employment. The passage money, $7 per head, was paid by the banker with the understanding that this was to be deducted from their wages. The agent of the banker paid $25 a month rent for 10 huts, but charged each laborer $1 a month, which for 215 men was $215 a month. All supplies had to be bought at the shanty store, the penalty for disobedience being a fine of $5.

33

"A HUNGARIAN GIRL'S IMPRESSIONS OF AMERICA" (1913)

Most immigrants came to America for economic reasons (some fled for political or religious reasons) and dreamed of living a good life. The immigrant experience, however, was often vastly different from the dream. Faced with a multitude of obstacles to overcome, immigrants took the most menial of jobs, lived in squalid housing, and were subject to exploitation and discrimination. For many, the key to survival was how quickly they could assimilate—"Americanize"—and learn the ways of America while retaining part of the Old World. The selection below is a Hungarian girl's commentary on her immigrant experience that was published in the popular magazine, *The Outlook*.

Questions to Consider: For this girl, what Old World beliefs and customs persisted in America? Were they a hindrance or an assist in her adjustment to life in America? What were some of the obstacles this girl had to overcome? Why did the strike change her views? Is this a "typical" immigrant experience?

I always dreamed of coming to America, it seems. We lived in the small country town of Ujhely, in Hungary, my mother, my father, six brothers, two sisters, and myself. Two brothers came first, then I was the third child. Father was only a crockery peddler, and sickly, and we were very poor. In that town if families are well off they live upstairs, and the poor live downstairs. We lived underneath a family like that, and their children would not speak to us. . . . When I heard people

"A Hungarian Girl's Impressions of America: A True Story Told by a White-goods Striker to Gertrude Barnum," *The Outlook* 104 (17 May 1913): 111-114.

talk about America, where all people are equal, I thought, "That is the place I will go." . . .

. . . When I came into my steerage cabin it was not clean at all, and two married women and another girl all slept in it besides me. We could not breathe, and it was rough, and we were sick. But when I was outside I was better, and kept on building dreams. The townspeople at home had warned me that Freedom was bad for girls, and said they got spoiled in a free country. I just took an oath I would not be like such bad girls, and I always kept that afterwards. . . .

. . . My heart was beating fast to get to the great America. Instead of seeing a beautiful city, we were pushed into a big dark room in crowds, just like beasts. Every one was talking in different languages, and all were worried or angry. It was a terrible place, with such a smell! And a rough matron pushed you away if you tried to ask questions. There were no windows and no light in this barn. No mattresses to sleep on. I thought it was prison, and we could not tell any one anything. Two days I was kept there in fear. . . .

. . . Finally they let me go out and I saw crowds in the city, but not like I had expected to see them. There were poor people, I saw them. But we rode on the elevated train and I liked that, and I talked and talked to the man. When I noticed push-carts and dirty little poor children and old, sad people, I would be sad again. But when I saw how high the buildings were, I thought, "Almost every one must be rich, only a few poor, and only at first." I thought the higher up you lived the richer you must be. Such a child I was.

My aunt lived in a little dark place. . . . My aunt took me to a white-goods shop and told them I would work for nothing to learn. It was noisy and hard to learn and America was so different. . . . I was ashamed, always making such mistakes at the machine, and I ached sharp pains in my back. After the third week they paid me a dollar, and then I was rich and my hopes climbed up fast again. It was a foot-power machine and a dirty shop without air, and we worked until 7:30 at night. I tried to console myself and say "it's no shame to be a working-girl," and I tried to comfort my pride. When pay-day came, I began to get two and three dollars. I changed from one shop to another after I got courage, and I made four dollars and four dollars and a half, and began to pay more board; all the back board I paid, and tried to catch up to the present. There was not a cent to send home, and there was all the ticket-money I owed yet. I tell you it was enough! Different from a dream! A strange city, a strange language, even the money strange. In the other factories it was worse, because no one showed you, or helped you, or cared how you made out. They called me "greenhorn;" that was the first English word I learned. . . . I only prayed that the examiner would take my work when I finished it and not throw it back to me to be ripped. That is the worst thing, the way a girl shivers before the examiner. They scold you fierce. . . .

Afterwards I learned to work well and fast and make six and seven dollars. I paid the rest of the ticket-money and sent a little home. I was sixteen, seventeen, then. . . .

Then I kept on sending money home every week, and it was such a little, so different from what I promised. I even began to think, "What do I care what happens to me? My life is spoiled, anyway; I was nineteen, but old; no hope for me any more. I might make some money on the street and send it home, and it would be better for the other children." Oh, yes, I thought of it very often before the strike. I could not think of any other good of me living, getting more pale and quiet all the time. I tried to study and learn, but to make nine or ten dollars you work hard, and you are too tired.

Now, you see, it was just in time I heard about the strike. That was a wonderful thing! Really from a child I always knew I had something better in me, if I got a chance. But up to the strike I never knew what I could do. We were inspired then! Everything we suffered was explained, the awful shops and the awful places we had to live. At the strike meetings we learned we could stand up for ourselves and our sisters. In all my life those five weeks will shine out the best. Everything was explained just as it is. All the wrongs we suffer, and how we can change this. We sympathized with each other and were not each one alone and for herself. I heard the great people speak about the Labor Movement. We got courage for picketing, and were arrested, and froze, and did not mind it; and fought for our cause, and saw a hope in America. I knew then it was the labor movement that could change the shops and the wages. . . . It was like a miracle when we won the strike. We laughed and cried together. The people had helped us, but we knew we did most of it ourselves. That was what helped us most. My pride was satisfied, because I could be somebody after all, and do something. . . . Even what we got in wages and shorter hours was not the thing. It is pride, and hope, and self-respect you get. You know you are not a machine, but as good as the best.

Now I believe in America getting more like what I hear, back in Hungary. America is the best country, after all!

— · — · — · — · — · — · — · — · — · — · — · — · — · — · — · — · — · — · — · —

PART II

DEVELOPMENT OF THE MODERN NATION

IMPERIALISM

1

The social Darwinist attitudes that supported economic exploitation and white Anglo-Saxon superiority in the United States combined to buttress a new imperialism abroad. Though traditionally expansionistic, the United States had previously confined its ambitions to the North American continent. During the 1890s, however, the "closing" of the frontier, a search for new economic opportunities, national pride, and competition with European rivals caused many Americans to champion a more aggressive policy overseas. America's new role in world affairs became a matter of serious debate by the turn of the century. The next several documents show the varying sentiments, both foreign and domestic, concerning the new imperialism.

34

THE SINKING OF THE *MAINE* (1898)

In 1895, the Cuban revolution against Spain flared up again. Spain sent troops under General Valeriano Weyler to quell the revolt, and he began a policy of "reconcentrado," assembling peasants into camps before laying waste to the countryside. The revolt was bloody and savage on both sides. Sensational American newspapers, especially William Randolph Hearst's *New York Journal* and Joseph Pulitzer's *New York World,* began publishing lurid—and often exaggerated—accounts and drawings of Spanish atrocities in an effort to increase circulation. This "yellow journalism" only created more American interest and sympathy in the Cuban revolt. When riots broke out in Havana, Cuba, in 1898 and it looked like American citizens might be endangered, the U.S. battleship *Maine* arrived in the harbor, supposedly on a courtesy call. On February 15, 1898, the *Maine* exploded and sank with the loss of 260 sailors. Rumors circulated that Spain sunk the battleship, and the tabloid newspapers blared headlines accusing Spain while clamoring for war. The selection below is the *New York Journal's* editorial on the sinking of the *Maine.*

Questions to Consider: Why is the *Maine* an "object lesson" to the *New York Journal?* According to the editorial, why should the United States intervene in Cuba? Is the justification sound? Who does the *New York Journal* blame for the destruction of the *Maine?* How did the *Maine's* destruction move the United States closer to war with Spain?

The prudent, proper and patriotic policy for the United States Government to adopt in dealing with the Cuban question is not changed by the disaster to the Maine. What the Journal said months ago is perfectly applicable to the situation today. It is the duty of the United States to intervene in Cuba, not because an American war ship has been destroyed in Havana harbor by a suspicious "accident," but because every dictate of national self-protection, every impulse of humanity compels such intervention.

The disaster to the Maine is an object lesson to the Administration rather than a present cause for war. If the inquiry which begins this week shall show it to have been the result of the faulty construction of the vessel, or of carelessness, it of course offers no reason for attack upon Spain. If it be shown to be the work of irresponsible individuals, malignant fanatics or murderous Weylerites the United States will demand full reparation and a money indemnity from Spain, the refusal of which would necessarily lead to war. If, what is almost incredible, the explosion should be shown to have been caused with connivance or by the act of responsible Spanish officers, a declaration of war would be instant and the war would be one of chastisement and revenge.

"Enforce Peace in Cuba," *New York Journal,* 21 February 1898, 10.

There are countless reasons to believe that the second hypothesis will be supported by the finding of the court of inquiry; but, even so, reliance upon it would defer tediously the time of American intervention in Cuba. After the time spent in investigation would come the delay attendant upon diplomatic correspondence with a nation which never does to-day what it can put off until to-morrow. That is why the disaster to the Maine is not to be regarded as an immediate cause for war.

But it is an object lesson which the Administration may well heed. For two years the Spaniards have carried on in Cuba a warfare which has outraged humanity and violated the laws of civilized nations. They have destroyed American property and imprisoned and murdered American citizens. The navy of the United States has been forced to do police duty on the seas that the Spaniards might prosecute their outrages the more securely. The commerce of the United States with Cuba has been destroyed. American vessels have been illegally fired upon and the United States flag insulted. To-day the revolution is no nearer suppression than it ever was. Spanish power in Cuba is a myth—it extends just far enough to give Spanish officials an opportunity to enrich themselves by plundering their own troops.

These reasons why the United States should intervene have existed ever since the McKinley Administration came into power. Had the right course been promptly taken the Spaniards would have been driven out of Cuba at probably a cost to the United States in lives than the "accident" to the Maine entailed. Are we to wait now until the ship sent to take the place of the Maine also meets with an "accident"? Shall we give Spain time to complete her projected alliance with the Spanish-American republics against the United States?

The result of the inquiry at Havana may make instant war with Spain inevitable. But the reasons why the United States should insure peace in their hemisphere by enforcing peace in Cuba would be as forceful to-day if the gallant Maine and her noble crew were still floating in Havana harbor.

35

AN ANTI-IMPERIALIST PERSPECTIVE (1899)

Congress declared war against Spain in April 1898 to establish Cuban independence, but the opening battle of the war was fought halfway around the world when Commodore George Dewey attacked the Spanish fleet in Manila, Philippines. The Spanish surrendered Manila to the Americans, while Filipino insurgent leader Emilio Aguinaldo, working with the Americans, liberated the countryside and established a temporary government. The war's end left the Philippines under joint American-Filipino control, but the future of the country was in the hands of Congress. The Philippine annexation issue—perhaps the most important foreign policy decision of the time—became hotly debated, as the sides were sharply drawn between imperialists and anti-imperialists. Among the first to denounce annexation was George F. Hoar, an aged four-term Republican senator

"Acquisition of Territory," *Congressional Record*, 55th Congress, 3rd Session, (9 January 1899), 493-503.

from Massachusetts. Hoar's political career spanned nearly 50 years: he helped form the Republican party, he oversaw the Republican party's shift to support business, and he denounced the popular election of senators. His speech, excerpted below, was given as the Senate considered ratifying the Treaty of Paris, which would officially end the war and make the Philippines an American possession.

Questions to Consider: For what reasons does George F. Hoar oppose the annexation of the Philippines? What does he fear about Philippine annexation? Why does Hoar believe the imperialists are hypocrites? How does Hoar's anti-imperialist stance compare with Beveridge's imperialistic position in "The New Manifest Destiny" (Document 36)?

M r. President, the persons who favor the ratification of this treaty without conditions and without amendment differ among themselves certainly in their views, purposes, and opinions . . . . In general, the state of mind and the utterance of the lips are in accord. If you ask them what they want, you are answered with a shout: "Three cheers for the flag! Who will dare haul it down? Hold on to everything you can get. The United States is strong enough to do what it likes. The Declaration of Independence and the counsel of Washington and the Constitution of the United States have grown rusty and musty. They are for little countries and not for great ones. There is no moral law for strong nations. America has outgrown Americanism." . . .

If you can not take down a national flag where it has once floated in time of war, were we disgraced when we took our flag down in Mexico, and in Vera Cruz, or after the invasion of Canada; England was dishonored when she took her flag down after she captured this capital; and every nation is henceforth pledged to the doctrine that where ever it puts its military foot or its naval power with the flag over it, that must be a war to the death and to extermination or the honor of the state is disgraced by the flag of that nation being withdrawn. . . .

Now Mr. President, there are Senators here yet hesitating as to what their action may be in the future, who will tell you that they loathe and hate this doctrine that we may buy nations at wholesale; that we may acquire imperial powers or imperial regions by conquest; that we may make vassal states and subject peoples without constitutional restraint, and against their will, and without any restraint but our own discretion. . . .

The Monroe Doctrine is gone. Every European nation, every European alliance, has the right to acquire dominion in this hemisphere when we acquire it in the other. The Senator's doctrine put anywhere in practice will make our beloved country a cheap-jack country, raking after the cart for the leaving of European tyranny. . . .

Our fathers dreaded a standing army; but the Senator's doctrine put in practice anywhere, now or hereafter, renders necessary a standing army, to be reenforced by a powerful navy. Our fathers denounced the subjection of any people whose judges were appointed or whose salaries were paid by a foreign power; but the Senator's doctrine, whenever it shall be put in practice, will entail upon us a national debt larger than any now existing on the face of the earth, larger than any ever known in history.

Our fathers dreaded the national taxgatherers; but the doctrine of the Senator from Connecticut, if it be adopted, is sure to make our national taxgatherers the most familiar visitant to every American home. . . .

. . . My proposition, summed up in a nut shell is this: I admit you have the right to acquire territory for constitutional purposes, and you may hold land and govern men on it for the constitutional purpose of a seat of government or for the constitutional purpose of admitting it as a State. I deny the right to hold land or acquire any property for any purpose not contemplated by the Constitution. The government of foreign people against their will is not a constitutional purpose, but a purpose expressly forbidden by the Constitution. Therefore I deny the right to acquire this territory and to hold it by the Government for that purpose. . . .

Now, I claim that under the Declaration of Independence you can not govern a foreign territory, a foreign people, another people than your own, that you can not subjugate them and govern them against their will, because you think it is for their good, when they do not: because you think you are going to give them the blessings of liberty. You have no right at the cannon's mouth to impose on an unwilling people your Declaration of Independence and your Constitution and your notions of freedom and notions of what is good. . . .

But read the account of what is going on in Iloilo. The people there have got a government, with courts and judges, better than those of the people of Cuba, who, it was said, had a right to self-government, collecting their customs; and it is proposed to turn your guns on them, and say "We think that our notion of government is better than the notion you have got yourselves." I say that when you put that onto them against their will and say that freedom as we conceive it, not freedom as they conceive it, public interest as we conceive it, not as they conceive it, shall prevail and that if it does not we are to force it on them at the cannon's mouth—I say that the nation which undertakes that plea and says it is subduing these men for their good, will encounter the awful and terrible rebuke, "Beware of the leaven of the Pharisees, which is hypocrisy."

36

THE NEW MANIFEST DESTINY (1900)

In the Philippine annexation debates, one of the most forceful advocates of imperialism was Albert J. Beveridge, a first-term Republican senator from Indiana. Known for his powerful political oratory and notions of Anglo-Saxon supremacy before arriving in the Senate, Beveridge broke with tradition and gave a major speech as a freshman senator. In order to obtain information about the Philippine

"Policy Regarding the Philippines," *Congressional Record,* 56th Congress, 1st Session, (9 January 1900), 704-712.

issue, Beveridge traveled to the islands and made a personal investigation. This inquiry added credibility to his annexation position. Excerpted below is Beveridge's eloquent Senate speech on the question of Philippine annexation. Beveridge served two terms in the Senate and was often considered one of the original "Progressive" Republicans. He lost a reelection bid in 1911, and became a distinguished historian. His best work was *The Life of John Marshall* (four volumes), which received the Pulitzer Prize for historical biography.

—

·⁓ **Questions to Consider:** According to Albert J. Beveridge, why should the United States annex the Philippines? Are his reasons valid? How does Beveridge address the issues of constitutional authority and the intent of the founding fathers? Was the Philippines as important as Beveridge suggests? Compare Beveridge's reasons for annexation with Hoar's ("An Anti-Imperialist Perspective," Document 35) opposition.

—

Mr. President, the times call for candor. The Philippines are ours forever, "territory belonging to the United States," as the Constitution calls them. And just beyond the Philippines are China's illimitable markets. We will not retreat from either. We will not repudiate our duty in the archipelago. We will not abandon our opportunity in the Orient. We will not renounce our part in the mission of our race, trustee, under God, of the civilization of the world. And we will move forward to our work, not howling out regrets like slaves whipped to their burdens, but with gratitude for a task worthy of our strength, and thanksgiving to Almighty God that He has marked us as His chosen people, hence forth to lead in the regeneration of the world.

This island empire is the last land left in all the oceans. If it should prove a mistake to abandon it, the blunder once made would be irretrievable. If it proves a mistake to hold it, the error can be corrected when we will. Every other progressive nation stands ready to relieve us.

But to hold it will be no mistake. Our largest trade henceforth must be with Asia. The Pacific is our ocean. More and more Europe will manufacture the most it needs, secure from its colonies the most it consumes. Where shall we turn for consumers of our surplus? Geography answers the question. China is our natural customer. She is nearer to us than to England, Germany, or Russia, the commercial powers of the present and the future. They have moved nearer to China by securing permanent bases on her borders. The Philippines give us a base at the door of all the East.

Lines of navigation from our ports to the Orient and Australia; from the Isthmian Canal to Asia; from all Oriental ports to Australia, converge at and separate from the Philippines. They are a self-supporting, dividend-paying fleet, permanently anchored at a spot selected by the strategy of Providence, commanding the Pacific. And the Pacific is the ocean of the commerce of the future. Most future wars will be conflicts for commerce. The power that rules the Pacific, therefore, is the power that rules the world. And, with the Philippines, that power is and will forever be the American Republic. . . .

Here, then, Senators, is the situation. Two years ago there was no land in all this world which we could occupy for any purpose. Our commerce was daily turning toward the Orient, and geography and trade developments made necessary our commercial empire over the Pacific. And in that ocean we had no commercial, naval, or military base. To-day we have one of the three great ocean possessions on the globe, located at the most commanding commercial, naval, and military points in the eastern seas, within hail of India, shoulder to shoulder with China, richer in its own resources than any equal body of land on the entire globe, and peopled by a race which civilization demands shall be improved. Shall we abandon it? That man little knows the common people of the Republic, little understands the instincts of our race, who thinks we will not hold it fast and hold it forever, administering just government by simplest methods. . . .

But Senators, it would be better to abandon this combined garden and Gibraltar of the Pacific, and count our blood and treasure already spent a profitable loss, than to apply any academic arrangement of self-government to these children. They are not capable of self-government. How could they be? They are not of a self-governing race. They are Orientals, Malays, instructed by Spaniards in the latter's worst estate.

They know nothing of practical self-government except as they have witnessed the weak, corrupt, cruel, and capricious rule of Spain. What magic will anyone employ to dissolve in their minds and characters those impressions of governors and governed which three centuries of misrule has created? What alchemy will change the oriental quality of their blood and set the self-government currents of the American pouring through their Malay veins? How shall they, in the twinkling of an eye, be exalted to the heights of self-governing peoples which required a thousand years, Anglo-Saxon though we are? . . .

No one need fear their competition with our labor. No reward could beguile, no force compel, these children of indolence to leave their trifling lives for the fierce and fervid industry of high wrought America. The very reverse is the fact. One great problem is the necessary labor to develop these islands—to build the roads, open the mines, clear the wilderness, drain the swamps, dredge the harbors. The natives will not supply it. . . .

Senators in opposition are estopped from denying our constitutional power to govern the Philippines as circumstances may demand, for such power is admitted in the case of Florida, Louisiana, Alaska. How, then, is it denied in the Philippines? Is there a geographical interpretation to the Constitution? Do degrees of longitude fix constitutional limitations? Does a thousand miles of ocean diminish constitutional power more than a thousand miles of land? . . .

Mr. President, this question is deeper than any question of party politics; deeper than any question of the isolated policy of our country even; deeper even than any question of constitutional power. It is elemental. It is racial. God has not been preparing the English-speaking and Teutonic peoples for a thousand years for nothing but vain and idle self-contemplation and self-admiration. No! He has made us the master organizers of the world to establish a system where chaos reigns. He has given us the spirit of progress to overwhelm the forces of reaction throughout the earth. He has made us adept in government that we may administer government among savage and senile peoples. Were it not for such a force as this the world would relapse into barbarism and night. And of all our race He has marked the American people as His chosen nation to finally lead in the regeneration of the world. This is the divine mission of America, and it holds for us all the profit, all the glory, all the happiness possible to man. We are the trustees of the world's programs, guardians of its righteous peace. The judgment of the Master is upon us: "Ye have been faithful over a few things; I will make you ruler over many things."

What shall history say of us? Shall it say that we renounced that holy trust, left the savage to his base condition, the wilderness to the reign of waste, deserted duty, abandoned glory, forget our sordid profits even, because we feared our strength and read the charter of our powers with the doubter's eye and the quibbler's mind? Shall it say that, called by events to captain and command the proudest, ablest, purest race of history in history's noblest work, we declined that great commission? Our fathers would not have had it so. No! They founded no paralytic government, no sluggard people, passive while the world's work calls them. They established no reactionary nation. They unfurled no retreating flag. . . .

Mr. President and Senators, adopt the resolution offered, that peace may quickly come and that we may begin our saving, regenerating, and uplifting work. . . . Reject it, and the world, history, and the American people will know where to forever fix the awful responsibility for the consequences that will surely follow such failure to do our manifest duty. How dare we delay when our soldiers' blood is flowing?

37

THE OPEN DOOR NOTES (1899)

The victory over Spain (1898) had thrust America into the role of major world power and provided the opportunity to exercise influence. The prospect of unlimited trade with China was threatened by the other major powers' "spheres of influence" in China and the possibility they could choke off all American trade through tariffs or special trade restrictions. Realizing the United States wanted to establish a foothold in China, the British proposed a joint statement on equal trade opportunity for all nations. Like the earlier Monroe Doctrine, the United States refused, preferring to issue its own statement. Secretary of State John Hay, borrowing heavily from a memorandum that William Rockhill, an Asian diplomatic specialist, had written, sent a series of notes to the European nations and Japan announcing the Open Door policy. A former secretary for Lincoln and a career diplomat, Hay boldly announced that the major world powers had accepted the Open Door Notes even though the responses were at best vague. The selection that follows is the dispatch sent to the German government in Berlin. The other notes were almost identical.

"Correspondence Concerning American Commercial Rights in China," *Papers Relating to the Foreign Relations of the United States, 1899* (Washington, DC, 1901), 129-30.

·⁓ **Questions to Consider:** How did the Open Door policy propose to resolve the European "spheres of influence" in China? Why was the international response vague? Besides trade with China, what did the United States hope to obtain through the Open Door Notes? Were the Open Door Notes successful?

A t the time when the Government of the United States was informed by that of Germany that it had leased from His Majesty the Emperor of China the port of Kiao-chao and the adjacent territory in the province of Shantung, assurances were given to the ambassador of the United States at Berlin by the Imperial German minister for foreign affairs that the rights and privileges insured by treaties with China to citizens of the United States would not thereby suffer or be in anywise impaired within the area over which Germany had thus obtained control.

More recently, however, the British Government recognized by a formal agreement with Germany the exclusive right of the latter country to enjoy in said leased area and the contiguous "sphere of influence or interest" certain privileges, more especially those relating to railroads and mining enterprises; but as the exact nature and extent of the rights thus recognized have not been clearly defined, it is possible that serious conflicts of interest may at any time arise not only between British and German subjects within said area, but that the interests of our citizens may also be jeopardized thereby.

Earnestly desirous to remove any cause of irritation and to insure at the same time to the commerce of all nations in China the undoubted benefits which should accrue from a formal recognition by the various powers claiming "spheres of interest" that they shall enjoy perfect equality of treatment for their commerce and navigation within such "spheres," the Government of the United States would be pleased to see His German Majesty's Government five formal assurances, and lend its cooperation in securing like assurances from the other interested powers, that each, within its respective sphere of whatever influence—

First. Will in no way interfere with any treaty port or any vested interest within any so-called "sphere of interest" or leased territory it may have in China.

Second. That the Chinese treaty tariff of the time being shall apply to all merchandise landed or shipped to all such ports as are within said "sphere of interest" (unless they be "free ports"), no matter to what nationality it may belong, and that duties so leviable shall be collected by the Chinese Government.

Third. That it will levy no higher harbor dues on vessels of another nationality frequenting any port in such "sphere" than shall be levied on vessels of its own nationality, and no higher railroad charges over lines built, controlled, or operated within its "sphere" or merchandise belonging to citizens or subjects of other nationalities transported through such "sphere" than shall be levied on similar merchandise belonging to its own nationals transported over equal distances.

The liberal policy pursued by His Imperial German Majesty in declaring Kiao-chao a free port and in aiding the Chinese Government in the establishment there of a custom-house are so clearly in line with the proposition which this Government is anxious to see recognized that it entertains the strongest hope that Germany will give its acceptance and hearty support.

The recent ukase of His Majesty the Emperor of Russia declaring the port of Ta-lien-wan open during the whole of the lease under which it is held from China to the merchant ships of all nations, coupled with the categorical assurances made to this Government by His Imperial Majesty's representative at this capital at the time and since repeated to me by the present Russian ambassador, seem to insure the support of the Emperor to the proposed measure. Our ambassador at the Court of St. Petersburg has in consequence been instructed to submit it to the Russian Government and to request their early consideration of it. A copy of my instruction on the subject to Mr. Tower is herewith inclosed for your confidential information.

The commercial interests of Great Britain and Japan will be so clearly served by the desired declaration of intentions, and the views of the Governments of these countries as to the desirability of the adoption of measures insuring the benefits of equality of treatment of all foreign trade throughout China are so similar to those entertained by the United States, that their acceptance of the propositions herein outlined and their cooperation in advocating their adoption by the other powers can be confidently expected. . . .

38

"A COLOMBIAN VIEW OF THE PANAMA CANAL QUESTION" (1903)

Since the 1840s, Americans had considered constructing a central American canal to facilitate inter-ocean transportation, but little was done until the 20th century. A French company—*Compagnie Universelle du Canal de Panama*—obtained the rights to build a canal in the Colombian province of Panama in 1881, but the effort ended in bankruptcy. When an American commission recommended construction of a canal in Nicaragua, representatives of the defunct French company, who held the rights to a Panama canal, lobbied Congress to adopt their route. When the group, led by Philippe Bunau-Varilla, lowered their asking price for the rights to build in Panama from $109 million to $40 million, Congress authorized construction of a Panama canal. In early 1903, Congress ratified the Hay-Herran Treaty and presented it to the Colombian government. The treaty authorized an American canal zone 10 miles wide for $10 million and an annual payment of $250,000. As the Colombian government considered the treaty, Raúl Pérez, Colombia's ambassador to the United States, published the excerpted article that follows in *The North American Review*. While not representing Colombia's official position, the article indicates apprehension over America's intervention as well as Colombia's potential loss from the canal.

'⁓ **Questions to Consider:** For what reasons does Raúl Pérez oppose the Hay-Herran Treaty? Does he oppose the canal? Which groups in Colombia support

Raúl Pérez, "A Colombian View of the Panama Canal Question," *The North American Review* 177 (July 1903): 63-68.

the canal treaty? Why? What does Pérez propose as the basis of a better treaty for Colombia? What happened to Colombia's interest in the canal a few months after this article appeared?

———

The most important matter to be settled with regard to opening the canal is that of exactly defining the status of the party that will carry on the enterprise. It is evident at a glance that there is a wide difference between a private corporation, such as the *Compagnie Universelle du Canal de Panama,* and the powerful government to the United States of America. The Company has been doing and was to do business under the protection of the Colombian laws, subject to those laws in every detail; being considered simply as any other "juridical person"—that is, any Colombian citizen. . . .

If the substitution of the United States government for the *Compagnie Universelle* were once affected, and the consequent transference of rights carried out, would the United States submit to be considered merely a "juridical person," with no more rights than any other Colombian citizen carrying on business in Colombian territory, under protection of the Colombian Laws and subject to those laws in every respect? Such is not the spirit of the Herran-Hay treaty; and, even if it were, Colombians would have plausible reasons for misgivings or apprehensions on that point. No one willing to consider the situation with absolute impartiality can criticise those who desire that the status of Panama Canal builders should be most clearly defined, particularly in a case where a World Power is to be the builder. . . .

Let it be well understood that the Colombians . . . are decidedly favorable to the opening of the canal by the United States, should the negotiations be concluded in a manner that would result in real and lasting good to their country. . . .

The ten millions of dollars that Colombia would receive as the only compensation is considered inadequate, and the same would be the case if the sum were increased to fifty millions. This may sound preposterous on first consideration, but not to those who know that the money would be distributed among the dictator's clique and the religious orders . . . .

There is also a very erroneous impression to the effect that the canal when completed will have a great beneficial influence on our country. The conditions as they exist to-day place Colombia in the position of the owner of a bridge, over which an immense traffic is constantly passing. There are many steamship lines converging on the ports of Panama and Colon that load and unload there enormous quantities of merchandise in transit, while large numbers of passengers are compelled to stop at both ends of the trans-Isthmian railroad. . . . Such will not be the case when the canal is opened. Steamers will go through as rapidly as possible, the passengers dreading the unhealthy climate. There will be no loading of cargoes. . . .

The facts stated are perfectly well known to Colombians, who from the time of Bolivar have imagined that within the narrow strip linking the two American continents, Colombia held her great trump card. It would be an unspeakable disappointment to them to see that advantage fall into other hands, with no return but a few millions of dollars to be employed not for but against their welfare and prosperity. Indeed, so strong is this sentiment that it seems more patriotic to feel that no compensation at all would be preferable. There are many who maintain that a seizure of the Isthmus by a world Power would be more satisfactory, inasmuch as Colombians would be in a position to repeat in all coming years the phrase: *"Tout est perdu, fors L'honneur."* The rights of Colombia in that case would hold good forever, and the day might come when they would be revindicated; but no such hope could be entertained if the dishonest band of clericals, who act as the government of Colombia, give a seemingly legal consent to the transaction.

The members of that band are in favor of the canal . . . simply because they see the possibility of securing ten millions of dollars to be applied to their own purposes. They argue more or less thus: "The Isthmus is a segregated limb of the country where we have not full sway. We may just as well abandon it in exchange for ten millions of dollars with which to establish our uncontested dominion in the rest of the territory."

The other enthusiastic supporters of the canal treaty as it stands are the short-sighted inhabitants of the Isthmus, who long to kill the goose that lays the golden eggs. They see in the near future a boom for their region—excavation contracts, which they imagine will be as profitable as were those of the good old times of the *Compagnie Universelle;* an increase in the value of property; thousands of people coming to make their fortunes, and all the business opportunities attending an undertaking of this kind. . . .

What the Colombians would like to do about the canal would be to have their country hold a permanent interest in the enterprise as a partner of the United States, deriving an income that would benefit not a few officials and one political party but all the people for generations to come. There is no reason why a partnership of that nature could not be successfully carried out, in the same way as a partnership between individuals. All details could be deliberately and safely settled between the two countries to the entire satisfaction of both, bearing in mind that a century in the life of a nation counts no more than one year in the life of a man, and that the canal must be of vast consequence for ages. The desire to cut the canal open as rapidly as possible is praiseworthy, but it is more important to lay first the solid foundations of the transaction and establish the exact limitations of the rights of those concerned, so as to avoid all possible friction in the future.

39

ROOSEVELT COROLLARY TO THE MONROE DOCTRINE (1904)

The victory in the Spanish-American War thrust the United States into the new position of world power, but it was problems in the Western Hemisphere that attracted American interests. Many Caribbean countries were plagued with

"Theodore Roosevelt, Fourth Annual Message," *The State of the Union Messages of the Presidents, 1790-1966: Vol. 2. 1861-1904*, ed. Fred L. Israel (New York: Chelsea House Publishers, 1967), 2134-2135.

political instability, and violent revolutions often broke out. Compounding the problem was the poor financial state of these countries. Concerned with stability in the region, and wary that hostile foreign powers might use military force to collect debts from these countries and establish a presence in the hemisphere, President Theodore Roosevelt intervened in the domestic affairs of neighboring countries to provide stability and order. This intervention also created investment opportunities for American bankers and businessmen. Such shortsighted activities became a pattern and helped create a legacy of distrust between Latin American nations and the United States. In his 1904 annual message to Congress, excerpted below, Roosevelt offered an explanation for intervention in his famous "corollary" to the Monroe Doctrine.

Questions to Consider: Under what circumstances would the United States intervene in a Caribbean Basin country's affairs? What are the purposes of such intervention? What are the potential problems of exercising such "international police power"? Are there elements of the Roosevelt Corollary to the Monroe Doctrine in America's role in the "new world order" of the 1990s (Document 99)?

It is not true that the United States feels any land hunger or entertains any projects as regards the other nations of the Western Hemisphere save such as are for their welfare. All that this country desires is to see the neighboring countries stable, orderly, and prosperous. Any country whose people conduct themselves well can count upon our hearty friendship. If a nation shows that it knows how to act with reasonable efficiency and decency in social and political matters, if it keeps order and pays its obligations, it need fear no interference from the United States. Chronic wrongdoing, or an impotence which results in a general loosening of the ties of civilized society, may in America, as elsewhere, ultimately require intervention by some civilized nation, and in the Western Hemisphere the adherence of the United States to the Monroe Doctrine may force the United States, however reluctantly, in flagrant cases of such wrongdoing or impotence, to the exercise of an international police power. If every country washed by the Caribbean Sea would show the progress in stable and just civilization which with the aid of the Platt amendment Cuba has shown since our troops left the island, and which so many of the republics in both Americas are constantly and brilliantly showing, all question of interference by this Nation with their affairs would be at an end. Our interests and those of our southern neighbors are in reality identical. They have great natural riches, and if within their borders the reign of law and justice obtains, prosperity is sure to come to them. While they thus obey the primary laws of civilized society they may rest assured that they will be treated by us in a spirit of cordial and helpful sympathy. We would interfere with them only in the last resort, and then only if it became evident that their inability or unwillingness to do justice at home and abroad had violated the rights of the United States or had invited foreign aggression to the detriment of the entire body of American nations. It is a mere truism to say that every nation, whether in America or anywhere else, which desires to maintain its freedom, its independence, must ultimately realize that the right of such independence can not be separated from the responsibility of making good use of it.

In asserting the Monroe Doctrine, in taking such steps as we have taken in regard to Cuba, Venezuela, and Panama, and in endeavoring to circumscribe the theater of war in the Far East, and to secure the open door in China, we have acted in our own interest as well as in the interest of humanity at large. There are, however, cases in which, while our own interests are not greatly involved, strong appeal is made to our sympathies. Ordinarily it is very much wiser and more useful for us to concern ourselves with striving for our own moral and material betterment here at home than to concern ourselves with trying to better the condition of things in other nations. We have plenty of sins of our own to war against, and under ordinary circumstances we can do more for the general uplifting of humanity by striving with heart and soul to put a stop to civic corruption, to brutal lawlessness and violent race prejudices here at home than by passing resolutions about wrongdoing elsewhere. Nevertheless there are occasional crimes committed on so vast a scale and of such peculiar horror as to make us doubt whether it is not our manifest duty to endeavor at least to show our disapproval of the deed and our sympathy with those who have suffered it. The cases must be extreme in which such a course is justifiable. There must be no effort made to remove the mote from our brother's eye if we refuse to remove the beam from our own. But in extreme cases action may be justifiable and proper. What form the action shall take must depend upon the circumstances of the case; that is, upon the degree of the atrocity and upon our power to remedy it. The cases in which we could interfere by force of arms as we interfered to put a stop to intolerable conditions in Cuba are necessarily very few.

—·—

The Progressive Movement

2

     The polarization of society into rich and poor, assimilable and unassimilable in the late 19th century prompted many middle-class Americans into action. The reformers who emerged to cure these ills came to be known as the progressives. Eschewing the laissez faire approach of the past, the movement believed that through the expansion of democracy, active government, and the regulation of business to create opportunity, a new class of well-trained professionals could solve society's problems. Although some contemporaries criticized the progressives' efforts as radical, the leaders of the movement actually sought a more centrist approach in solving these problems. The next group of documents illustrates the problems facing and solutions advocated by the progressives.

40

AN INSIDER'S VIEW OF HULL HOUSE

One of the initial efforts to bring about progressive reform came from individuals such as Jane Addams, who helped establish the settlement house movement in America. Part of a first generation of college-educated women, Addams declined marriage and motherhood and devoted her life to the poor and to social reform. In 1889, she and college friend Ellen Starr bought the Hull House mansion in a Chicago immigrant neighborhood and created a model settlement house that offered services to the poor in the neighborhood: playground, nursery, kindergarten, library, night school for adults, and some job training. But Addams realized that such neighborhood activities were futile unless laws were reformed to address larger problems, so she campaigned to pass state and local laws that would improve conditions in the urban neighborhoods. Addams publicized Hull House and social reform with lecture tours and writing. Hilda S. Polacheck, the author of the excerpted selection below, was a Polish immigrant who discovered Hull House and its offerings. Her account presents a unique insider's view of Hull House and the services it provided for immigrants in the neighborhood. Polacheck credits Hull House, and especially Jane Addams, with making her life in America better.

Questions to Consider: What did Hull House provide immigrants and urban dwellers? Why? How could they finance such an operation? Why did Hilda Polacheck frequently visit and work at Hull House? What was Hull House's impact on the urban neighborhood? Are there similar institutions in contemporary American cities?

She took me up a flight of stairs and then down a flight and we came to the Labor Museum. The museum had been opened a short time before and it was a very special addition to the work at Hull-House and very dear to her heart. As I look back, and this may be wishful thinking, I feel that she sensed what I needed most at that time. . . .

There were many classes connected with the Labor Museum. Here we could learn how to cook and sew and also learn about millinery and embroidery. . . .

There was still another function that the Labor Museum filled. Miss Addams found that there was a definite feeling of superiority on the part of children of immigrants toward their parents. As soon as the children learned to speak English, they were prone to look down on those who could not speak the language. I am grateful that I never had that feeling toward my parents, but I often talked to play-mates who would disdainfully say: "Aw, she can't talk English."

Hilda Satt Polacheck, *I Came a Stranger: The Story of a Hull-House Girl,* ed. Dena J. Polacheck Epstein (Urbana, IL, 1989), 63-67, 70-73, 91-92, 102. Copyright 1989 The Trustees of the University of Illinois. Reprinted by permission.

I recall having an argument with a girl whose mother could speak German, French, Russian, and Polish but had not yet learned to speak English. That girl did not realize that her mother was a linguist. To her, the mother was just a greenhorn.

For such children the Labor Museum was an eye-opener. When they saw crowds of well-dressed Americans standing around admiring what Italian, Irish, German, and Scandinavian mothers could do, their disdain for their mothers often vanished.

The Labor Museum did not solve all the problems of immigrant parents and their children. There were many problems that were not easy to solve. Children, by going to school and to work, did come in contact with forces in American life and had a better chance of becoming Americanized. But I am sure the Labor Museum reduced the strained feelings on the part of immigrants and their children. . . .

I soon branched out into other activities. I joined a reading class that was conducted by Miss Clara Landsberg. . . .

. . . She opened new vistas in reading for me. In her class we would be assigned a book, which we were to read during the week and then discuss the following session of the class. The class met once a week. I not only read the assigned books but every book I could borrow. Dickens, Scott, Thackeray, Louisa May Alcott, Victor Hugo, Alexander Dumas, and many others now became my friends. The daily monotony of making cuffs was eased by thinking of these books and looking forward to evenings at Hull-House.

For ten years I spent most of my evenings at Hull-House. The first three years of that time I saw Jane Addams almost every night. As more and more people found their way to this haven of love and understanding, she began to relegate the work to other people and to seek rest at the home of friends. But her presence was always felt, whether she was there in person or in spirit. . . .

Bad housing of the thousands of immigrants who lived near Hull-House was the concern of Jane Addams. Where there were alleys in back of the houses, these alleys were filled with large wooden boxes where garbage and horse manure were dumped. In most cases these boxes did not have covers and were breeding places for flies and rats. The city gave contracts to private scavengers to collect the garbage. Its responsibility seemed to end there. There was no alley inspection and no one checked on these collectors.

When Jane Addams called the attention of the health department to the unsanitary conditions, she was told that the city had contracted to have the garbage collected and it could do nothing else. When the time came to renew contracts for garbage collection, Miss Addams, with the backing of some businessmen, put in a bid to collect garbage. Her bid was never considered, but she was appointed garbage inspector for the ward. I have a vision of Jane Addams, honored by the great of the world, acclaimed as the first citizen of Chicago, following a filthy garbage truck down an alley in her long skirt and immaculate white blouse. . . .

Being allowed to teach English to immigrants at Hull-House did more for me than anything that I imparted to my students. It gave me a feeling of security that I so sorely needed. What added to my confidence in the future was that my class was always crowded and the people seemed to make good progress. From time to time Jane Addams would visit the class to see what I was doing, and she always left with that rare smile on her face; she seemed to be pleased. . . .

But to come back to the subject of textbooks, since there were none, I decided to use the Declaration of Independence as a text. It was a distinct success. The students did not find the words difficult; so in addition to learning English, we all learned the principles of Americanism.

I next introduced the manual on naturalization and the class learned English while studying how to become a citizen. It was all very exciting and stimulating.

My students were now beginning to confide in me. Classes at Hull-House were never just classes where people came to learn a specific subject. There was a human element of friendliness among us. Life was not soft or easy for any of them. They worked hard all day in shops and factories and made this valiant effort to learn the language of their adopted country. At times they needed real help, and they knew that somewhere in this wonderful house on Halsted Street they would get it. . . .

As time went on, I discovered that Hull-House was the experimental laboratory for Jane Addams's interests and services. To create opportunities for young people of the neighborhood, to bring a little sunshine into otherwise bleak lives of older immigrants, to point out the evils of miserable housing; in short, to tell Chicago what its responsibility to the poor was, was just first aid to the problem. She traveled through America spreading the gospel of a better life than she had found on South Halsted Street. As a result, social settlements sprang up all over the country. Chicago became dotted with playgrounds. Social centers were added to these playgrounds and became the responsibility of the city government.

41

BOSS GOVERNMENT AT WORK (1903)

In the early 20th century, a group of investigative journalists began writing exposés about the social, political, and economic problems of the nation. They considered their work scientific and objective. President Theodore Roosevelt contemptuously nicknamed them "muckrakers" from a character in John Bunyan's *Pilgrim's Progress* who "could look no way but downward with a muckrake in his hands" as he dug up filth rather than see more important issues. The beginning of muckraking journalism is often associated with a *McClure's Magazine* 1902-1903 series of Lincoln Steffens' articles on municipal corruption in various American cities. The articles, later collected in a book, *The Shame of the Cities*, focused national attention on the problem and helped bring about reform. Steffens spent his career as a reporter and editor with New York newspapers and magazines and prided himself on objective reporting that was not self-righteous. The final article in the *McClure's* series, which is excerpted on the next page,

Lincoln Steffens, *Shame of the Cities* (New York, 1904), 279-94, 302-303. Originally published as "New York: Good Government to the Test," *McClure's Magazine* 22 (November 1903): 84-92.

focused on the Democratic party machine—Tammany Hall—in New York City and how this boss government operated.

———

Questions to Consider: Why does Lincoln Steffens marvel at Tammany's blatant dishonesty? How does this boss government obtain and preserve political power? Why does Steffens consider Tammany leaders as bad for the people? Why is Steffens fearful of "municipal reform"? How is this boss government rule broken?

———

Tammany is bad government; not inefficient, but dishonest; not a party, not a delusion and a snare, hardly known by its party name—Democracy; having little standing in the national councils of the party and caring little for influence outside of the city. Tammany is Tammany, the embodiment of corruption. All the world knows and all the world may know what it is and what it is after. For hypocrisy is not a Tammany vice. Tammany is for Tammany, and the Tammany men say so. Other rings proclaim lies and make pretensions; other rogues talk about the tariff and imperialism. Tammany is honestly dishonest. Time and time again, in private and in public, the leaders, big and little, have said they are out for themselves and their own; not for the public, but for "me and my friends"; not for New York, but for Tammany. Richard Croker said under oath once that he worked for his own pockets all the time, and Tom Grady, the Tammany orator, has brought his crowds to their feet cheering sentiments as primitive, stated with candor as brutal. The man from Mars would say that such an organization, so self-confessed, could not be very dangerous to an intelligent people. Foreigners marvel at it and at us, and even Americans—Pennsylvanians, for example—cannot understand why we New Yorkers regard Tammany as so formidable. I think I can explain it. Tammany is corruption with consent; it is bad government founded on the suffrages of people. . . . Tammany rules, when it rules, by right of the votes of the people of New York. . . .

Tammany's democratic corruption rests upon the corruption of the people, the plain people, and there lies its great significance; its grafting system is one in which more individuals share than any I have studied. The people themselves get very little; they come cheap, but they are interested. Divided into districts, the organization subdivides them into precincts or neighborhoods, and their sovereign power, in the form of votes, is brought up by kindness and petty privileges. They are forced to a surrender, when necessary, by intimidation, but the leader and his captains have their hold because they take care of their own. They speak pleasant words, smile friendly smiles, notice the baby, give picnics up the River or the Sound, or a slap on the back; find jobs, most of them at the city's expense, but they have also news-stands, peddling privileges, railroad and other business places to dispense, they permit violations of the law, and, if a man has broken the law without permission, see him through the court. Though a blow in the face is as readily given as a shake of the hand, Tammany kindness is real kindness, and will go far, remember long, and take infinite trouble for a friend.

The power that is gathered up thus cheaply, like garbage, in the districts is concentrated in the district leader, who in turn passes it on through a general committee to the boss. This is a form of living government, extra-legal, but very actual, and, though the beginnings of it are purely democratic, it develops at each stage into an autocracy. . . .

Tammany leaders are usually the natural leaders of the people in these districts, and they are originally good-natured, kindly men. No one has a more sincere liking than I for some of those common but generous fellows; their charity is real, at first. But they sell out their own people. They do give them coal and help them in their private troubles, but, as they grow rich and powerful, the kindness goes out of the charity and they not only collect at their saloons or in rents—cash for their "goodness"; they not only ruin fathers and sons and cause the troubles they relieve; they sacrifice the children in the schools; let the Health Department neglect the tenements, and, worst of all, plant vice in the neighborhood and in the homes of the poor.

This is not only bad; it is bad politics; it has defeated Tammany. Woe to New York when Tammany learns better. Honest fools talk of the reform of Tammany Hall. It is an old hope, this, and twice it has been disappointed, but it is not vain. That is the real danger ahead. The reform of a corrupt ring means, as I have said before, the reform of its system of grafting and a wise consideration of certain features of good government. . . .

42

THE JUNGLE (1906)

Early in the 20th century, some individuals questioned the quality of food and medicine production in America. The "embalmed beef" scandal of the Spanish-American War, involving tainted provisions for troops, and muckraking exposés of patent medicines and the "beef trust" had alerted the American people that some problems existed. But when Upton Sinclair's novel *The Jungle* was published in January 1906, it created an immediate furor. The novel was intended to advocate socialism as it depicted the difficult life of Lithuanian immigrant Jurgis Rudkus and his friends in the fictitious Packingtown. Sinclair also included some descriptions of conditions in the meatpacking houses where Jurgis worked. It was these shocking descriptions, some of which are excerpted below, that appalled the American people. President Theodore Roosevelt read the book, then sent two agents to investigate Chicago's meatpacking houses to learn if Sinclair's depiction was accurate—and it was. Within six months the Pure Food and Drug Act was passed. Sinclair later wrote about his novel: "I aimed at the public's heart and by accident hit it in the stomach."

Upton Sinclair, *The Jungle* (New York, 1906), 115-120.

·⌐ **Questions to Consider:** Which is more shocking, the work conditions or the preparation of meat for the American consumers? Why? Why did the American people tolerate such food production? How could government regulation resolve the situation?

S o Jurgis learned a few things about the great and only Durham canned goods, which had become a national institution. They were regular alchemists at Durham's; they advertised a mushroom catsup, and the men who made it did not know what a mushroom looked like. They advertised "potted chicken,"—and it was like the boarding-house soup of the comic papers, through which a chicken had walked with rubbers on. Perhaps they had a secret process for making chickens chemically—who knows? Said Jurgis's friends; the things that went into the mixture were tripe, and the fat of pork, and beef suet, and hearts of beef, and finally the waste ends of veal, when they had any. They put these up in several grades, and sold them at several prices; but the contents of the cans all came out of the same hopper. And then there was "potted game" and "potted grouse," "potted ham" and "devilled ham"—de-vyled, as the men called it. "De-vyled" ham was made out of the waste ends of smoked beef that were too small to be sliced by the machines; and also tripe, dyed with chemicals so that it would not show white; and trimmings of hams and corned beef; and potatoes, skins and all; and finally the hard cartilaginous ingenious mixture was ground up and flavoured with spices to make it taste like something. Anybody who could invent a new imitation had been sure of a fortune from old Durham. . . .

There was another interesting set of statistics that a person might have gathered in Packingtown—those of the various afflictions of the workers. When Jurgis had first inspected the packing plants with Szedvilas, he had marvelled while he listened to the tale of all the things that were made out of the carcasses of animals, and of all the lesser industries that were maintained there; now he found that each one of these lesser industries was a separate little inferno, in its way as horrible as the killing beds, the source and fountain of them all. The workers in each of them had their own peculiar diseases. And the wandering visitor might be sceptical about all the swindles, but he could not be sceptical about these, for the worker bore the evidence of them about on his own person—generally he had only to hold out his hand.

There were the men in the pickle rooms, for instance, where old Antanas had gotten his death; scarce a one of these that had not some spot of horror on his person. Let a man so much as scrape his finger pushing a truck in the pickle rooms, and he might have a sore that would put him out of the world; all the joints in his fingers might be eaten by the acid, one by one. Of the butchers and floorsmen, the beef-goners and trimmers, and all those who used knives, you could scarcely find a person who had the use of his thumb; time and time again the base of it had been slashed, till it was a mere lump of flesh against which the man pressed the knife to hold it. The hands of these men would be criss-crossed with cuts, until you could no longer pretend to count them or to trace them. They would have no nails—they had worn them off pulling hides; their knuckles were swollen so that their fingers spread out like a fan. There were men who worked in the cooking rooms, in the midst of steam and sickening odours, by artificial light; in these rooms the germs of tuberculosis might live for two years, but the supply was renewed every hour. There were the beef-luggers, who carried two-hundred-pound quarters into the refrigerator cars—a fearful kind of work, that began at four o'clock in the morning, and that wore out the most powerful men in a few years. There were those who worked in the chilling rooms, and whose special disease was rheumatism; the time limit that a man could work in the chilling rooms was said to be five years. There were the wool-pluckers, whose hands went to pieces even sooner than the hands of the pickle men; for the pelts of the sheep had to be painted with acid to loosen the wool, and then the pluckers had to pull out this wool with their bare hands, till the acid had eaten their fingers off. There were those who made the tins for the canned meat; and their hands, too, were a maze of cuts, and each cut represented a chance for blood poisoning. Some worked at the stamping machines, and it was seldom that one could work long there at the pace that was set, and not give out and forget himself, and have a part of his hand chopped off. There were the "hoisters," as they were called, whose task it was to press the lever which lifted the dead cattle off the floor. They ran along upon a rafter, peering down through the damp and the steam; and as old Durham's architects had not built the killing room for the convenience of the hoisters, at every few feet they would have to stoop under a beam, say four feet above the one they ran on; which got them into the habit of stooping, so that in a few years they would be walking like chimpanzees. Worst of any, however, were the fertilizer-men, and those who served in the cooking rooms. These people could not be shown to the visitor, for the odour of a fertilizer-man would scare any ordinary visitor at a hundred yards; and as for the other men, who worked in tank rooms full of steams, and in some of which there were open vats near the level of the floor, their peculiar trouble was that they fell into the vats; and when they were fished out, there was never enough of them left to be worth exhibiting—sometimes they would be overlooked for days, till all but the bones of them had gone out to the world as Durham's Pure Leaf Lard!

--- --- --- --- --- --- --- --- --- --- --- --- ---

43

"THE PRINCIPLES OF SCIENTIFIC MANAGEMENT"
(1912)

An aspect of the Progressive Era that altered traditional production methods, redefined worker-management relations, and would be applied to government operations was efficiency through scientific management. While business had long sought efficiency, it was Frederick W. Taylor who developed and implemented a

U.S. Congress, House, *Hearings Before the Special Committee of the House of Representatives to Investigate the Taylor and Other Systems of Shop Management under the Authority of House Resolution 90* (Washington, DC, 1912), 3: 1377-1508.

practical management system. Taylor began work as a common laborer, became a steel mill engineer, but resigned in 1893 to start a consulting firm that specialized in "Systematizing Shop Management and Manufacturing Costs." After years of observing manufacturing conditions and methods, Taylor concluded that by scientific study of every individual step in a manufacturing process, information on the production capabilities of machine and man could be obtained, and when this information was properly applied, the animosity between worker and management would dissolve and a more efficient operation would result. Taylor's new system was called "Scientific Management"; he applied it in a variety of businesses, but its successful use in the Bethlehem Steel Company brought him fame. In 1901, he decided to devote his life to scientific management: he published on the topic and gave his services freely to any company willing to accept his system. In 1911, Taylor was called before a special congressional committee on new management systems. His excerpted testimony is below.

—

Questions to Consider: What is scientific management? What is required for it to succeed? How would workers and management view Taylor's new system? How does scientific management compare with the description of labor relations in "The Impact of Mechanization" (Document 14)? Is Taylor's proposed system used today?

—

But under scientific management absolutely every element in the work of every man in your establishment, sooner or later, becomes the subject of exact, precise, scientific investigation and knowledge to replace the old, "I believe so," and "I guess so." Every motion, every small fact becomes the subject of careful, scientific investigation. . . .

I want to clear the deck, sweep away a good deal of rubbish first by pointing out what scientific management is not.

Scientific management is not any efficiency device, not a device of any kind for securing efficiency; nor is it any bunch or group of efficiency devices. It is not a new system of figuring costs; it is not a new scheme of paying men; it is not a piecework system; it is not a bonus system; it is not a premium system; it is no scheme for paying men; it is not holding a stop watch on a man and writing things down about him; it is not time study; it is not motion study nor an analysis of the movements of men; it is not the printing and ruling and unloading of a ton or two of blanks on a set of men and saying, "Here's your system; go use it." It is not divided foremanship or functional foremanship; it is not any of the devices which the average man calls to mind when scientific management is spoken of. The average man thinks of one or more of these things when he hears the words "scientific management" mentioned, but scientific management is not any of these devices. I am not sneering at cost-keeping systems, at time study, at functional foremanship, nor at any new and improved scheme of paying men, nor at any efficiency devices, if they are really devices that make for efficiency. I believe in them; but what I am emphasizing is that these devices in whole or in part are not scientific management; they are useful adjuncts to scientific management, so are they also useful adjuncts of other systems of management.

In its essence, scientific management involves a complete mental revolution on the part of the workingman engaged in any particular establishment or industry—a complete mental revolution on the part of these men as to their duties toward their work, toward their employers. And it involves the equally complete mental revolution on the part of those on the management's side—the foreman, the superintendent, the owner of the business, the board of directors—a complete mental revolution on their part as to their duties toward their fellow workers in the management, toward their workmen, and toward all of their daily problems. And without this complete mental revolution on both sides scientific management does not exist. . . .

The great revolution that takes place in the mental attitudes of the two parties under scientific management is that both sides take their eyes off the division of the surplus as the all important matter, and together turn their attention toward increasing the size of the surplus until this surplus becomes so large that it is unnecessary to quarrel over how it shall be divided. . . .

. . . This, gentlemen, is the beginning of the great mental revolution which constitutes the first step toward scientific management. It is along this line of complete change in the mental attitude of both sides; of the substitution of peace for war; the substitution of hearty brotherly cooperation for contention and strife; of both pulling hard in the same direction instead of pulling apart; of replacing suspicious watchfulness with mutual confidence; of becoming friends instead of enemies; it is along this line, I say, that scientific management must be developed.

. . . There is, however, one more change in viewpoint which is absolutely essential to the existence of scientific management. Both sides must recognize as essential the substitution of exact scientific investigation and knowledge for the old individual judgment or opinion, either of the workingmen or the boss, in all matters relating to the work done in the establishment. And this applies both as to the methods to be employed in doing the work and the time in which each job should be done.

Scientific management cannot be said to exist, then, in any establishment until after this change has taken place in the mental attitude of both the management and the men, both as to their duty to cooperate in producing the largest possible surplus and as to the necessity for substituting exact scientific knowledge for opinions or the old rule-of-thumb or individual knowledge.

These are two absolutely essential elements of scientific management.

44

THE NEW NATIONALISM OF THEODORE ROOSEVELT (1912)

Disappointed with William Howard Taft's conservative nature and his unwillingness to pursue progressive policies, former President Theodore Roosevelt began challenging Taft's position while offering a new brand of progressivism.

"Roosevelt Would Give People Right to Recall Judges' Decisions: Favors Initiative and Referendum, Carefully Safeguarded," *The Ohio State Journal* (Columbus, OH), 22 February 1912, 4.

Roosevelt gave a series of speeches throughout the country in which he gradually formulated his program—the "New Nationalism." Roosevelt called for expanding the federal government's powers to control and regulate big business, new measures of direct democracy, and a program of labor and social legislation. In February 1912, Roosevelt addressed the Ohio Constitutional Convention and offered one of the most clear explanations of the "New Nationalism." The speech is excerpted below. Several days after the address, Roosevelt announced he would seek the Republican party's presidential nomination in 1912. When the Republicans chose Taft, Roosevelt bolted the party and established the Progressive or Bull Moose party that used the "New Nationalism" as its platform.

Questions to Consider: What are the various roles of government according to Theodore Roosevelt? How does Roosevelt propose to expand democracy? For what purposes? What cautions does he offer about these democratic features?

This is the reason why I have for so many years insisted, as regards our national government, that it is both futile and mischievous to endeavor to correct the evils of big business by an attempt to restore business conditions as they were in the middle of the last century, before railways and telegraphs rendered larger business organizations both inevitable and desirable. . . .

All business into which the element of monopoly in any way or degree enters, and where it proves in practice impossible totally to eliminate this element of monopoly, should be carefully supervised, regulated and controlled by governmental authority; and such control should be exercised by administrative, rather than judicial officers. No effort should be made to destroy a big corporation merely because it is big, merely because it has shown itself a particularly efficient business instrument.

But we should not fear, if necessary, to bring the regulation of big corporations to the point of controlling conditions so that the wage-worker shall have a wage more than sufficient to cover the basic cost of living, and hours of labor not so excessive as to wreck his strength by the strain of unending toil and leave him unfit to do his duty as a good citizen in the community. Where regulation by competition (which is, of course, preferable), proves insufficient, we should not shrink from bringing governmental regulation to the point of control of monopoly prices if it should ever become necessary to do so, just as in exceptional cases railway rates are now regulated. . . .

The people have nothing whatever to fear from giving any public servant power so long as they retain their own power to hold him accountable for his use of the power they have delegated to him. You will get the best service where you elect only a few men, and where each man has his duties and responsibilities, and is obliged to work in the open, so that the people who know who he is and what he is doing, and have the information that will enable them to hold him to account for his stewardship.

I believe in providing for direct nominations by the people, including therein direct presidential primaries for the election of delegates to the national nominating conventions. Not as a matter of theory, but as a matter of plain and proved experience, we find that the convention system, while it often records the popular will, is also often used by adroit politicians as a method of thwarting the popular will. In other words, the existing machinery for nominations is cumbrous, and is not designed to secure the real expression of a majority of the people, but we do not like to acquiesce in a nomination secured by adroit political management in defeating the wish of the majority of people.

I believe in the election of United States senators by direct vote. Just as actual experience convinced our people that presidents should be elected (as they are now in practice, although not in theory) by direct vote of the people instead of by indirect vote through an untrammeled electoral college, so actual experience has convinced us that senators should be elected by direct vote of the people instead of indirectly through the various legislatures.

I believe in the initiative and the referendum, which should be used not to destroy representative government, but to correct it whenever it become misrepresentative. Here again I am concerned not with theories but with actual facts. If in any state the people are themselves satisfied with their present representative system, then it is, of course, their right to keep that system unchanged; and it is nobody's business but theirs.

But in actual practice it has been found in very many states that legislative bodies have not been responsive to the popular will. Therefore I believe that the state should provide for the possibility of direct popular action in order to make good such legislative failure.

The power to invoke such direct action, both by initiative and referendum, should be provided in such fashion as to prevent its being wantonly or too frequently used. I do not believe that it should be made the easy or ordinary way of taking action. In the great majority of cases it is far better that action on legislative matters should be taken by those specifically delegated to perform the task. . . . But where the men thus delegated fail to perform their duty, then it should be in the power of the people themselves to perform the duty. . . .

I do not believe in adopting the recall save as a last resort, when it has become clearly evident that no other course will achieve the desired result. But either the recall will have to be adopted or else it will have to be made much easier than it now is to get rid, not merely of a bad judge, but of a judge who, however virtuous, has grown so out of touch with social needs and facts that he is unfit longer to render good service on the bench. . . .

When the supreme court of the state declares a given statute unconstitutional, because in conflict with the state or the national constitution, its opinion should be subject to revision by the people themselves. Such an opinion ought always to be created with great respect by the people, and unquestionably in the majority of cases would be accepted and followed by them. But actual experience has shown the vital need of the people reserving to themselves the right to pass upon such opinion. . . .

I do not say that the people are infallible. But I do say that the American people are more often sound in their decisions than is the case with any of the governmental bodies to whom, for their convenience, they have delegated portions of their power. If this is not so, then there is no justification for the existence of our government; and if it is so, then there is no justification for refusing to give the people the real, and not merely the nominal, ultimate decision on questions of constitutional law. . . . [S]o I hold that now the American people as a whole have shown themselves wiser than the courts in the way they have approached and dealt with such vital questions of our day as those concerning the proper control of the big corporations and of securing their rights to industrial workers.

45

"WHY WOMEN SHOULD VOTE" (1910)

In the several decades after the Seneca Falls Convention (1848), women argued that suffrage was a natural right, a position that threatened male political dominance and was therefore denied. At the dawn of the 20th century, the woman suffrage campaign languished, but a less threatening expediency argument emerged to help revive the movement. Frustrated with combating state and local politicians to bring about social improvement, the settlement house women realized they needed the vote in order to challenge the politicians and to make America better. The best known settlement house woman was Jane Addams, who published the excerpted article below in the *Ladies Home Journal* in 1910. Addams placated the middle-class female audience of this magazine by arguing that the woman's domain remained the home and cultural affairs, but that women voting could help with the larger problems of social housekeeping. With this argument (and others like it)—coupled with new publicity generated by the actions of radical suffragettes, a revitalized moderate suffragist organization, and women's good deeds in wartime—public support for woman suffrage grew rapidly. In 1920, the Nineteenth Amendment, granting women the right to vote, was ratified.

—

Questions to Consider: How does Jane Addams argue that woman suffrage is an extension of the traditional female duties? Is the argument valid? In what ways does Addams soften the perceived threat to male political power? How would women and men react to this article?

—

This paper is an attempt to show that many women today are failing to discharge their duties to their own households properly simply because they do not perceive that as society grows more complicated it is necessary that woman shall extend her sense of responsibility to many things outside of her own home if she would continue to preserve the home in its entirety. One could illustrate in many ways. A woman's simplest duty, one would say, is to keep her house clean and wholesome and to feed her children properly. Yet if she lives in a tenement house, as so many of my neighbors do, she cannot fulfill these simple obligations by her own efforts

Jane Addams, "Why Women Should Vote," *Ladies Home Journal* 27 (January 1910): 21-22.

because she is utterly dependent upon the city administration for the conditions which render decent living possible. . . . In a crowded city quarter, however, if the street is not cleaned by the city authorities no amount of private sweeping will keep the tenement free from grime; if the garbage is not properly collected and destroyed a tenement-house mother may see her children sicken and die of diseases from which she alone is powerless to shield them, although her tenderness and devotion are unbounded. . . . In short, if woman would keep on with her old business of caring for her house and rearing her children she will have to have some conscience in regard to public affairs lying quite outside of her immediate household. The individual conscience and devotion are no longer effective. . . .

If women follow only the lines of their traditional activities there are certain primary duties which belong to even the most conservative women, and which no one woman or group of women can adequately discharge unless they join the more general movements looking toward social amelioration through legal enactment.

The first of these . . . is woman's responsibility for the members of her own household that they may be properly fed and clothed and surrounded by hygienic conditions. The second is a responsibility for the education of children: (a) that they may be provided with good schools; (b) that they may be kept free from vicious influences on the street; (c) that when working they may be protected by adequate child-labor legislation.

(a) The duty of a woman toward the schools which her children attend is so obvious that it is not necessary to dwell upon it. But even this simple obligation cannot be effectively carried out without some form of social organization as the mothers' school clubs and mothers' congresses testify, and to which the most conservative women belong because they feel the need of wider reading and discussion concerning the many problems of childhood. It is, therefore, perhaps natural that the public should have been more willing to accord a vote to women in school matters than in any other, and yet women have never been members of a Board of Education in sufficient numbers to influence largely actual school curriculi. . . .

(b) But women are also beginning to realize that children need attention outside of school hours; that much of the petty vices in cities is merely the love of pleasure gone wrong, the overrestrained boy or girl seeking improper recreation and excitement. It is obvious that a little study of the needs of children, a sympathetic understanding of the conditions under which they go astray, might save hundreds of them. Women traditionally have had an opportunity to observe the plays of children and the needs of youth, and yet in Chicago, at least, they had done singularly little in this vexed problem of juvenile delinquency until they helped to inaugurate the Juvenile Court movement a dozen years ago. . . .

(c) As the education of her children has been more and more transferred to the school, so that even children four years old go to the kindergarten, the woman has been left in a household of constantly-narrowing interests, not only because the children are away, but also because one industry after another is slipping from the household into the factory. . . . Because many thousands of those working in factories and shops are girls between the ages of fourteen and twenty-two there is a necessity that older women should be interested in the conditions of industry.

The very fact that these girls are not going to remain in industry permanently makes it more important that some one should see to it that they shall not be incapacitated for their future family life because they work for exhausting hours and under insanitary conditions.

. . . If conscientious women were convinced that it was a civic duty to be informed in regard to these grave industrial affairs, and then to express the conclusions which they had reached by depositing a piece of paper in a ballot-box, one cannot imagine that they would shirk simply because the action ran counter to old traditions. . . .

This is, perhaps, the attitude of many busy women who would be glad to use the ballot to further public measures in which they are interested and for which they have been working for years. It offends the taste of such a woman to be obliged to use indirect "influence" when she is accustomed to well-bred, open action in other affairs, and she very much resents the time spent in persuading a voter to take her point of view, and possibly to give up his own, quite as honest and valuable as hers, although different because resulting from a totally different experience. Public-spirited women who wish to use the ballot, as I know them, do not wish to do the work of men nor to take over men's affairs. They simply want an opportunity to do their own work and to take care of those affairs which naturally and historically belong to women, but which are constantly being overlooked and slighted in our political institutions. . . .

In closing, may I recapitulate that if woman would fulfill her traditional responsibility to her own children; if she would educate and protect from danger factory children who must find their recreation on the street; if she would bring the cultural forces to bear upon our materialistic civilization; and if she would do it all with the dignity and directness fitting one who carries on her immemorial duties, then she must bring herself to the use of the ballot—that latest implement for self-government. May we not fairly say that American women need this implement in order to preserve the home?

MAKING THE WORLD SAFE FOR DEMOCRACY

3

The values of the progressive movement were expressed on a wider scale when the United States entered the First World War. Government-employed professionals using a centrist approach to solve problems now directed their methods against the United States' foreign enemies. The ensuing crusade to save democracy set off a similar movement at home, in which those who lacked this progressive sense of patriotism, particularly leftists, were subject to persecution by both the government and private citizens. The dislocation that followed the war only heightened the sense of urgency perceived by many Americans, many of whom yearned for a return to a simpler time. The following set of documents captures the various moods and issues of the time.

46

WOODROW WILSON'S DECLARATION OF WAR
MESSAGE (1917)

When the First World War broke out in June 1914, President Woodrow Wilson gave the routine declaration of neutrality and urged Americans to be "impartial in thought as well as action." This would prove difficult to maintain. As the largest neutral nation with huge economic resources available, the United States was vulnerable to efforts to control trade from both sides in the conflict. The British, whose surface fleet controlled the Atlantic, were very successful at maintaining trade with the United States. To counter British naval supremacy and throttle trade with Great Britain, the Germans began submarine warfare. The U-boat violated traditional naval warfare by sinking merchant ships without warning. When American lives were lost, especially when the passenger liner *Lusitania* was sunk in 1915, the Wilson administration protested and the Germans agreed to limit their submarine attacks. In late January 1917, in an attempt to win the war, the Germans announced unrestricted submarine warfare against any ship bound for Great Britain. Several American ships were sunk in February and March. Even though he was reelected in 1916 on the slogan "He kept us out of war," Wilson asked Congress for a declaration of war on April 2, 1917. Excerpted below is Wilson's war message.

Questions to Consider: Why is Woodrow Wilson asking for a declaration of war? Why is it significant that Wilson wants war declared against the German government, but not the German people? What is the purpose of America's war effort? Are there any similarities between the design of Roosevelt's Corollary to the Monroe Doctrine (Document 39) and the mission of Woodrow Wilson's war effort?

The present German submarine warfare against commerce is a warfare against mankind.

It is a war of all nations. American ships have been sunk, American lives taken, in ways which it has stirred us very deeply to learn of, but the ships and people of other neutral and friendly nations have been sunk and overwhelmed in the waters in the same way. There has been no discrimination. The challenge is to all mankind. Each nation must decide for itself how it will meet it. The choice we make for ourselves must be made with a moderation of counsel and a temperance of judgment befitting our character and our motives as a nation. We must put excited feeling away. Our motive will not be revenge or the victorious assertion of the physical might of the nation, but only the vindication of right, of human right, of which we are only a single champion. . . .

With a profound sense of the solemn and even tragical character of the step I am taking and of the grave responsibilities which it involves, but in unhesitating

---

"Address by the President of the United States," *Congressional Record*, 65th Congress, 1st Session, (2 April 1917), 102-104.

obedience to what I deem my constitutional duty, I advise that the Congress declare the recent course of the Imperial German Government to be in fact nothing less than war against the government and people of the United States; that it formally accept the status of belligerent which has thus been thrust upon it; and that it take immediate steps, not only to put the country in a more thorough state of defense but also to exert all its power and employ all its resources to bring the Government of the German Empire to terms and end the war. . . .

Our object now, as then, is to vindicate the principles of peace and justice in the life of the world as against selfish and autocratic power and to set up among the really free and self-governed peoples of the world such a concert of purpose and of action as will henceforth ensure the observance of those principles. Neutrality is no longer feasible or desirable where the peace of the world is involved and the freedom of its peoples, and the menace to that peace and freedom lies in the existence of an autocratic government backed by an organized force which is controlled wholly by their will, not the will of their people. We have seen the last of neutrality in such circumstances. We are at the beginning of an age in which it will be insisted that the same standards of conduct and of responsibility for wrong done shall be observed among nations and their governments that are observed among the individual citizens of civilized states.

We have no quarrel with the German people. We have no feeling toward them but one of sympathy and friendship. It was not upon their impulse that their government acted in entering this war. It was not with their previous knowledge or approval. It was a war determined as wars used to be determined in the old, unhappy days when peoples nowhere [were] consulted by their rulers and wars were provoked and waged in the interest of dynasties or of little groups of ambitious men who were accustomed to use their fellowmen as pawns and tools. . . .

The world must be made safe for democracy. Its peace must be planted upon the tested foundations of political liberty. We have no selfish ends to serve. We desire no conquest, no domination. We seek no indemnities for ourselves, no material compensation for the sacrifices we shall freely make. We are but one of the champions of the rights of mankind. We shall be satisfied when those rights have been made as secure as the faith and the freedom of nations can make them. . . .

It will be all the easier for us to conduct ourselves as belligerents in a high spirit of right and fairness because we act without animus, not in enmity toward a people or with the desire to bring any injury or disadvantage upon them, but only in armed opposition to an irresponsible government which has thrown aside all considerations of humanity and of right and is running amuck. We are, let me say again, the sincere friends of the German people, and shall desire nothing so much as the early reestablishment of intimate relations of mutual advantage between us—however hard it may be between them, for the time being, to believe that this is spoken from our hearts. We have borne with their present government through all these bitter months because of that friendship,—exercising a patience and forebearance which would otherwise have been impossible. We shall, happily, still have an opportunity to prove that friendship in our daily attitude and actions toward the millions of men and women of German birth and native sympathy who live among us and share our life, and we shall be proud to prove it toward all who are in fact loyal to their neighbors and to the Government in the hour of test. They are, most of them, as true and loyal Americans as if they had never known any other fealty or allegiance. . . .

It is a distressing and oppressive duty, gentlemen of Congress, which I have performed in thus addressing you. There are, it may be, many months of fiery trial and sacrifice ahead of us. It is a fearful thing to lead this great peaceful nation into war, into the most terrible and disastrous of all wars, civilization itself seeming to be in the balance. But the right is more precious than peace, and we shall fight for the things which we have always carried nearest our hearts,—for democracy, for the right of those who submit to authority to have a voice in their own governments, for the rights and liberties of small nations, for a universal dominion of right by such a concert of free peoples as shall bring peace and safety to all nations and make the world itself at last free. To such a task we can dedicate our lives and our fortunes, everything that we are and everything that we have, with the pride of those who know that the day has come when America is privileged to spend her blood and her might for the principles that gave her birth and happiness and the peace which she has treasured. God helping her, she can do no other.

47

THE QUESTION OF FIRST AMENDMENT RIGHTS
(1919)

America's entry into the First World War produced widespread nationalism among the American people. The Woodrow Wilson administration helped mold this reaction when it launched an extraordinarily successful propaganda campaign to rally support for the war crusade. Capitalizing on this popular mood and eager to protect war mobilization, Congress passed the Espionage Act (1917), which imposed severe penalties on persons found guilty of obstructing the war effort. Despite the patriotic fervor, some individuals and groups opposed the war, with certain members of the Socialist party the most conspicuous. In 1917, Socialist Charles Schenck was arrested and found guilty of violating the Espionage Act. He appealed the decision to the Supreme Court, where Justice Oliver Wendell Holmes, Jr., delivered the court's opinion in *Schenck v. U.S.* Holmes devoted his entire life to studying the law, becoming one of the great legal minds of the 20th century who was best known for his liberal dissenting opinions on the Court. Holmes argued that interpretations of the law should be based not simply on legal precedents but on the conditions of the time. In the selection taken from *Schenck v. U.S.*, Holmes introduces the "clear and present danger" test for limitations on free speech.

Questions to Consider: How had Charles Schenck violated the Espionage Act?

Schenck v. United States, 249 *US Reports* 47-53 (1919).

Were the Socialist leaflets that menacing? How does Oliver Wendell Holmes, Jr., interpret the First Amendment in this case? Do you agree? What are the consequences of such a decision?

———

This is an indictment in three counts. The first charges a conspiracy to violate the Espionage Act of June 15, 1917, by causing and attempting to cause insubordination, etc., in the military and naval forces of the United States, and to obstruct the recruiting and enlistment service of the United States, when the United States was at war with the German Empire; to wit, that the defendant wilfully conspired to have printed and circulated to men who had been called and accepted for military service under the Act of May 18, 1917, a document set forth and alleged to be calculated to cause such insubordination and obstruction. The count alleges overt acts in pursuance of the conspiracy, ending in the distribution of the document set forth. The second count alleges a conspiracy to commit an offense against the United States; to wit, to use the mails for the transmission of matter declared to be nonmailable by title 12, of the Act of June 15, 1917. . . . The third count charges an unlawful use of the mails for the transmission of the same matter and otherwise as above. The defendants were found guilty on all the counts. They set up the 1st Amendment to the Constitution, forbidding Congress to make any law abridging the freedom of speech or of the press, and, bringing the case here on that ground, have argued some other points also of which we must dispose.

It is argued that the evidence, if admissible, was not sufficient to prove that the defendant Schenck was concerned in sending the document. According to the testimony Schenck said he was general secretary of the Socialist party and had charge of the Socialist headquarters from which the documents were sent. He identified a book found there as the minutes of the executive committee of the party. The book showed a resolution of August 13, 1917, that 15,000 leaflets should be printed on the other side of one of them in use, to be mailed to men who had passed examination boards, and for distribution. Schenck personally attended to the printing . . . and there was a resolve that Comrade Schenck be allowed $125 for sending the leaflets through the mail. He said that he had about fifteen or sixteen thousand printed. . . . Without going into confirmatory details that were proved, no reasonable man could doubt that the defendant Schenck was largely instrumental in sending the circulars about. . . .

The document in question, upon its first printed side, recited the 1st section of the 13th Amendment, said that the idea embodied in it was violated by the Conscription Act, and that a conscript is little better than a convict. In impassioned language it intimated that conscription was despotism in its worst form and a monstrous wrong against humanity, in the interest of Wall street's chosen few. It said: "Do not submit to intimidation;" but in form at least confined itself to peaceful measures, such as a petition for the repeal of the act. The other and later printed side of the sheet was headed, "Assert Your Rights." It stated reasons for alleging that anyone violated the Constitution when he refused to recognize "your right to assert your opposition to the draft," and went on: "If you do not assert and support your rights, you are helping to deny or disparage rights which it is the solemn duty of all citizens and residents of the United States to retain." It described the arguments on the other side as coming from cunning politicians and a mercenary capitalist press, and even silent consent to the Conscription Law as helping to support an infamous conspiracy. It denied the power to send our citizens away to foreign shores to shoot up the people of other lands, and added that words could not express the condemnation such cold-blooded ruthlessness deserves, etc., etc., winding up, "You must do your share to maintain, support, and uphold the rights of the people of this country." Of course the document would not have been sent unless it had been intended to have some effect, and we do not see what effect it could be expected to have upon persons subject to the draft except to influence them to obstruct the carrying of it out. . . .

But it is said, suppose that that was the tendency of this circular, it is protected by the 1st Amendment to the Constitution. Two of the strongest expressions are said to be quoted respectively from well-known men. It well may be that the prohibition of laws abridging the freedom of speech is not confined to previous restraints, although to prevent them may have been the main purpose. . . . We admit that in many places and in ordinary times the defendants, in saying all that was said in the circular, would have been within their constitutional rights. But the character of every act depends upon the circumstances in which it is done. The most stringent protection of free speech would not protect a man in falsely shouting fire in a theater, and causing a panic. It does not even protect a man from an injunction against uttering words that may have all the effect of force. The question in every case is whether the words used are used in such circumstances and are of such a nature as to create a clear and present danger that they will bring about substantive evils that Congress has a right to prevent. It is a question of proximity and degree. When a nation is at war many things that might be said in time of peace are such a hindrance to its effort that their utterance will not be endured so long as men fight, and that no court could regard them as protected by any constitutional right. It seems to be admitted that if an actual obstruction of the recruiting service were proved, liability for words that produced that effect might be enforced. The Statute of 1917 punishes conspiracies to obstruct as well as actual obstruction. If the act (speaking, or circulating a paper), its tendency and the intent with which it is done, are the same, we perceive no ground for saying that success alone warrants making the act a crime. . . .

Judgments affirmed.

48

A SOLDIER'S VIEW OF THE WAR (1918)

The First World War introduced new military technology, yet both sides

Captain Arthur P. Terry, Diary, August–September 1918, Arthur P. Terry Collection, Box 1, Folder 1, George C. Marshall Research Foundation, Lexington, VA.

employed age-old military tactics. The result was massive losses for all belligerents as the conflict stagnated into trench fighting (where battles were often fought to gain yards), and a war of attrition developed. The nature of the war changed in 1917 when Russia withdrew from the fighting (they signed a peace treaty with Germany), and the United States entered the war. The American Expeditionary Force (AEF) landed in France in June 1917, but the bulk of American troops did not arrive until early 1918. American participation was minimal until the Germans launched a massive offensive in March 1918, which the Americans helped repel. One of the nearly two million Americans who fought in the war was Captain Arthur P. Terry of Wytheville, Virginia. Terry entered the army shortly after graduation from Virginia Polytechnical Institute in 1916 and arrived in France in May 1918. His excerpted diary accounts present war from the soldier's perspective in the battles of Saint-Mihiel and Meuse-Argonne in 1918.

——

·⌐ **Questions to Consider:** What are Captain Arthur Terry's views of the war? What is the tone of his diary account? What seems to be Terry's preoccupation in these excerpts? What is his attitude about trench warfare?

——

August 6th

Yesterday Bob Patterson and I with thirty-five non-commissioned officers and a British Gas Officer were on our way to the front to witness a gas wave attack which was being launched last night by the British. The British Officer was for some reason very anxious to get to the lines before night fall. In going up we crossed over the heights to the right of Blairville and as we reached the top we were seen by a battery of German artillery, who opened fire on us. Two shots, three inch shells, struck on each side of the path where we were walking but fortunately they were "duds." Lying on my stomach I could have touched where both shells struck. One of the men took oath to the fact that one of the shells passed between his legs. We ran to some trenches near by, where we had to remain from five o'clock until nine. We timed them and every seven minutes the enemy put over on the trenches a salvo of three inch shells. We escaped by simply outguessing the Germans by changing our positions, and too by "digging in." Several times officers were covered up by the earth thrown up by the bursting shells. Those were four long hours and in an exceedingly hot place. We expected every moment to be the last with some or all of us. . . .

August 11th

We had quite a hot time last night. Colonel Parks and I were at the front and he had just sent out five patrols to try to get a German prisoner. They had not captured one in over three weeks. We wanted one so as to make him talk and get the dope on who was opposing us and what they were doing. Our patrols had just gone out when a message was received from the observation post reporting a great deal of activity in the German lines, and that he thought a relief was being made. We then ordered the artillery to open up, and in a minute—well it was wonderful but awful. With the opening of our guns "Jerry" sent up flares and rockets which lit up the entire country for miles. Then he retalliated [sic] with his guns. It was just one continuous roar with the screeching and whistling of the shells as they passed over. We were very anxious of our patrols but as the night passed on all of them checked in with no one hurt or missing. . . .

September 25th

That night in Bois de Borrus—it can never be forgotten! It was ten forty-five; the regiment was forming in columns of squads when suddenly the silence of the night was broken by the now familiar hissing and whistling of an approaching shell; then the whole woods seemed to rock from a terrific explosion. Who will ever forget that moment? The crash of the shells; the cries of caution in the dark; the loud commands; for a time it seemed that we would die like rats in a trap. The first shell carried its death toll—it killed the first sergeant and the N. C. O's in a platoon of L Company. One of the men in Company F, in dodging a shell, fell by the side of me; just then the shell exploded, and he cried out "Mama." His cry was evidently a premonition of death, for we found him with a part of his head blown away. During the trying minutes which were ours here a very peculiar incident occurred. In jumping into a trench in dodging one of the shells a man of Company B landed on the legs of two other men, breaking one leg for each of them. In going to the head of the column with a message for Major Emory I had a very narrow escape. I had been jumping in and out of the trenches from the shells. At the end of the trench was a drain pool about fifteen feet deep, the bottom of which was filled with loose rock. It was dark and I could not see in it; over came a shell and I dived into it. The fall knocked me unconscious, but upon regaining same a few minutes later I fired my pistol and yelled for help. . . .

49

OPPOSITION TO THE LEAGUE OF NATIONS (1919)

When the peace conference convened in France in 1919, President Woodrow Wilson attended and took an active role in negotiations in the hope of preserving his proposed idealistic blueprint for peacemaking, the Fourteen Points. The resulting Treaty of Versailles contained little of the original Fourteen Points except a League of Nations, which Wilson believed would correct the mistakes of the peace treaty. The heart of the new League of Nations was Article 10, which urged league members "to respect and preserve" the territory of members from external aggression. When Wilson submitted the treaty to the U.S. Senate for ratification, it came under the close scrutiny of Henry Cabot Lodge, chair of the Foreign Relations Committee. Born in Massachusetts and Harvard educated (he earned a Ph.D. in political science),

"League of Nations," *Congressional Record,* 66th Congress, 1st Session, part 4, (12 August 1919), 3778-3784.

Lodge was known for his clear and forceful arguments in the 37 years he served in Congress. In a speech on the Senate floor, which is excerpted below, Lodge offered his reasons for opposing the Treaty of Versailles (and the League of Nations). The Senate would defeat the treaty ratification in two separate votes.

--

·- **Questions to Consider:** For what reasons does Henry Cabot Lodge oppose the treaty? What changes would he make in the treaty? How does he propose to maintain world peace? Is that possible? Is Lodge an isolationist?

--

I object in the strongest possible way to having the United States agree, directly or indirectly, to be controlled by a league which may at any time, and perfectly lawfully and in accordance with the terms of the covenant, be drawn in to deal with internal conflicts in other countries, no matter what those conflicts may be. We should never permit the United States to be involved in any internal conflict in another country, except by the will of her people expressed through the Congress which represents them.

With regard to wars of external aggression on a member of the league, the case is perfectly clear. There can be no genuine dispute whatever about the meaning of the first clause of article 10. In the first place, it differs from every other obligation in being individual and placed upon each nation without the intervention of the league. Each nation for itself promises to respect and preserve as against external aggression the boundaries and the political independence of every member of the league. . . .

Any analysis of the provisions of this league covenant, however, brings out in startling relief one great fact. Whatever may be said, it is not a league of peace; it is an alliance, dominated at the present moment by five great powers, really by three, and it has all the marks of an alliance. The development of international law is neglected. The court which is to decide disputes brought before it fills but a small place. The conditions for which this league really provides with the utmost care are political conditions, not judicial questions, to be reached by the executive council and the assembly, purely political bodies without any trace of a judicial character about them. Such being its machinery, the control being in the hands of political appointees whose votes will be controlled by interest and expedience it exhibits that most marked characteristic of an alliance—that its decisions are to be carried out by force. Those articles upon which the whole structure rests are articles which provide for the use of force; that is, for war. This league to enforce peace does a great deal for enforcement and very little for peace. It makes more essential provisions looking to war than to peace for the settlement of disputes. . . .

Taken altogether, these provisions for war present what to my mind is the gravest objection to this league in its present form. We are told that of course nothing will be done in the way of warlike acts without the assent of Congress. If that is true let us say so in the covenant. But as it stands there is no doubt whatever in my mind that American troops and American ships may be ordered to any part of the world by nations other than the United States, and that is a proposition to which I for one can never assent. . . .

Those of us, Mr. President, who are either wholly opposed to the league, or who are trying to preserve the independence and the safety of the United States by changing the terms of the league, and who are endeavoring to make the league, if we are to be a member of it, less certain to promote war instead of peace have been reproached with selfishness in our outlook and with a desire to keep our country in a state of isolation. So far as the question of isolation goes, it is impossible to isolate the United States. . . . But there is a wide difference between taking a suitable part and bearing a due responsibility in world affairs and plunging the United States into every controversy and conflict on the face of the globe. By meddling in all the differences which may arise among any portion or fragment of humankind we simply fritter away our influence and injure ourselves to no good purpose. . . .

. . . In the prosecution of the war we gave unstintedly American lives and American treasure. When the war closed we had 3,000,000 men under arms. We were turning the country into a vast workshop for war. We advanced ten billions to our allies. We refused no assistance that we could possibly render. All the great energy and power of the Republic were put at the service of the good cause. We have not been ungenerous. We have been devoted to the cause of freedom, humanity, and civilization everywhere. Now we are asked, in the making of peace, to sacrifice our sovereignty in important respects, to involve ourselves almost without limit in the affairs of other nations and to yield up policies and rights which we have maintained throughout our history. We are asked to incur liabilities to an unlimited extent and furnish assets at the same time which no man can measure. I think it is not only our right but our duty to determine how far we shall go. . . .

No doubt many excellent and patriotic people see a coming fulfillment of noble ideals in the words "league for peace." We all respect and share these aspirations and desires, but some of us see no hope, but rather defeat, for them in this murky covenant. For we, too have our ideals, even if we differ from those who have tried to establish a monopoly of idealism. Our first ideal is our country, and we see her in the future, as in the past, giving service to all her people and to the world. Our ideal of the future is that she should continue to render that service of her own free will. She has great problems of her own to solve, very grim and perilous problems, and a right solution, if we can attain to it, would largely benefit mankind. We would have our country strong to resist a peril from the West, as she has flung back the German menace from the East. We would not have our politics distracted and embittered by the dissensions of other lands. We would not have our country's vigor exhausted or her moral force abated, by everlasting meddling and muddling in every quarrel, great and small, which afflicts the world. Our ideal is to make her ever stronger and better and finer, because in that way alone, as we believe, can she be of the greatest service to the world's peace and to the welfare of mankind.

50

"WHAT IS BEHIND THE NEGRO UPRISINGS?" (1919)

The First World War created both opportunity and despair for African Americans. In the years before the war, some blacks left the segregationist South and moved to the North for economic opportunity and the hope of a better life. When the war created labor shortages, however, this "Great Migration" of African Americans swelled, as several hundred thousand moved to the North to work in war industries. Blacks were also drafted into the Army, and segregated units fought in Europe. With the conclusion of peace, the return of the troops, and the economic readjustment, racial tensions increased dramatically during the summer of 1919, and numerous race riots and racial confrontations occurred in what some called "The Red Summer." The fledgling National Association for the Advancement of Colored People (NAACP), formed by white and black intellectuals in 1909-1910 to combat segregation and discrimination, launched a publicity campaign to explain the riots, advocate rights for African Americans, and demonstrate that race relations was a national problem. Spearheaded by journalist Herbert J. Seligmann, the NAACP's publicity director, articles were published in many prominent national magazines. The selection below is Seligmann's article in *Current Opinion*.

Questions to Consider: According to Herbert J. Seligmann, why did African Americans move to the North during the war? Why does the South and the North view race relations differently? How did the war change the racial situation? Why does Seligmann believe race relations is a national problem? Is he correct?

The movement of the Negroes from the South to the North has had something of the quality of a race migration. For Negroes who left the South were coming from one civilization to another. The war was less the cause of migration than an opportunity for thousands of Negroes in whom a desire to leave the South had been growing to gratify the impulse. The most conservative estimates place the number of migrant Negroes during the war at half a million. Mainly, that migration took place in the northern industrial centers like Chicago, Pittsburgh, St. Louis and Philadelphia, and it is in those centers that the North has come to recognize the presence of a national race problem. Having been invited by labor agents and by the manifest economic opportunity created by the cessation of immigration from Europe; impelled to go North as well by denial of fundamental justice in the South, the Negro came, and it was as a result of this stimulated migration that the North found difficulty in absorbing these additions to its indus-

Herbert J. Seligmann, "What is Behind the Negro Uprisings?" *Current Opinion* 67 (September 1919): 154-155.

trial population. The abnormal expansion of the Negro population during the war years in cities like Chicago raised issues which the North had never before had to face. When colored people moved into white residential districts, there began to be talk of "segregation" and white property owners' associations indulged in incendiary language at meetings which were often secret. The influx of unionized colored men caused feeling among white unionists, notably among the stockyard workers of Chicago, and the North found itself with an incipient race problem in organized labor.

The riots in Washington and Chicago following upon disturbances in Pennsylvania and a strained situation throughout the South, with riots barely averted in Memphis and Birmingham, have forced upon the attention of the country the fact that the relation of the races is a national problem. The Negro does not constitute that problem, but the attitude of the white man towards him. The white South is still very largely envisaging that problem in terms of "racial inferiority," "social inequality," "Negro criminality," and "rape." In the North the problem, as was well shown by the riot in Chicago, beginning Sunday, July 27, and continuing for three days, is almost entirely economic. Hoodlums and perverts can, of course, be relied upon to make racial or any other superficial difference between men the occasion of brutal assault and bloody violence. But in Chicago the words most often used in accounting for the bitter feeling which existed were not "Negro criminality," "brutal assaults upon women," but "decline of real estate value," "invasion of white residential districts by Negroes," "housing," "friction between union men and unorganized Negroes."

North and South, then, both share the national race problem, but each has to face it in different phases. In a number of southern newspapers there was shown a disposition to crow over the disorders in the North, to point the finger of scorn at those northern critics who had been condemning mob violence, lynching, and in general the treatment of the Negro in the South. Many letters were written to northern papers and published predicting that as a consequence of the disorders the North would have to deal with the race problem as they have been dealt with in the South, that the North would have come to segregation and Jim Crowism. But better public sentiment in the South is coming to realize that the problem there is one of education. . . . It is becoming increasingly illogical, after the Negro's services in the war and the intensified feeling of self-respect as a United States citizen which he gained in the course of those services, to continue to treat the Negro race as a subject race to be exploited on the farm and in industry and to be patronized in lieu of giving him the rights of citizenship.

The civilization of the South has been a Jim Crow civilization. That is, the Negro has not only been denied equal treatment in the courts, proper policing, lighting, and housing, but, as oft-cited statistics show, provision for education of his children and for his health has been in many sections lamentably deficient. The means used to "keep the Negro in his place" in the South has been lynching and mob violence or a threat of violence, a form of Prussianism which is coming to be increasingly condemned by Southerners themselves. Temporarily at least, the reflex of the Negro's increasing prosperity as a result of the war, his feeling that he must have his rights even if it is necessary to fight for them, have intensified race hatred throughout the South. It is not unlikely that there will be a number of severe clashes. Eventually it will be necessary to recognize his status as a citizen upon which the Negro is going to insist and to cooperate with him through proper education and sanitation.

51

THE RED SCARE (1920)

A series of labor strikes convulsed the country in 1919, and, influenced by the Bolshevik Revolution in Russia, the American public came to believe that these strikes were the beginning of a communist revolution. When the Post Office discovered nearly 40 bombs addressed to various prominent officials (one was delivered and it exploded), many Americans were further convinced of a pending communist revolt. These perceived communist tactics, the wartime hysteria against all things German (and foreign), the intolerance of dissenting opinions, and fervent nationalism all combined for an easy shift into the Red Scare. And recently appointed Attorney General A. Mitchell Palmer led the witch hunt to remove the "Reds." Palmer was a Pennsylvania Quaker, a three-term congressman, a superb lawyer, and a Woodrow Wilson confidant who distrusted aliens and hoped to become president. Under Palmer's direction, the Justice Department launched a series of "raids" that rounded up nearly 5,000 radicals and aliens, even deporting 249 individuals without benefit of a court hearing. Riding the crest of popular support, Palmer published the excerpted article below in the respected magazine *The Forum* to justify the raids.

Questions to Consider: What made the "Reds" so threatening to America? What was in jeopardy? Is his argument convincing? What does he ask the American people to do? How does his position compare with those found in "The Question of First Amendment Rights" (Document 47), "The Ku Klux Klan's Perspective" (Document 53), and "Closing the Golden Door" (Document 54)?

L ike a prairie-fire, the blaze of revolution was sweeping over every American institution of law and order a year ago. It was eating its way into the homes of the American workman, its sharp tongues of revolutionary heat were licking the altars of the churches, leaping into the belfry of the school bell, crawling into the sacred corners of American homes, seeking to replace marriage vows with vows of libertine laws, burning up the foundations of society.

Robbery, not war, is the ideal of communism. This has been demonstrated in Russia, Germany, and in America. As a foe, the anarchist is fearless of his own life, for his creed is a fanaticism that admits no respect of any other creed. Obviously it

---

A. Mitchell Palmer, "The Case Against the 'Reds,'" *The Forum* 63 (February 1920): 173-185.

is the creed of any criminal mind, which reasons always from motives impossible to clean thought. Crime is the degenerate factor in society.

Upon these two basic certainties, first that the "Reds" were criminal aliens, and secondly that the American Government must protect crime, it was decided that there could be no nice distinctions between the theoretical ideals of the radicals and their actual violations of our national laws. . . .

My information showed that communism in this country was an organization of thousands of aliens, who were the direct allies of Trotzky. Aliens of the same misshapen cast of mind and indecencies of character, and it showed that they were making the same glittering promises of lawlessness, of criminal autocracy to Americans, that they had made to the Russian peasants. How the Department of Justice discovered upwards of 60,000 of these organized agitators of the Trotzky doctrine in the United States, is the confidential information upon which the Government is now sweeping the nation clean of such alien filth. . . .

One of the chief incentives of the present activity of the Department of Justice against the "Reds" has been the hope that American citizens will, themselves, become voluntary agents for us, in a vast organization for mutual defense against the sinister agitation of men and women aliens, who appear to be either in the pay or under the criminal spell of Trotzky and Lenine. . . .

Behind, and underneath, my own determination to drive from our midst the agents of Bolshevism with increasing vigor and with greater speed, until there are no more of them left among us, so long as I have the responsible duty of that task, I have discovered the hysterical methods of these revolutionary humans with increasing amazement and suspicion. In the confused information that sometimes reaches the people, they are compelled to ask questions which involve the reasons for my acts against the "Reds." I have been asked, for instance, to what extent deportation will check radicalism in this country. Why not ask what will become of the United States Government if these alien radicals are permitted to carry out the principles of the Communist Party as embodied in its so-called laws, aims and regulations?

There wouldn't be any such thing left. In place of the United States Government we should have the horror and terrorism of bolsheviki tyranny such as is destroying Russia now. Every scrap of radical literature demands obedience to the instincts of criminal minds, that is, to the lower appetites, material and moral. The whole purpose of communism appears to be a mass formation of the criminals of the world to overthrow the decencies of private life, to usurp property that they have not earned, to disrupt the present order of life regardless of health, sex or religious rights. By a literature that promises the wildest dreams of such low aspirations, that can occur only to the criminal minds, communism distorts our social law.

The chief appeal communism makes is to "The Worker." If they can lure the wage-earner to join their own gang of thieves, if they can show him that he will be rich if he steals, so far they have succeeded in betraying him to their own criminal course. . . .

It has been inferred by the "Reds" that the United States Government, by arresting and deporting them, is returning to the autocracy of Czardom, adopting the system that created the severity of Siberian banishment. My reply to such charges is, that in our determination to maintain our government we are treating our alien enemies with extreme consideration. To deny them the privilege of remaining in the country which they have openly deplored as an unenlightened community, unfit for those who prefer the privileges of Bolshevism, should be no hardship. It strikes me as an odd form of reasoning that these Russian Bolsheviks who extol the Bolshevik rule, should be so unwilling to return to Russia. The nationality of most of the alien "Reds" is Russian and German. There is almost no other nationality represented among them.

It has been impossible in so short a space to review the entire menace of the internal revolution in this country as I know it, but this may serve to arouse the American citizen to its reality, its danger, and the great need of united effort to stamp it out, under our feet, if needs be. It is being done. The Department of Justice will pursue the attack of these "Reds" upon the Government of the United States with vigilancy, and no alien, advocating the overthrow of existing law and order in this country, shall escape arrest and prompt deportation.

It is my belief that while they have stirred discontent in our midst, while they have caused irritating strikes, and while they have infected our social ideas with the disease of their own minds and their unclean morals, we can get rid of them! and not until we have done so shall we have removed the menace of Bolshevism for good.

THE RETURN TO "NORMALCY"

4

During the 1920s, America withdrew from the world and attempted to return to a simpler, pre-progressive time. The decade proved to be one of paradoxes. For many Americans, the time was one of abundance, where great fortunes were made, unprecedented mobility was enjoyed through the use of the automobile, and a new morality evolved. For other Americans, the decade had a far harsher reality. The reemergence of nativism led to persecution of ethnic, religious, and racial minorities. In the countryside, farmers who had enjoyed boom years a decade earlier stood on the brink of financial ruin. The following documents bring the decade's many inconsistencies into sharp relief.

52

FARM PROBLEMS IN SOUTH DAKOTA (1922)

The first two decades of the 20th century is often considered the golden age of American agriculture. Many farmers experienced moderate prosperity because of increased demand for farm commodities, rising land values, and rapidly rising farm prices. The First World War provided the most significant boost by increasing demand and prices for American farm products. But these prosperous times ended abruptly in 1920 when postwar deflation caused agricultural prices to plummet (wheat went from $2.50 a bushel to $1.00, and cotton fell from $.35 a pound to $.13), and the world demand evaporated. Caught between dropping farm prices and escalating operating costs, the American farmer was hit extremely hard and many families lost their farms in bank foreclosures. Alarmed at the depression sweeping agricultural America, many farm spokesmen appealed to Congress for federal relief. Appearing before the House Committee on Agriculture in 1922 was Tom Ayres, manager of the South Dakota Nonpartisan League, who presented the following account of agricultural conditions in South Dakota.

―――

·⌐ **Questions to Consider:** According to Tom Ayres, what was the agricultural situation in South Dakota? What happened to produce those conditions? Whom does he blame? What does he suggest as remedies? What happens to agriculture over the next 20 years? How does Ayres' depiction compare to that described in "The Credit System of the South" (Document 20) and the "Populist Party Platform" (Document 24)?

―――

The condition of the agricultural population of South Dakota is such as to demand immediate constructive relief. The condition of the farmers of my State, no matter what may be said by boosters and boomers, or by politicians seeking to mitigate or soften present conditions, is about as desperate as it could well be. If a devastating drought, or a hurricane, or any other calamity had befallen people it could not have put them in a much worse position to meet their basic obligations and live. Their mortgages and taxes are now so heavy that they can not be met by the sale of their products. Interest is not being paid, notes are being extended, and interest compounded at high rates. The crops at the present levels scarcely pay the taxes on the land. Most of the farmers, outside of the comparatively few, who are fortunate enough to own their land free of encumberance, are remaining on the land because they have nowhere else to go. They are able to get a grubstake to carry them along. So far as it is possible, the banks are furnishing the grubstake, extending paper and urging the farmers to remain on the land, look after the mortgaged live stock and the mortgaged crops, hoping against hope that

―――――――――――

"Statement of Mr. Tom Ayres," *Stabilizing Prices of Farm Products, Hearings before the House Committee on Agriculture,* 67th Congress, 3rd & 4th Sessions, Series O (Second Supplement), (29 November 1922), 14.

there may be a turn in the tide of affairs which will save the farmers as well as themselves.

Here is a State, one-third of which is composed of the best agricultural land in the northwest. It had had an industrious and conservative farming population. Since I began my residence in South Dakota—nearly 39 years ago—the farmers and their families have worked in season and out of season, faithfully, diligently, and intelligently. The land is well improved in most cases, but it is mortgaged now for more than it would sell for. This presents a situation that ought to challenge the attention of lawmakers and statisticians and economists. It is an indictment against our present marketing system of the worst possible character. These farmers have not been extravagant. They have worked from 4 o'clock in the morning during the busy season until late at night and still their obligations have grown instead of diminishing, while their taxes have increased. The farmers are now at a point where they are simply staying and suffering because they know not what else to do. A part of the farming population is angry—the other part is hopeless. They have lost faith in popular government and in their own ability to remedy affairs through political action or cooperative effort. The present marketing system has stolen three crops from them already and left them in a position where the fourth crop may be stolen with equal facility but with more tragic results.

It is safe to say that one-fourth of the land must be foreclosed upon within the next year or carried over through extensions by the mortgage holders, who may prefer to have their buildings inhabited rather than to find new tenants. If the present condition of affairs continues for another year or two, nothing can avert wholesale foreclosure.

For the last year I have travelled by automobile 10,000 miles, covering every part of the State of South Dakota, a considerable portion of the State of North Dakota, and parts of Minnesota and Nebraska, and I find this same situation existing everywhere.

It will do no good to formulate new schemes for loaning money at cheap rates to these farmers. The War Finance Corporation scheme was a fiasco, so far as the farmers are concerned. It enabled the banks to take a rake-off for handling War Finance Corporation loans, but it did not enhance the equities in the mortgaged property, and the farmers found themselves as bad off or worse than before. I have witnessed, in probably 100 cases, men, women, and little children working in the fields. In instances I have seen women driving plows, hay racks, and mowing machines, carrying an infant in one arm and driving with the other arm. This has been done in a desperate effort to "get by," and still they do not get by.

What is needed is a living price for the productions of these people. What they demand and what they should have is a stabilized price for their labor. We have stabilized the banking business; we have stabilized the manufacturing business by tariff duties; we are proposing with all the power of a great administration behind it to stabilize the shipping industry; we have stabilized the returns of the transportation companies, but we have allowed the great basic industry of the Nation to be despoiled, starved, and enslaved by a hideous system that is as stupid as it is criminal. What the agricultural industry needs and should have is storage for the surplus products, cheap transportation, and cheap credits to hold such products until they can be sold in an orderly way on the foreign and domestic markets. As soon as this is accomplished, cooperative societies of buyers and sellers, foreign and domestic, will be induced to get together on a basis which will destroy gambling and offer substantial relief to consumers; place the agricultural industry on a living basis. . . .

53

THE KU KLUX KLAN'S PERSPECTIVE (1926)

In 1915, William J. Simmons revived the Ku Klux Klan. Patterned after the group formed during Reconstruction, the new Klan languished until a promotional campaign, several well publicized investigations, and America's disillusionment following the First World War combined to boost membership into the millions (estimates range from three to eight million). Appealing to America's nativistic tendencies and fears, the Klan spread beyond the South and became a powerful national organization that influenced state and local politics, conducted parades of members wearing white robes and hoods, and held rallies where crosses were burned. In 1922, a revolt removed Simmons as Klan leader and a dentist from Dallas, Texas, Hiram W. Evans, became the Klan's new Imperial Wizard. Evans oversaw much of the Klan's spectacular rise and its decline. In 1926, he published an article, excerpted below, in the respected *North American Review* that explained the Klan's purpose and moral agenda for America.

·⌐ **Questions to Consider:** What is the purpose of the Ku Klux Klan? How does it plan to carry out its goals? What does the Klan oppose? What is the Klan's position on African Americans and "aliens"? Who would join the Klan? Why? Did the Klan achieve the agenda that Hiram Evans outlines in this article?

The Ku Klux Klan, in short, is an organization which gives expression, direction and purpose to the most vital instincts, hopes and resentments of the old stock Americans, provides them with leadership, and is enlisting and preparing them for militant, constructive action toward fulfilling their racial and national destiny. . . .

There are three of these great racial instincts, vital elements in both the historic and the present attempts to build an America which shall fulfill the aspirations and justify the heroism of the men who made the nation. These are the instincts of loyalty to the white race, to the traditions of America, and to the spirit of Protestantism, which has been an essential part of Americanism ever since the days of Roanoke and Plymouth Rock. They are condensed into the Klan slogan: "Native, white, Protestant supremacy."

Hiram Wesley Evans, "The Klan's Fight For Americanism," *North American Review* 223 (March-April-May 1926): 33-61. (Copyright 1926 by the *North American Review*.) Reprinted by permission.

First in the Klansman's mind is patriotism—America for Americans. He believes religiously that a betrayal of Americanism or the American race is treason to the most sacred of trusts, a trust from his fathers and a trust from God. He believes, too, that Americanism can only be achieved if the pioneer stock is kept pure. . . .

Americanism, to the Klansman, is a thing of the spirit, a purpose and a point of view, that can only come through instinctive racial understanding. It has, to be sure, certain defined principles, but he does not believe that many aliens understand those principles, even when they use our words in talking about them. Democracy is one, fairdealing, impartial justice, equal opportunity, religious liberty, independence, self-reliance, courage, endurance, acceptance of individual responsibility as well as individual rewards for effort, willingness to sacrifice for the good of his family, his nation and his race before anything else but God, dependence on enlightened conscience for guidance, the right to unhampered development—these are fundamental. But within the bounds they fix there must be the utmost freedom, tolerance, liberalism. In short, the Klansman believes in the greatest possible diversity and individualism within the limits of the American spirit. But he believes also that few aliens can understand that spirit, that fewer try to, and that there must be resistance, intolerance even, toward anything that threatens it, or the fundamental national unity based upon it.

The second word in the Klansman's trilogy is "white." The white race must be supreme, not only in America but in the world. This is equally undebatable, except on the ground that the races might live together, each with full regard for the rights and interests of others, and that those rights and interests would never conflict. Such an idea, of course, is absurd; the colored races today, such as Japan, are clamoring not for equality but for their supremacy. . . . The world has been so made that each race must fight for its life, must conquer, accept slavery or die. The Klansman believes that the whites will not become slaves, and he does not intend to die before his time.

Moreover, the future of progress and civilization depends on the continued supremacy of the white race. . . . Until the whites falter, or some colored civilization has a miracle of awakening, there is not a single colored stock that can claim even equality with the white; much less supremacy.

The third of the Klan principles is that Protestantism must be supreme; that Rome shall not rule America. The Klansman believes this not merely because he is a Protestant, nor even because the Colonies that are now our nation were settled for the purpose of wresting America from the control of Rome and establishing a land of free conscience. He believes it also because Protestantism is an essential part of Americanism; without it America could never have been created and without it she cannot go forward. Roman rule would kill it.

Protestantism contains more than religion. It is the expression in religion of the same spirit of independence, self-reliance and freedom which are the highest achievements of the Nordic race. . . .

Let it be clear what is meant by "supremacy." It is nothing more than power of control, under just laws. It is not imperialism, far less is it autocracy or even aristocracy of a race or stock of men. What it does mean is that we insist on our inherited right to insure our own safety, individually and as a race, to secure the future of our children, to maintain and develop our racial heritage in our own, white, Protestant, American way, without interference. . . .

And we deny that either bigotry or prejudice enters into our intolerance or our narrowness. We are intolerant of everything that strikes at the foundations of our race, our country or our freedom of worship. We are narrowly opposed to the use of anything alien—race, loyalty to any foreign power or to any religion whatever— as a means to win political power. . . . This is our intolerance; based on the sound instincts which have saved us many times from the follies of the intellectuals. We admit it. More and worse, we are proud of it. . . .

The Negro, the Klan considers a special duty and problem of the white American. He is among us through no wish of his; we owe it him and to ourselves to give him full protection and opportunity. But his limitations are evident; we will not permit him to gain sufficient power to control our civilization. Neither will we delude him with promises of social equality which we know can never be realized. The Klan looks forward to the day when the Negro problem will have been saved on some much saner basis than miscegenation, and when every State will enforce laws making any sex relations between a white and a colored person a crime.

For the alien in general we have sympathy, opportunity, justice, but no permanent welcome unless he becomes truly American. It is our duty to see that he has every chance for this, and we shall be glad to accept him if he does. We hold no rancor against him; his race, instincts, training, mentality and whole outlook of life are usually widely different from ours. We cannot blame him if he adheres to them and attempts to convert us to them, even by force. But we must see that he can never succeed. . . .

54

CLOSING THE GOLDEN DOOR (1924)

The First World War had slowed immigration to a trickle, but in the first year following the war nearly 800,000 people, mostly from southern and eastern Europe, entered the country. The flood of immigrants to America had resumed in earnest. Many Americans, consumed with strong nativistic tendencies following the war and reacting to the labor strikes, bombings, and the Red Scare, believed these immigrants brought radical ideas and alien customs that threatened American institutions and way of life. They could also take jobs from Americans. Alarmed at the sudden rush in immigration and swept up in the nativistic surge, Congress passed the Emergency Immigration Act of 1921, which limited by quota the number of immigrants from any country. Three years later, Congress passed a more restrictive immigration law. Excerpted on the next page is Commissioner General of Immigration W. W. Husband's annual report for 1924, which compared the two immigration quota laws by country.

W. W. Husband, *Annual Report of the Commissioner General of Immigration to the Secretary of Labor* (Washington, DC: Government Printing Office, 1924), 24, 27.

·⤳ **Questions to Consider:** The stricter Act of 1924 affected which countries or regions the most? Why? How were the quotas established for each act? Why is the selection of the census year important? Would the Immigration Restriction League (Document 31) approve of these laws? What long-term impact would this law have on the United States?

It will undoubtedly be considered that the most important event in the immigration history of the fiscal year was the passage of the act of May 26, officially known as the "Immigration Act of 1924." This legislation supplants the so-called quota limit act of May 19, 1921. . . .

It will be remembered that the quota limit act of May 1921, provided that the number of aliens of any nationality admissible to the United States in any fiscal year should be limited to 3 per cent of the number of persons of such nationality who were resident in the United States according to the census of 1910, it being provided that not more than 20 per cent of any annual quota could be admitted in any one month. Under the act of 1924 the number of each nationality who may be admitted annually is limited to 2 per cent of the population of such nationality resident in the United States according to the census of 1890, and not more than 10 per cent of any annual quota may be admitted in any month except in cases where such quota is less than 300 for the entire year.

Under the Act of May 1921, the quota area was limited to Europe, the Near East, Africa, and Australasia. The countries of North and South America, with adjacent islands, and countries immigration from which was otherwise regulated, such as China, Japan, and other countries within the Asiatic barred zone, were not within the scope of the quota law. Under the new act, however, immigration from the entire world, with the exception of the Dominion of Canada, Newfoundland, the Republic of Mexico, the Republic of Cuba, the Republic of Haiti, the Dominican Republic, the Canal Zone, and independent countries of Central and South America, is subject to quota limitations. . . .

The quotas from various countries or regions of birth allotted under the act of May, 1921, the old quota law, and the act of 1924 are shown in the following compilation:

Country or region of birth	Act of 1921	Act of 1924
Albania	288	100
Armenia (Russian)	230	124
Austria	7,342	785
Belgium	1,563	512
Bulgaria	302	100
Czechoslovakia	14,357	3,073
Danzig	301	228
Denmark	5,619	2,789
Esthonia	1,348	124
Finland	3,921	471

Continued . . .

Country or region of birth	Act of 1921	Act of 1924
France	5,729	3,954
Germany	67,607	51,227
Great Britain, Ireland	77,342	34,007
Greece	3,063	100
Hungary	5,747	473
Iceland	75	100
Irish Free State[1]	—	28,567
Italy	42,057	3,845
Latvia	1,540	142
Lithuania	2,629	344
Luxemburg	92	100
Netherlands	3,607	1,648
Norway	12,202	6,453
Poland	30,977	5,982
Portugal	2,465	503
Rumania	7,419	603
Russia	24,405	2,248
Spain	912	131
Sweden	20,042	9,561
Switzerland	3,752	2,081
Yugoslavia	6,426	671
Palestine	57	100
Syria	882	100
Turkey	2,654	100
Australia	279	121
New Zealand and Pacific Islands	80	100
All others	492	3,100
TOTAL	357,803	164,667

[1]Included in Great Britain, under Act of 1921.

55

THE NEW WOMAN (1927)

The 1920s witnessed the emergence of the "new woman." Having achieved suffrage with the Nineteenth Amendment, some women turned their attention to other feminine issues—such as political equality, economic independence, and improved relations between the sexes—to broaden their reform efforts, but this movement lacked cohesion. Some radical feminists advocated an equal rights

Dorothy Dunbar Bromley, "Feminist—New Style," *Harper's Monthly Magazine* 155 (October 1927): 552-560. (Copyright (c) 1927 by *Harper's Magazine*.) All rights reserved. Reprinted from the October issue by special permission.

amendment, individualism, female solidarity, and equality with men while retaining differences from men. Other women pursued reforms in the workplace and acceptance from men. Some young women—the "flappers"—received considerable press coverage for their revolution in morals: they wore lipstick, cut their hair short, smoked, drank alcohol, dressed in short skirts, attended wild parties, and sought sexual freedom. While other women, stagnating in male-dominated marriages that relegated them to care for the household and children, hoped to improve relations in the home. The new woman, then, worked for different agendas and with contrasting methods to challenge the prevailing convention. In an article published in *Harper's Monthly Magazine*, Dorothy Dunbar Bromley promoted the "Feminist—New Style," a woman who understood the roots of feminism and was willing to make changes in her life.

Questions to Consider: What is the purpose of Dorothy Dunbar Bromley's article? What is the new style of feminist? How does she differ from old feminists and new feminists? What does the new style feminist advocate? How would men react to Bromley's article? How does Bromley's argument compare with Betty Friedan's in "The Problem that Has No Name" (Document 80)?

"Feminism" has become a term of opprobrium to the modern young woman. For the word suggests either the old school of fighting feminists who wore flat heels and had very little feminine charm, or the current species who antagonize men with their constant clamor about maiden names, equal rights, woman's place in the world, and many another cause . . . *ad infinitum*. . . .

But what of the constantly increasing group of young women in their twenties and thirties who are truly modern ones, those who admit that a full life calls for marriage and children as well as a career? These women if they launch upon marriage are keen to make a success of it and an art of child-rearing. But *at the same time* they are moved by an inescapable inner compulsion to be individuals in their own right. And in this era of simplified housekeeping they see their opportunity, for it is obvious that a woman who plans intelligently can salvage some time for her own pursuits. Furthermore, they are convinced that they will be better wives and mothers for the breadth they gain from functioning outside the home. In short, they are highly conscious creatures who feel obliged to plumb their own resources to the very depths, despite the fact that they are under no delusions as to the present inferior status of their sex in most fields of endeavor.

Numbers of these honest, spirited young women have made themselves heard in article and story. But since men must have things pointed out to them in black and white, we beg leave to enunciate the tenets of the modern woman's credo. Let us call her "Feminist—New Style."

First Tenet. Our modern young woman freely admits that American women have so far achieved but little in the arts, sciences, and professions as compared with men. . . .

But it remains true that a small percentage of women have proved the capacity, even the creative power of the feminine mind. Or have they not rather proved the fallacy of drawing a hard and fast distinction between the quality of men's minds and the quality of women's minds? . . .

Second Tenet. Why, then, does the modern woman care about a career or a job if she doubts the quality and scope of women's achievement to date? There are three good reasons why she cares immensely: first, she may be of that rare and fortunate breed of persons who find a certain art, science, or profession as inevitable a part of their lives as breathing; second, she may feel the need of a satisfying outlet for her energy whether or not she possesses creative ability; third, she may have no other means of securing her economic independence. And the latter she prizes above all else, for it spells her freedom as an individual, enabling her to marry or not marry, as she chooses, to terminate a marriage that has become unbearable, and to support and educate her children if necessary. . . .

Third Tenet. She will not, however, live for her job alone, for she considers that a woman who talks and thinks only shop has just as narrow a horizon as the housewife who talks and thinks only husband and children—perhaps more so, for the latter may have a deeper understanding of human nature. She will therefore refuse to give up all of her personal interests, year in and year out, for the sake of her work. . . .

Fourth Tenet. Nor has she become hostile to the other sex in the course of her struggle to orient herself. On the contrary, she frankly likes men and is grateful to more than a few for the encouragement and help they have given her.

In the business and professional world, for instance, Feminist—New Style has observed that more and more men are coming to accord women as much responsibility as they show themselves able to carry. She and her generation have never found it necessary to bludgeon their way, and she is inclined to think that certain of the pioneers would have got farther if they had relied on their ability rather than on their militant methods. . . .

Fifth Tenet. By the same corollary, Feminist—New Style professes no loyalty to women *en masse,* although she staunchly believes in individual women. Surveying her sex as a whole, she finds their actions petty, their range of interests narrow, their talk trivial and repetitious. As for those who set themselves up as leaders of the sex, they are either strident creatures of so little ability and balance that they have won no chance to "express themselves" (to use their own hackneyed phrase) in a man-made world; or they are brilliant, restless individuals who too often battle for women's rights for the sake of personal glory. . . .

Sixth Tenet. There is, however, one thing which Feminist—New Style envies Frenchwomen, and that is their sense of "chic." Indeed, she is so far removed from the early feminists that she is altogether baffled by the psychology which led some of them to abjure men in the same voice with which they aped them. Certainly their vanity must have been anaesthetized, she tells herself, as she pictures them with their short hair, so different from her own shingle, and dressed in their unflattering mannish clothes—quite the antithesis of her own boyish effects which are subtly designed to set off feminine charms. . . .

Seventh Tenet. Empty slogans seem to Feminist—New Style just as bad taste as masculine dress and manners. They serve only to prolong the war between the sexes and to prevent women from learning to think straight. Take these, for instance, "Keep your maiden name." "Come out of the kitchen." "Never darn a sock." . . .

Eighth Tenet. As for "free love," she thinks that it is impractical rather than immoral. With society organized as it is, the average man and woman cannot carry on a free union with any degree of tranquillity.

Incidentally, she is sick of hearing that modern young women are cheapening themselves by their laxity of morals. As a matter of fact, all those who have done any thinking, and who have any innate refinement, live by an aesthetic standard of morals which would make promiscuity inconceivable. . . .

Ninth Tenet. She readily concedes that a husband and children are necessary to the average woman's fullest development, although she knows well enough that women are endowed with varying degrees of passion and of maternal instinct. . . .

But no matter how much she may desire the sanction of marriage for the sake of having children, she will not take any man who offers. First of all a man must satisfy her as a lover and a companion. And second, he must have the mental and physical traits which she would like her children to inherit. . . .

This business of combining two careers presents its grave difficulties. In fact, it is a bigger job than any man has ever attempted. But because it is a big job, and because she has seen a few women succeed at it, Feminist—New Style will rise to the challenge. . . .

Tenth Tenet. But even while she admits that a home and children may be necessary to her complete happiness, she will insist upon *more freedom and honesty within the marriage relation.* . . .

Finally, Feminist—New Style proclaims that men and children shall no longer circumscribe her world, although they may constitute a large part of it. She is intensely self-conscious whereas the feminists were intensely sex-conscious. Aware of possessing a mind, she takes a keen pleasure in using that mind for some definite purpose; and also in learning to think clearly and cogently against a background of historical and scientific knowledge. . . . She knows that it is her American, her twentieth-century birth right to emerge from a creature of instinct into a full-fledged individual who is capable of molding her own life. And in this respect she holds that she is becoming man's equal.

If this be treason, gentlemen, make the most of it.

56

THE IMPACT OF THE AUTOMOBILE (1926)

The most significant social and economic development of the 1920s was the automobile. It speeded transportation, created a movement for improved roads, helped accelerate suburban sprawl, and provided a sense of independence for American youths. The Ford Motor Company, founded by Henry Ford in 1903,

Lawrence Abbott, "The Vices and Virtues of the Automobile," *The Outlook* 144 (15 December 1926): 491-492.

revolutionized the auto industry with the assembly line and mass production techniques used to make the Model T. Before stopping production of the "tin lizzie" after 20 years, Ford manufactured over 15 million Model Ts, selling them for as little as $290 in 1927. Other automobile makers adopted the mass production techniques, but fierce price competition and the large capital outlays required to maintain production reduced the number of companies from 253 in 1908 to 44 in 1929. The "Big Three" auto manufacturers—Ford, General Motors, and Chrysler—made 80 percent of the cars in the United States in the 1920s. In 1926, Lawrence Abbott, contributing editor to *The Outlook* magazine, published the following editorial on the social and economic impact of the automobile.

⸺

Questions to Consider: What economic developments related to the automobile still persist? What problems associated with the automobile expressed in this editorial still persist? What social changes did the automobile bring about?

⸺

Five of us were on our way to Pinehurst, North Carolina, for a little December golf. The party was composed of a manufacturer of an important and Nationally known automobile accessory, an expert on National advertising, an influential financier and industrialist, a member of the bar whose specialty is in the field of taxation and the administration of large estates, and the writer of these lines—all being New Yorkers. After dinner, as we were seated in the compartment of one of the group, the conversation happened to turn to the automobile and the part it has played in the development of modern civilization. The discussion interested me, and perhaps it may interest my readers, so I venture to report it as well as can:

The Manufacturer. I sometimes wonder how long the country can continue to absorb the incredible number of automobiles produced annually. Are you men aware that there are more automobiles owned and operated in the United States than in all the other countries of the world put together? On top of that fact place the fact that new cars are being turned out under the system of mass production by the hundreds of thousand every year, and you can form some idea of the top-heaviness which the industry is facing.

The Financier. I don't see anything to worry about yet. The purchasing power of the American people is steadily growing. They are buying automobiles out of past or future savings, and I am inclined to think that an automobile is a better thing for the average family to put its savings into than gewgaws[1] and furbelows[2].

Myself. What do you mean by future savings?

The Financier. I mean the system of installment buying, which has been carried to a higher state of perfection in the automobile industry than in any other trade. When a man buys a car, pays so much down, and agrees to pay the balance in monthly installments, he at once becomes a saver. He has to.

⸺

[1]Something gaudy and useless, a trinket.
[2]A bit of showy trimming or finery, such as a ruffle on a woman's shirt.

The Advertising Expert. Yes; but the trouble is that he is constantly tempted to buy other things on the same basis—an oil burner for his furnace, perhaps, or an electric refrigerator, or a radio outfit. Why, you can even get your house painted on the installment plan nowadays!

The Financier. True enough. Like every other good thing, the system can be carried to a foolish and even a dangerous extreme. But this is a fault of administration, and is not inherent in the system itself. A proper credit-inspection organization can prevent over-extension of credit in retail buying just as it can in mortgages or bank loans.

The Advertising Expert. Of course, it is to my self-interest to have the automobile industry extended. They are great advertisers. But I sometimes think automobiling is overdone. At any rate, automobiles have emphasized certain social vices.

Myself. Such as what?

The Advertising Expert. Such as congestion of traffic, indifference to fatal accidents, extravagance, and, above all, waste of time and other forms of dissipation among the young people. President _____ of the University of _____ told me the other day that the automobile was the bane of his life. At six o'clock in the evening he might know that his students were where they belong, on the campus. At eight o'clock they might be fifty miles away at some disreputable road-house, while the university authorities were in utter ignorance of how they were conducting themselves. If he could have his way, he said, he would abolish the automobile for undergraduates.

Myself. You must offset those vices by two very great social virtues which the automobile has contributed to American civilization—good roads and good cookery. Good roads are not merely of economic value, but they have greatly aided the distribution of intelligence and culture. They have made consolidated schools possible, to which the children are brought in automobiles. The auto is rapidly driving out the one-room cross-roads country school, where the acme of education was "readin', 'ritin' and 'rithmetic." The farm boy or girl now often has at command a good library or a good laboratory, thanks to good roads and automobiles. As to cookery, the country-wide improvement in the cooking and purveying of food can be realized only by those whose business took them to our country villages thirty and forty years ago.

The Manufacturer. Right you are. When I was a traveling salesman, forty years ago, it was almost impossible, outside of the best and most progressive cities, to buy a palatable meal in a public place. Salesmen used to arrange their itineraries so as to get to certain towns on Saturday night where they could be sure of a decent meal on Sunday. Now every village that is reached by automobiles has a place where you can get palatable food, even if it is nothing more than a "hot dog" stand. Good roads and good food are transforming this country; we owe that to the automobile. . . .

57

AMERICAN INDIVIDUALISM (1928)

Herbert Hoover had a long and distinguished career as a government worker before seeking the Presidency in 1928. Born in Iowa and raised a Quaker, Hoover became a wealthy engineer-businessman before age 40. He headed the Food Administration during the First World War and used voluntary methods and a propaganda campaign to raise food production while reducing civilian consumption. Hoover served as secretary of commerce under Presidents Warren G. Harding and Calvin Coolidge and transformed the insignificant department into one of the most dynamic agencies of the federal government: he helped promote new markets for business, developed industrial standardization, and established regulations for the infant radio and aviation industries. Hoover was well known to Americans, had established a reputation as a brilliant administrator, and was a successful businessman when he ran for president against Democratic candidate Al Smith in 1928. Many argued Hoover would "engineer" the country to continued prosperity. Hoover concluded his presidential campaign in New York with the excerpted speech below. It embodied Herbert Hoover's belief in American individualism as well as the Republican party's philosophy in the 1920s.

Questions to Consider: According to Herbert Hoover, why did America have a strong economy in the 1920s? What is Hoover's "American System"? Why does Hoover fear government involvement in the economy? Is his argument valid? Was Hoover's philosophy of "rugged individualism" workable in the Great Depression? How does Hoover's speech compare with "The Reagan Revolution" (Document 93)?

When the war closed, the most vital of all issues both in our own country and throughout the world was whether governments should continue their wartime ownership and operation of many instrumentalities of production and distribution. We were challenged with a peace-time choice between the American system of rugged individualism and a European philosophy of diametrically opposed doctrines—doctrines of paternalism and state socialism. The acceptance of these ideas would have meant the destruction of self-government through centralization of government. It would have meant the undermining of the individual initiative and enterprise through which our people have grown to unparalleled greatness.

The Republican Party from the beginning resolutely turned its face away from these ideas and these war practices. . . . When the Republican Party came into full power it went at once back to our fundamental conception of the state and the rights and responsibilities of the individual. Thereby it restored confidence and

---

"Text of Hoover's Speech on Relation of Government to Industry," *The New York Times*, 23 October 1928, 2.

hope in the American people, it freed and stimulated enterprise, it restored the government to its position as an umpire instead of a player in the economic game. For these reasons the American people have gone forward in progress while the rest of the world has halted, and some of the countries have even gone backwards. . . .

There has been revived in this campaign, however, a series of proposals which, if adopted, would be a long step toward the abandonment of our American system and a surrender to the destructive operation of governmental conduct of commercial business. Because the country is faced with difficulty and doubt over certain national problems—that is prohibition, farm relief, and electrical power— our opponents propose that we must thrust government a long way into the businesses which give rise to these problems. In effect, they abandon the tenets of their own party and turn to state socialism as a solution for the difficulties presented by all three. It is proposed that we shall change from prohibition to the state purchase and sale of liquor. If their agricultural relief program means anything, it means that the Government shall directly or indirectly buy and sell and fix prices of agricultural products. And we are to go into the hydroelectric power business. In other words, we are confronted with a huge program of government in business.

There is, therefore, submitted to the American people a question of fundamental principle. That is: shall we depart from the principles of our American political and economic system, upon which we have advanced beyond all the rest of the world, in order to adopt methods based on principles destructive of its very foundations? And I wish to emphasize the seriousness of these proposals. I wish to make my position clear; for this goes to the very roots of American life and progress. . . .

Let us first see the effect upon self-government. When the Federal Government undertakes to go into commercial business it must at once set up the organization and administration of that business, and it immediately finds itself in a labyrinth, every alley of which leads to the destruction of self-government. . . .

Bureaucracy is ever desirous of spreading its influence and its power. You cannot extend the mastery of the Government over the daily working life of a people without at the same time making it the master of the people's souls and thoughts. Every expansion of Government in business means that Government in order to protect itself from the political consequences of its errors and wrongs is driven irresistibly without peace to greater and greater control of the nation's press and platform. Free speech does not live many hours after free industry and free commerce die.

It is a false liberalism that interprets itself into the government operation of commercial business. Every step of bureaucratizing the business of our country poisons the very roots of liberalism—that is, political equality, free speech, free assembly, free press, and equality of opportunity. It is the road not to more liberty, but to less liberty. Liberalism should be found not striving to spread bureaucracy but striving to set bounds to it. True liberalism seeks all legitimate freedom first in the confident belief that without such freedom the pursuit of all other blessings and benefits is vain. That belief is the foundation of all American progress, political as well as economic.

Liberalism is a force truly of the spirit, a force proceeding from the deep realization that economic freedom cannot be sacrificed if political freedom is to be preserved. Even if Governmental conduct of business could give us more efficiency instead of less efficiency, the fundamental objection to it would remain unaltered and unabated. It would destroy political equality. It would increase rather than decrease abuse and corruption. It would stifle initiative and invention. It would undermine the development of leadership. It would cramp and cripple the mental and spiritual energies of our people. It would extinguish equality and opportunity. It would dry up the spirit of liberty and progress. For these reasons primarily it must be resisted. For a hundred and fifty years liberalism has found its true spirit in the American system, not in the European systems. . . .

By adherence to the principles of decentralized self-government, ordered liberty, equal opportunity, and freedom to the individual, our American experiment in human welfare has yielded a degree of well-being unparalleled in all the world. It has come nearer to the abolition of poverty, to the abolition of fear of want, than humanity has ever reached before. Progress of the past seven years is the proof of it. This alone furnishes the answer to our opponents, who ask us to introduce destructive elements into the system by which this has been accomplished. . . .

I have endeavored to present to you that the greatness of America has grown out of a political and social system and a method of control of economic forces distinctly its own—our American system—which has carried this great experiment in human welfare farther than ever before in all history. We are nearer today to the ideal of the abolition of poverty and fear from the lives of men and women than ever before in any land. And I again repeat that the departure from our American system by injecting principles destructive to it which our opponents propose, will jeopardize the very liberty and freedom of our people, and will destroy equality of opportunity not alone to ourselves but to our children. . . .

PART III

THE EMERGENCE OF THE AMERICAN COLOSSUS

FDR AND THE NEW DEAL

1

The uneven prosperity of the 1920s vanished with the onset of the Great Depression. As America's leaders searched for a solution to the crisis, large numbers of Americans sank into poverty. Thousands of Americans imbued with the values of rugged individualism begged for food, while many others wandered the country in search of opportunity. The Great Depression gave the Democrats political control of the country. Behind the leadership of President Franklin D. Roosevelt, the government energetically sought a variety of means to revive the economy and restore hope to the American people. Despite these efforts, political opposition and ecological difficulties hampered these attempts. The following documents depict the despair of many Americans and the varying efforts undertaken to alleviate these conditions.

58

URBAN FAMILIES IN THE GREAT DEPRESSION
(1931)

The economic boom of the 1920s vanished with the stock market crash in October 1929, and the country slid into the Great Depression. While it did not cause the Great Depression, the crash revealed the unsound nature of business and helped trigger the economic collapse. Millions of workers lost their jobs as companies retrenched; prices dropped dramatically, but consumer spending virtually ceased. Thousands of businesses failed, and the banking system neared disintegration under the financial strain. At the nadir of the Great Depression, the standard of living had dropped by 50 percent, and over one-third of the work force was fully unemployed (some received shorter work hours but were considered employed). Among the people hardest hit were the urban poor and those living on the margin of poverty. As the depression worsened, Congress heard testimony from numerous individuals operating private relief agencies about conditions for urban residents. Dorothy Kahn, executive director of the Jewish Welfare Society of Philadelphia, Pennsylvania, testified before the Senate Subcommittee on Unemployment Relief in December 1931. Her excerpted statement below reveals the plight of the urban family in the midst of the Great Depression.

———

·⌐ **Questions to Consider:** What happened to urban families in Philadelphia? How did they react to these circumstances? According to Dorothy Kahn, what was the attitude of the unemployed? Why does she tell this to the Congressional committee? How are the problems of housing and unemployment resolved?

———

T HE CHAIRMAN: What happens to these families when they are evicted? MISS KAHN: The families in Philadelphia are doing a number of things. The dependence of families upon the landlords, who seem to have a remarkable willingness to allow people to live in their quarters, rent free, is something that has not been measured. I think the only indication of it is the mounting list of sheriff's sales where property owners are simply unable to maintain their small pieces of property because rents are not being paid. Probably most of you saw in the newspapers the account of the "organized" representation of the taxpayers recently, where they vigorously and successfully opposed a rise in local taxes, largely because of the fact that they are under a tremendous burden through nonpayment of rents. That, of course, is the least of the difficulties, although I think this is the point at which we ought to stress one of the factors that Mr. West and other speakers have brought out in their testimony, that is the effect on families of the insecu-

———

U.S. Congress, Senate, Subcommittee on Unemployment Relief, "Statement of Miss Dorothy Kahn," *Hearings before the Senate Subcommittee on Unemployment Relief, Senate Committee on Manufacturers,* 72nd Congress, 1st Session, (28 December 1931), 73–77.

rity of living rent free, and in addition to that, the effect on their attitude toward meeting their obligations. Some of us would not be surprised if rent paying became an obsolete custom in our community. There are also, of course, evictions and the evictions in Philadelphia are frequently accompanied not only by the ghastly placing of a family's furniture on the street, but the actual sale of the family's household goods by the constable. These families are, in common Philadelphia parlance, "sold out."

One of the factors that is never counted in all of the estimates of relief in this country is the factor of neighborliness. That factor of neighborliness is a point that I would like to stress here, because it seems to us who are close to this problem that this factor has been stretched not only beyond its capacity but beyond the limits of human endurance. We have no measure in Philadelphia to-day of the overcrowding that is a direct or indirect result of our inability to pay rent for families. Only the other day a case came to my attention in which a family of 10 had just moved in with a family of 6 in a 3-room apartment. However shocking that may be to the members of this committee, it is almost an every-day occurrence in our midst. Neighbors do take people in. They sleep on chairs, they sleep on the floor. There are conditions in Philadelphia that beggar description. There is scarcely a day that calls do not come to all of our offices to find somehow a bed or a chair. The demand for boxes on which people can sit or stretch themselves is hardly to be believed. . . .

Only the other day a man came to our office, as hundreds do day after day, applying for a job, in order not to have to apply for relief. I think we have already stressed the reluctance of individuals to accept relief, regardless of the source from which it comes. This man said to our worker: "I know you haven't any money to give us. I know there isn't enough money in the city to take care of the needs of everybody, but I want you to give me a job." Now, we have so many applications of that kind during the day that it has gotten to the point where we can scarcely take their names as they come in, because we have no facilities for giving jobs. In this particular case this individual interested me because when he heard that we had no jobs to give him, he said: "Have you anybody you can send around to my family to tell my wife you have no job to give me! Because she doesn't believe that a man who walks the street from morning till night, day after day, actually can't get a job in this town. She thinks I don't want to work." I think it is not necessary to dramatize the results of a situation like that. And there are thousands of them. It is only one illustration.

Another thing, it seems to me to be important to stress is the effect of this situation on the work habits of the next generation. I think it has not been brought out that in the early period of this so-called "depression" one of the most outstanding features of it was the fact that young people could get jobs even when old people of 40 years and over could not get jobs, and it has become quite customary for families to expect that their young members who are just coming of working age can replace the usual breadwinner, the father of the family. It is easy to forget about these young boys and girls reaching 14, 15, 16, 17, 18 years of age, who have had no work experience, and if we think of work not as merely a means of livelihood but as an aspect of our life and a part of our life, it has a good deal of significance that these young people are having their first work experience, and experience not with employment but with unemployment; that in addition to that they are looked to as potential breadwinners in the family; that they are under the same strain, the same onus that the father of the family is under, suspected of malingering, suspected of not wanting to work—all of these things which the average individual sees not as clearly as we see them in terms of millions of unemployed. . . .

59

THE GREAT DEPRESSION IN RURAL AMERICA
(1932)

The Republican party's campaign slogan for 1928 promised continued prosperity for the nation: "A chicken for every pot and a car in every garage." But the onslaught of the Great Depression shattered the prosperity associated with the Republican party. Besides the millions of people who lost their jobs and businesses, the American farmer faced a dire situation. Existing in a state of economic decline in the decade before the Great Depression, farmers witnessed further price declines and vanishing markets as the depression worsened. Many farmers either lost their farms to bank foreclosures or found it financially impractical to continue operations. In February 1932, when the Great Depression was near the bottom, Oscar Ameringer, a newspaper editor from Oklahoma, testified before the House Committee on Labor on unemployment in agriculture. His statement, excerpted below, divulges a near-desperate situation in rural America.

⌐ **Questions to Consider:** What was most shocking to Oscar Ameringer as he toured America? What does he believe are the twin problems facing farmers? Ameringer argues that a revolution was imminent. Why did it not occur? How does Ameringer's description compare with Tom Ayres' account ("Farm Problems in South Dakota," Document 52)?

During the last three months I have visited, as I have said, some 20 States of this wonderfully rich and beautiful country. Here are some of the things I heard and saw: In the State of Washington I was told that the forest fires raging in that region all summer and fall were caused by unemployed timber workers and bankrupt farmers in an endeavor to earn a few honest dollars as fire fighters. The last thing I saw on the night I left Seattle was numbers of women searching for scraps of food in the refuse piles of the principal market of that city. A number of Montana citizens told me of thousands of bushels of wheat left in the fields uncut on account of its low price that hardly paid for the harvesting. In Oregon I saw thousands of bushels of apples rotting in the orchards. Only absolute flawless apples were still salable, at from 40 to 50 cents a box containing 200 apples. At the

U.S. Congress, House, Committee on Labor, "Statement of Oscar Ameringer," *Hearings before the House Committee on Labor,* 72nd Congress, 1st Session, (February 1932), 97–99.

same time, there are millions of children who, on account of the poverty of their parents, will not eat one apple this winter.

While I was in Oregon the Portland Oregonian bemoaned the fact that thousands of ewes were killed by the sheep raisers because they did not bring enough in the market to pay the freight on them. And while Oregon sheep raisers fed mutton to the buzzards, I saw men picking for meat scraps in the garbage cans in the cities of New York and Chicago. I talked to one man in a restaurant in Chicago. He told me of his experience in raising sheep. He said that he had to kill 3,000 sheep this fall and thrown them down the canyon, because it cost $1.10 to ship a sheep, and then he could not afford to feed the sheep, and he would not let them starve, so he just cut their throats and threw them down the canyon.

The roads of the West and Southwest teem with hungry hitchhikers. The camp fires of the homeless are seen along every railroad track. I saw men, women, and children walking over the hard roads. Most of them were tenant farmers who had lost their all in the late slump in wheat and cotton. Between Clarksville and Russellville, Ark., I picked up a family. The woman was hugging a dead chicken under a ragged coat. When I asked her where she had procured the fowl, first she told me she had found it dead in the road, and then added in grim humor, "They promised me a chicken in the pot, and now I got mine."

In Oklahoma, Texas, Arkansas, and Louisiana I saw untold bales of cotton rotting in the fields because the cotton pickers could not keep body and soul together on 35 cents paid for picking 100 pounds. The farmers cooperatives who loaned the money to the planters to make the crops allowed the planters $5 a bale. That means 1,500 pounds of seed cotton for the picking of it, which was in the neighborhood of 35 cents a pound. A good picker can pick about 200 pounds of cotton a day, so that the 70 cents would not provide enough pork or beans to keep the picker in the field, so that there is fine staple cotton rotting down there by the hundreds and thousands of tons.

As a result of this appalling overproduction on the one side and staggering underconsumption on the other side, 70 per cent of the farmers of Oklahoma were unable to pay the interests on their mortgages. Last week one of the largest and oldest mortgage companies in that State went into the hands of the receiver. In that and other states we have now the interesting spectacle of farmers losing their farms by foreclosure and mortgage companies losing their recouped holdings by tax sales.

The farmers are being pauperized by the poverty of industrial populations and the industrial populations are being pauperized by the poverty of farmers. Neither has the money to buy the product of the other, hence we have overproduction and underconsumption at the same time in the same country.

I have not come here to stir you in a recital of the necessity for relief for our suffering fellow citizens. However, unless something is done for them and done soon, you will have a revolution on hand. And when the revolution comes it will not come from Moscow, it will not be made by the poor communists whom our police are heading up regularly and efficiently. When the revolution comes it will bear the label "Laid in the U.S.A." and its chief promoters will be the people of American stock.

60

FRANKLIN D. ROOSEVELT'S FIRST INAUGURAL ADDRESS (1933)

The dominant issue in the presidential election in 1932 was the Great Depression. The Republicans renominated Herbert Hoover, who campaigned defensively on his record, while the Democrats selected New York Governor Franklin Delano Roosevelt, who offered few specific proposals to end the depression but radiated confidence as he pledged a New Deal for the American people. Roosevelt won the presidency in a landslide (472 electoral votes to 59), and the Democrats gained control of both houses of Congress. But in the four long months between the election and inauguration—soon remedied when the Twentieth Amendment moved the inauguration from March 4 to January 20—the Great Depression worsened: unemployment increased, more businesses failed, and there were numerous "runs" on banks, as panicked depositors withdrew life savings, which forced some banks to close their doors. On inauguration day, 80 percent of America's banks were closed (either by declared state holiday or by failure), and the country was near economic ruin. Roosevelt's inaugural address, excerpted below, exuded a sense of vigor and action at a time when Americans suffered a crisis of confidence.

Questions to Consider: In what ways does Franklin Roosevelt seek to build the American people's confidence? What does Roosevelt believe are the significant problems facing the nation? How does he propose to solve them? For what purposes does Roosevelt refer to the crisis as similar to war?

President, Mr. Chief Justice, my friends:
   This is a day of national consecration, and I am certain that my fellow-Americans expect that on my induction into the Presidency I will address them with a candor and a decision which the present situation of our nation impels.

   This is pre-eminently the time to speak the truth, the whole truth, frankly and boldly. Nor need we shrink from honestly facing conditions in our country today. This great nation will endure as it has endured, will revive and will prosper.

   So first of all let me assert my firm belief that the only thing we have to fear is fear itself—nameless, unreasoning, unjustified terror which paralyzes needed efforts to convert retreat into advance.

   In every dark hour of our national life a leadership of frankness and vigor has met with that understanding and support of the people themselves which is essential to victory. I am convinced that you will again give that support to leadership in these critical days.

"Text of the Inaugural Address; President for Vigorous Action," *The New York Times*, 5 March 1933, 1, 3.

In such a spirit on my part and on yours we face our common difficulties. They concern, thank God, only material things. Values have shrunken to fantastic levels; taxes have risen; our ability to pay has fallen, government of all kinds is faced by serious curtailment of income; the means of exchange are frozen in the currents of trade; the withered leaves of industrial enterprise lie on every side; farmers find no markets for their produce; the savings of many years in thousands of families are gone.

More important, a host of unemployed citizens face the grim problem of existence, and an equally great number toil with little return. Only a foolish optimist can deny the dark realities of the moment.

Yet our distress comes from no failure of substance. We are stricken by no plague of locusts. Compared with the perils which our forefathers conquered because they believed and were not afraid, we have still much to be thankful for. Nature still offers her bounty and human efforts have multiplied it. Plenty is at our doorstep, but a generous use of it languishes in the very sight of the supply. . . .

Small wonder that confidence languishes, for it thrives only on honesty, on honor, on the sacredness of obligations, on faithful protection, on unselfish performance. Without them it cannot live.

Restoration calls, however, not for changes in ethics alone. This nation asks for action, and action now.

Our greatest primary task is to put people to work. This is no unsolvable problem if we face it wisely and courageously.

It can be accomplished in part by direct recruiting by the government itself, treating the task as we would treat the emergency of a war, but at the same time, through this unemployment, accomplishing greatly needed projects to stimulate and reorganize the use of our natural resources.

Hand in hand with this, we must frankly recognize the overbalance of population in our industrial centers and, by engaging on a national scale in the redistribution, endeavor to provide a better use of the land for those best fitted for the land.

The task can be helped by definite efforts to raise the values of agricultural products and with this the power to purchase the output of our cities.

It can be helped by preventing realistically the tragedy of the growing loss, through foreclosure, of our small homes and our farms.

It can be helped by insistence that the Federal, State and local governments act forthwith on the demand that their cost be drastically reduced.

It can be helped by the unifying of relief activities which are today often scattered, uneconomical and unequal. It can be helped by national planning for and supervision of all forms of transportation and of communications and other utilities which have a definitely public character.

There are many ways in which it can be helped, but it can never be helped merely by talking about it. We must act, and act quickly.

Finally, in our progress toward a resumption of work we require two safeguards against a return of the evils of the old order; there must be a strict supervision of all banking and credits and investments; there must be an end to speculation with other people's money, and there must be a provision for an adequate but sound currency.

These are the lines of attack. I shall presently urge upon a new Congress in special session detailed measure for their fulfillment, and I shall seek the immediate assistance of the several States.

Through this program of action we address ourselves to putting our own national house in order and making income balance outgo. . . .

I shall ask the Congress for the one remaining instrument to meet the crisis—broad executive power to wage a war against the emergency as great as the power that would be given me if we were in fact invaded by a foreign foe.

For the trust reposed in me I will return the courage and the devotion that befit the time. I can do no less.

We face the arduous days that lie before us in the warm courage of national unity; with the clear consciousness of seeking old and precious moral values; with the clean satisfaction that comes from the stern performance of duty by old and young alike.

We aim at the assurance of a rounded and permanent national life.

We do not distrust the future of essential democracy. The people of the United States have not failed. In their need they have registered a mandate that they want direct, vigorous action.

They have asked for discipline and direction under leadership. They have made me the present instrument of their wishes. In the spirit of the gift I take it.

In this dedication of a nation we humbly ask the blessing of God. May He protect each and every one of us! May He guide me in the days to come!

61

THE "SHARE OUR WEALTH" PLAN (1933)

Franklin Delano Roosevelt's first New Deal attempted to restore economic confidence in the American people, provide relief to the unemployed, revive the sagging agricultural and business enterprises, and put people to work. Uneven in its impact and often contradictory and improvised, the New Deal "experiment" enjoyed massive public support during its inception. The New Deal, however, brought only limited recovery, and, as the economic crisis waned, critics of the program emerged. Among the most prominent critics of Roosevelt and the New Deal was Louisiana Senator Huey P. Long. Nicknamed the "Kingfish," Long developed a fervent following from poor whites in Louisiana, was elected governor, and created a political machine that gave him almost dictatorial rule over the state. Elected senator in 1930, the demagogue used his popularity to spread his Share Our Wealth program, an implausibly simplistic plan that appealed to many Americans' resentment toward the wealthy. Long claimed membership in the Share Our Wealth clubs exceeded seven million. The 1933 Huey P. Long autobiography, *Everyman a King*, excerpted next, promised economic security for all Americans with the proposed Share Our Wealth Plan.

Huey P. Long, *Everyman a King: The Autobiography of Huey P. Long* (New Orleans: The National Book Company, 1933), 338–340. (1961 Copyright renewed by Russell B. Long. Reprinted with permission.)

·⌣ **Questions to Consider:** Why would many Americans support this plan? What would the people do to receive their share of the wealth? Would such a plan help the poor? How did Long's plan challenge the New Deal? With what effect?

The increasing fury with which I have been, and am to be, assailed by reason of the fight and growth of support for limiting the size of fortunes can only be explained by the madness which human nature attaches to the holders of accumulated wealth.

What I have proposed is:—

THE LONG PLAN

1. A capital levy tax on the property owned by any one person of 1% of all over $1,000,000; 2% of all over $2,000,000 etc., until, when it reaches fortunes of over $100,000,000, the government takes all above that figure; which means a limit on the size of any one man's fortune to something like $50,000—the balance to go to the government to spread out in its work among the people.
2. An inheritance tax which does not allow any one person to receive more than $5,000,000 in a lifetime without working for it, all over that amount to go to the government to be spread among the people for its work.
3. An income tax which does not allow any one man to make more than $1,000,000 in one year, exclusive of taxes, the balance to go to the United States for general work among the people.

The foregoing program means all taxes paid by the fortune holders at the top and none at the bottom; the spreading of wealth among all the people and the breaking up of a system of Lords and Slaves in our economic life. It allows the millionaires to have, however, more than they can use for any luxury they can enjoy on earth. But, with such limits, all else can survive.

That the public press should regard my plan and effort as a calamity and me as a menace is no more than should be expected, gauged in the light of past events. According to Ridpath, the eminent historian:

"The ruling classes always possess the means of information and the process by which it is distributed. The newspaper of modern times belongs to the upper man. The under man has no voice; or if, having a voice, he cries out, his cry is lost like a shout in the desert. Capital, in the places of power, seizes upon the organs of public utterance, and howls the humble down the wind. Lying and misrepresented are the natural weapons of those who maintain an existing vice and gather the usufruct of crime."

—Ridpath's History of the World, page 410

In 1932, the vote for my resolution showed possibly a half dozen other Senators back of it. It grew in the last Congress to nearly twenty Senators. Such growth through one other year will mean the success of a venture, the completion of everything I have undertaken,—the time when I can and will retire from the stress and fury of my public life, maybe as my forties begin,—a contemplation so serene as to appear impossible.

That day will reflect credit on the States whose Senators took the early lead to spread the wealth of the land among all the people.

Then no tear dimmed eyes of a small child will be lifted into the saddened face of a father or mother unable to give it the necessities required by its soul and body for life; then the powerful will be rebuked in the sight of man for holding that which they cannot consume, but which is craved to sustain humanity; the food of the land will feed, the raiment clothe, and the houses shelter all the people; the powerful will be elated by the well being of all, rather than through their greed.

Then, those of us who have pursued that phantom of Jefferson, Jackson, Webster, Theodore Roosevelt and Bryan may hear wafted from their lips in Valhalla:

EVERY MAN A KING

62

THE "DUST BOWL" (1935)

The Great Plains region of Oklahoma, the Texas Panhandle, Kansas, Colorado, and New Mexico is known for its sparse rainfall, thin soil, high winds, and expanse of natural prairie grasses. During the late-19th and early 20th centuries, the prairie grasses adequately supported the ranching industry, but during the First World War, farmers, enticed by high grain prices and using tractors, plowed up millions of acres of the grass cover to plant wheat. They helped create an environmental tragedy. In the mid-1930s, a drought struck the region, and without the natural root system to keep the soil in place, high winds loosened the top soil and swirled it into great dust clouds called "black blizzards." As the article in *Literary Digest* made clear to its readers, the continued winds wreaked havoc in what became known as the "Dust Bowl." Nearly 60 percent of the area's population was driven out, and many, called "Okies," moved to cities on the West Coast.

Questions to Consider: What are the short-term effects of the "Dust Bowl"? The long-term effects? What helped create this environmental tragedy? What would drought relief programs do?

Recurrent dry winds continued last week to spread a suffocating pall over more than a dozen States. AAA [Agricultural Adjustment Administration] officials said continuation of the great siege from the air would mean a new drought-relief

---

"Dust and the Nation's 'Bread-Basket,'" *Literary Digest* 119 (20 April 1935): 10.

grant. The Independent Kansas City *Star*, however, minimized the extent of the duststorms and their effect. Kansas City, it said, "sits in a vast empire of green, extending in every direction."

Others reported the sun hidden in several localities. Lands laid bare by the plow in the old cow-country to grow wheat during the War were surrendering top-soil to every breeze. People and animals were finding it difficult to breathe. Housewives were taping their windows to keep out the wind-blown soil, made so fine that it could sift in. Cow-country families were reported fighting their way eastward through the choking pall. Trains, struggling through, were several hours late.

"Noon was like night," said Walter Knudsen, Conductor of the Santa Fe Navajo, when the train reached Chicago six hours behind time. "There was no sun, and, at times, it was impossible to see a yard. The engineer could not see the signal-lights."

R.G. Goetze, Conductor of the Rock Island Colorado Express, which arrived in Chicago two and a half hours late, said, according to the Associated Press, which also had quoted Conductor Knudsen: "There was a heavy coating of dust on the streets when we left Denver. Then it snowed. The mixture put a plaster on the sides of the train."

In several places schools closed, and business was at a standstill. In Memphis, people covered their faces with handkerchiefs. Arkansas was covered by haze of dust. In Texas, birds feared to take wing. Texas State Senators put on surgical-masks. "Point of order," shouted Senator Ben G. Oneal of Wichita Falls, "the Governor is trying to gag the Senate."

The brunt of the storm, reports indicate, fell on Western Kansas, East Colorado and Wyoming, Western Oklahoma, virtually all of Texas, and parts of New Mexico. Dust swirled over Missouri, Iowa, and Arkansas, crossed the Mississippi, and sifted down on Illinois, Indiana, Kentucky, Tennessee, and Louisiana.

Kenneth Welch, relief-administrator in Baca County, Colorado, reported that "dust-pneumonia is rapidly increasing among children." Scores of women and children had been sent out of the country.

Report had it, too, that some live stock had suffocated in Kansas. There was said to be a staggering crop-damage.

Walter Barlow of Amarillo, Texas, a grain-elevator operator, estimated that the wheat-crop damage in the Texas Panhandle was between $18,000,000 and $20,000,000. Harry B. Cordell, President of the Oklahoma State Board of Agriculture, said the last of that State's wheat-planting had virtually been destroyed by dust-storms of the last forty-eight hours. Government reports showed that much land in the nation's "bread-basket" was being abandoned.

Meanwhile, the Government was moving to expand its drought-relief program. Officials were planning to use $150,000,000 of work-relief money. Ten years, said Secretary of Agriculture Henry A. Wallace, would be required to make the program effective. Grass and other cover-crops, and tree-belts, will have to be planted; dams and terraces be constructed.

63

AN EDITORIAL ON THE NATIONAL LABOR RELATIONS ACT (1935)

After two years in operation, Franklin Roosevelt's first New Deal was in jeopardy. It was limited in its promotion of economic recovery, faced growing opposition, and the Supreme Court began declaring some New Deal legislation unconstitutional. In the summer of 1935, Roosevelt launched the so-called second New Deal, a new set of initiatives designed to achieve economic and social gains for the middle and working classes. One of the most important pieces of legislation in this effort was the National Labor Relations Act (1935), which provided certain guarantees to labor in the hope they could achieve better work conditions and higher pay. Among the intended beneficiaries was the American Federation of Labor (AFL), the largest labor union in the country. AFL President William Green, who had served as the union's leader since 1924, published the excerpted editorial below in the AFL journal, *American Federationist,* to inform rank and file members about the new law and what it meant for some laborers.

—

Questions to Consider: Why does William Green state that this act begins "a new chapter in the history of American labor"? What is the function of the National Labor Relations Board? What power does it possess? Is that important? Why is Green guardedly optimistic about this new labor law? How does labor react to this new law?

—

The National Labor Relations Act, known also as the Wagner-Connery Act, became law on July 5, 1935.

The enactment of this measure, long and bitterly fought by organized employers, marks the beginning of a new chapter in the history of American Labor. Great responsibility rests with Labor and management alike to see that these new pages in the annals of our industrial relations are not marred by a record of strife bred by misunderstanding, misrepresentation, and deliberate flouting of the law.

Every representative of labor should make a careful study of the provisions of this Act, and thoroughly understand their meaning, if he is to give full measure of service expected of him by his fellow-workers. . . .

In the statement issued upon his signing of the act, President Roosevelt said:

> This Act defines, as a part of our substantive law, the right of self-organization of employees in industry for the purpose of collective bargaining, and provides methods by which the government can safeguard that legal right. It establishes a National Labor Relations Board to hear and determine cases in which it is charged that this legal right is abridged or denied, and to hold fair elections to ascertain who are the chosen representatives of employees.

William Green, "National Labor Relations Act," *American Federationist* 42 (August 1935): 814–821. (Reprinted by permission of the American Federation of Labor.)

A better relationship between labor and management is the high purpose of this Act. By assuring the employees the right of collective bargaining it fosters the development of the employment contract on a sound and equitable basis. By providing an orderly procedure for determining who is entitled to represent the employees, it aims to remove one of the chief causes of wasteful economic strife. By preventing practices which tend to destroy the independence of labor, it seeks, for every worker within its scope, that freedom of choice and action which is justly his. . . .

In doing so, we must always remember that the scope of the Act is limited. It does not apply to all industry and labor, but is effective only when the violation of the legal right of independent self-organization would tend to burden or obstruct interstate commerce. . . .

The intent of the Act is:

1. to encourage the practice and procedure of collective bargaining;
2. to protect the exercise by workers of full freedom of association, self-organization, and designation of representatives of their own choosing, for the purpose of negotiating the terms and conditions of their employment or other mutual aid or protection.
3. Inasmuch as the denial by employers of the right of workers to organize and the refusal by employers to accept the procedure of collective bargaining lead to industrial unrest, with the necessary effect of obstructing the free flow of interstate commerce, it is the basic purpose of the Act to eliminate the causes of these obstructions of interstate commerce.

In order to establish these guarantees to the workers of their rights of collective bargaining and self-organization, the Act creates a National Labor Relations Board, with sufficient powers to enforce these rights. Briefly, the Board has authority to prevent the following practices by employers:

1. Interference, restraint or coercion of employees in the exercise of their rights established by this law.
2. Domination or interference with the formation or administration of any labor organization, of financial support of such organization.
3. Discrimination with regard to hire or tenure of employment, designed to discourage membership in any labor organization.
4. Discrimination against workers who file charges against their employers under the Act.
5. Refusal to bargain collectively with the freely chosen representatives of the employees.

In addition to this, the Act definitely establishes the principle of majority representation and specifically legalizes the union shop.

The Board is given adequate authority to investigate, through its power to subpoena witnesses and gain access to all pertinent evidence. To enforce its decisions, the Board is authorized to issue cease and desist order, enforceable in the Courts. In no instance will the Board attempt mediation.

The Act does not provide for arbitration, either voluntary or compulsory, nor does it deprive the workers of the right to strike.

The application of this Act is limited to firms whose business affects interstate commerce. Just exactly in what cases the law will apply remains to be decided by the National Labor Relations Board and affirmed by the Courts.

64

FRANCES PERKINS ENDORSES THE SOCIAL SECURITY ACT (1935)

The Social Security Act (1935) was passed as part of the second New Deal, and it became the most significant social program in America. Franklin Roosevelt called it the "supreme achievement" of the New Deal, and the act remains its enduring legacy. The act represented a break with previous American practices of voluntarism and individualism and placed protection of all citizens—with old-age insurance, unemployment compensation, disability pensions, and aid to dependents—under the government's auspices. Aware that Americans were traditionally suspicious of government social programs, an effort was made to inform the public about Social Security. In a national radio broadcast celebrating Labor Day 1935, Secretary of Labor Frances Perkins, the first woman to hold a Cabinet position, took the opportunity to explain and to endorse the Social Security Act. Excerpted below is her address.

Questions to Consider: What is the purpose of Social Security? Who was to benefit? Explain the relationship between the federal and state government in administering the Social Security program. Why is the act so significant? How does this act change the function of the federal government?

People who work for a living in the United States of America can join with all other good citizens on this forty-eighth anniversary of Labor Day in satisfaction that the Congress has passed the Social Security Act. This act establishes unemployment insurance as a substitute for haphazard methods of assistance in periods when men and women willing and able to work are without jobs. It provides for old aged pensions which mark great progress over the measures upon which we have hitherto depended in caring for those who have been unable to provide for the years when they no longer can work. It also provides security for dependent and crippled children, mothers, the indigent disabled and the blind.

Old people who are in need, unemployable, children, mothers and the sightless, will find systematic regular provisions for needs. The Act limits the Federal aid to not more than $15 per month in special cases and there is no requirement to

---

Frances Perkins, "The Social Security Act," *Vital Speeches of the Day* 1 (September 1935): 792–794.

allow as much as $15 from either State or Federal funds when a particular case has some personal provision and needs less than the total allowed.

Following essentially the same procedure, the Act as passed provides for Federal assistance to the States in caring for the blind, a contribution by the State of up to $15 a month to be matched in turn by a like contribution by the Federal Government. The Act also contains provision for assistance to the States in providing payments to dependent children under sixteen years of age. There also is provision in the Act for cooperation with medical and health organizations charged with rehabilitation of physically handicapped children. The necessity for adequate service in the fields of public and maternal health and child welfare calls for the extension of these services to meet individual community needs.

Consider for a moment those portions of the Act which, while they will not be effective this present year, yet will exert a profound and far-reaching effect upon millions of citizens. I refer to the provision for a system of old-age benefits supported by the contributions of employer and employees, and to the section which sets up the initial machinery for unemployment insurance.

Old-age benefits in the form of monthly payments are to be paid to individuals who have worked and contributed to the insurance fund in direct proportion to the total wages earned by such individuals in the course of their employment subsequent to 1936. The minimum monthly payment is to be $20, the maximum $85. These payments will begin in the year 1942 and will be to those who have worked and contributed. . . .

With the States rests now the responsibility of devising and enacting measures which will result in the maximum benefits to the American workman in the field of unemployment compensation. I am confident that impending State action will not fail to take cognizance of this responsibility. The people of the different States favor the program designed to bring them greater security in the future and their legislatures will speedily pass appropriate laws so that all may help to promote the general welfare.

Federal legislation was framed in the thought that the attack upon the problems of insecurity should be a cooperative venture participated in by both the Federal and State Governments, preserving the benefits of local administration and national leadership. It was thought unwise to have the Federal Government decide all questions of policy and dictate completely what the States should do. Only very necessary minimum standards are included in the Federal measure leaving wide latitude to the States. . . .

Our social security program will be a vital force working against the recurrence of severe depressions in the future. We can, as the principle of sustained purchasing power in hard times makes itself felt in every shop, store and mill, grow old without being haunted by the spectre of a poverty-ridden old age or of being a burden on our children.

The costs of unemployment compensation and old-age insurance are not actually additional costs. In some degree they have long been borne by the people, but irregularly, the burden falling much more heavily on some than on others, and none of such provisions offering an orderly or systematic assurance to those in need. The years of depression have brought home to all of us that unemployment entails huge costs to government, industry and the public alike.

Unemployment insurance will within a short time considerably lighten the public burden of caring for those unemployed. It will materially reduce relief costs in future years. In essence, it is a method by which reserves are built up during periods of employment from which compensation is paid to the unemployed in periods when work is lacking.

The passage of this act with so few dissenting votes and with so much intelligent public support is deeply significant of the progress which the American people have made in thought in the social field and awareness of methods of using cooperation through government to overcome social hazards against which the individual alone is adequate. . . .

ISOLATIONISM AND WORLD WAR II

2

By the late 1930s, the attention of the United States increasingly turned overseas. In both Europe and East Asia, states eager to seize territory and add to national glory had threatened the peace. America remained divided over whether it should become involved until being pulled into both European and Pacific theaters late in 1941 with the Japanese surprise attack on Pearl Harbor, Hawaii. The war forever changed American society. On the home-front, women replaced men in many occupations; on the battlefront, the skills of modern science were applied to create tools of massive destruction. The overwhelming majority of Americans heartily supported the war effort, despite the fact that thousands of their fellow citizens were deprived of their civil liberties. The following descriptions reveal some of the major issues and events of the war years.

65

ISOLATION FROM THE EUROPEAN WAR (1941)

When Europe erupted in war with Germany's invasion of Poland in September 1939, America, fearfully isolationist since the previous war, proclaimed neutrality. But when Germany swept over Europe leaving Great Britain fighting alone, a growing number of Americans came to believe that the United States should support Britain's battle, provided America did not wage war. Capitalizing on this shifting mood, President Franklin Roosevelt described the country as "the great arsenal of democracy" and proposed that Great Britain have unlimited access to American supplies. Congress complied with the Lend-Lease Act (1941), providing aid to Great Britain and drawing America closer to war. Opposed to the possible American intervention into the war, the America First Committee, comprising some prominent Midwestern businessmen and politicians, was organized in July 1940. Within one year, it claimed 450 chapters nationwide and a membership of several hundred thousand. National hero and aviator Charles A. Lindbergh was America First's most famous spokesman. One month after the passage of the Lend-Lease Act, Lindbergh addressed the New York chapter of the America First Committee. His speech, explaining the committee's position, is excerpted below.

- **Questions to Consider:** For what reasons does Charles Lindbergh oppose American intervention in this war? Is Lindbergh an isolationist? Did American citizens support the views of the America First Committee? Is military preparedness a deterrent to war?

I know I will be severely criticized by the interventionists in America when I say we should not enter a war unless we have a reasonable chance of winning. That, they will claim, is far too materialistic a standpoint. . . . But I do not believe that our American ideals, and our way of life, will gain through an unsuccessful war. And I know that the United States is not prepared to wage war in Europe successfully at this time. . . .

I have said before, and I will say again, that I believe it will be a tragedy to the entire world if the British Empire collapses. That is one of the main reasons why I opposed this war before it was declared, and why I have constantly advocated a negotiated peace. I did not feel that England and France had a reasonable chance of winning. France has now been defeated; and . . . it is now obvious that England is losing a war. I believe this is realized even by the British Government. But they have one last desperate plan remaining. They hope that they may be able to persuade us to send another American Expeditionary Force to Europe and to share with England militarily, as well as financially, the fiasco of this war.

Charles Lindbergh, "We Cannot Win This War for England," *Vital Speeches of the Day* 7 (May 1941): 424–426.

I do not blame England for this hope, or for asking for our assistance. . . .

. . . But we in this country have a right to think of the welfare of America first, just as the people in England thought first of their own country when they encouraged the smaller nations of Europe to fight against hopeless odds. When England asks us to enter this war, she is considering her own future, and that of her empire. In making our reply, I believe we should consider the future of the United States and that of the Western Hemisphere.

It is not only our right, but it is our obligation as American citizens to look at this war objectively and to weigh our chances for success if we should enter it. I have attempted to do this, especially from the standpoint of aviation; and I have been forced to the conclusion that we cannot win this war for England, regardless of how much assistance we send. . . .

. . . There is a policy open to this nation that will lead to success—a policy that leaves us free to allow our own way of life, and to develop our own civilization. It is not a new and untried idea. It was advocated by Washington. It was incorporated in the Monroe Doctrine. Under its guidance, the United States has become the greatest nation in the world.

It is based upon the belief that the security of a nation lies in the strength and character of its own people. It recommends the maintenance of armed forces sufficient to defend this hemisphere from attack by any combination of foreign powers. It demands faith in an independent American destiny. This is the policy of the America First Committee today. It is a policy not of isolation, but of independence; not of defeat, but of courage. It is a policy that led this nation to success during the most trying years of our history, and it is a policy that will lead us to success again.

We have weakened ourselves for many months, and still worse, we have divided our own people by this dabbling in Europe's wars. While we should have been concentrating on American defense we have been forced to argue over foreign quarrels. We must turn our eyes and our faith back to our own country before it is too late. . . .

The United States is better situated from a military standpoint than any other nation in the world. Even in our present condition of unpreparedness no foreign power is in a position to invade us today. If we concentrate on our own defenses and build the strength that this nation should maintain, no foreign army will ever attempt to land on American shores.

War is not inevitable for this country. Such a claim is defeatism in the true sense. No one can make us fight abroad unless we ourselves are willing to do so. No one will attempt to fight us here if we arm ourselves as a great nation should be armed. Over a hundred million people in this nation are opposed to entering the war. If the principles of democracy mean anything at all, that is reason enough for us to stay out. If we are forced into a war against the wishes of an overwhelming majority of our people, we will have proved democracy such a failure at home that there will be little use fighting for it abroad.

The time has come when those of us who believe in an independent American destiny must band together and organize for strength. . . .

. . . These people—the majority of hardworking American citizens, are with us. They are the true strength of our country. And they are beginning to realize as you and I, that there are times when we must sacrifice our normal interests in life in order to insure the safety and the welfare of our nation. . . .

If you believe in an independent destiny for America, if you believe that this country should not enter the war in Europe, we ask you to join the America First Committee in its stand. We ask you to share our faith in the ability of this nation to defend itself, to develop its own civilization, and to contribute to the progress of mankind in a more constructive and intelligent way than has yet been found by the warring nations of Europe. We need your support, and we need it now. The time to act is here. I thank you.

66

ROOSEVELT'S DECLARATION OF WAR MESSAGE
(1941)

For nearly a decade, the Japanese had been expanding into China while the United States worked to thwart the encroachment. Tensions between the two countries remained high, as negotiations either failed or were dismissed. When Japan imperialistically sought to consolidate all of East Asia under its domain in 1941, the United States responded with diplomatic pressure and economic embargoes on goods vital to the Japanese economy. Japanese leaders concluded that to preserve their empire they must fight the United States soon, so preparations were made to attack Pearl Harbor, Hawaii, and expand further in Asia. The United States had broken Japan's diplomatic secret code and knew that some attack was imminent, but the location was not known. American leaders guessed the attack would come in Southeast Asia (possibly Malaya), so only general warnings were sent to forces at Pearl Harbor. On Sunday morning, December 7, 1941, Japanese planes struck American forces at Pearl Harbor in two separate waves, crippling the Pacific fleet and killing over 2,000 Americans. The next day, President Franklin Roosevelt gave the following speech to a joint session of Congress.

·⌐ **Questions to Consider:** In what manner does Roosevelt characterize the actions of the Japanese? Why does he offer a listing of locations where the Japanese have attacked? How will the United States make "certain that this form of treachery shall never again endanger us"?

M r. Vice President, Mr. Speaker, members of the Senate and the House of Representatives:

"The President's Message," *The New York Times*, 9 December 1941, 1, 6.

Yesterday, Dec. 7, 1941—a date which will live in infamy—the United States of America was suddenly and deliberately attacked by naval and air forces of the empire of Japan.

The United States was at peace with that nation, and, at the solicitation of Japan, was still in conversation with its government and its Emperor looking toward the maintenance of peace in the Pacific.

Indeed, one hour after Japanese air squadrons had commenced bombing in the American island of Oahu the Japanese Ambassador to the United States and his colleague delivered to our Secretary of State a formal reply to a recent American message. And, while this reply stated that it seemed useless to continue the existing diplomatic negotiations, it contained no threat or hint of war or of armed attack.

It will be recorded that the distance of Hawaii from Japan makes it obvious that the attack was deliberately planned many days or even weeks ago. During the intervening time the Japanese Government has deliberately sought to deceive the United States by false statements and expressions of hope for continued peace.

The attack yesterday on the Hawaiian Islands has caused severe damage to American naval and military forces. I regret to tell you that very many American lives have been lost in addition. American ships have been reported torpedoed on the high seas between San Francisco and Honolulu.

Yesterday the Japanese Government also launched an attack against Malaya.

Last night Japanese forces attacked Hong Kong.

Last night Japanese forces attacked Guam.

Last night Japanese forces attacked the Philippine Islands.

Last night the Japanese attacked Wake Island.

And this morning the Japanese attacked Midway Island.

Japan has therefore undertaken a surprise offensive extending throughout the Pacific area. The facts of yesterday and today speak for themselves. The people of the United States have already formed their opinions and well understand the implications to the very life and safety of our nation.

As Commander in Chief of the Army and Navy, I have directed that all measures be taken for our defense, that always will our whole nation remember the character of the onslaught against us.

No matter how long it may take us to overcome this premeditated invasion, the American people, in their righteous might, will win through to absolute victory.

I believe that I interpret the will of the Congress and of the people when I assert that we will not only defend ourselves to the uttermost but will make it very certain that this form of treachery shall never again endanger us.

Hostilities exist. There is no blinking at the fact that our people, our territory and our interests are in grave danger.

With confidence in our armed forces, with the unbounding determination of our people, we will gain the inevitable triumph. So help us God.

I ask that the Congress declare that since the unprovoked and dastardly attack by Japan on Sunday, Dec. 7, 1941, a state of war has existed between the United States and the Japanese Empire.

67

LIFE IN A JAPANESE INTERNMENT CAMP (1942)

As World War II began, there were more than 100,000 people of Japanese descent living in the United States, mainly along the West Coast. After the surprise attack on Pearl Harbor, rumors spread that Japanese in America would hinder the war effort in "fifth column" (espionage or sabotage) actions. Reacting to old suspicions, ignorant fears, and racial prejudice toward all Asians, the federal government ordered Japanese Americans—regardless of loyalty or American citizenship—to abandon their homes and businesses and be placed in "Relocation Centers." Nearly 110,000 people were incarcerated in centers that resembled concentration camps: they were located in remote areas and had armed guards, barbed wire fencing, communal living arrangements in wooden barracks, and poor food. Among those relocated was Charles Kikuchi, an American-born child (Nisei) of Japanese immigrants (Issei), who kept a diary of his internment at Tanforan, a temporary assembly area in Southern California. Kikuchi's diary, excerpted below, reveals the tensions of life in the camp as well as his own torn loyalties between his family and Japanese ancestry and his American citizenship.

Questions to Consider: Why does Charles Kikuchi believe the internment will be harmful to the Japanese Americans? Why could Kikuchi see humor in some Americans' reaction to internment, yet be fearful of nativist groups like the Native Sons of the Golden West? Where were Kikuchi's loyalties? Were the "relocation camps" necessary?

S. F. Japanese Town certainly looks like a ghost town. All the stores are closed and the windows are bare except for a mass of "evacuation sale" signs. The junk dealers are having a roman holiday, since they can have their cake and eat it too. It works like this! They buy cheap from the Japanese leaving and sell dearly to the Okies coming in for defense work. Result, good profit. . . .

April 30, 1942, Berkeley

Today is the day that we are going to get kicked out of Berkeley. It certainly is degrading. I am down here in the control station, and I have nothing to do so I am jotting down these notes! The Army Lieutenant over there doesn't want any of the photographers to take pictures of these miserable people waiting for the Greyhound bus because he thinks that the American public might get a sympathetic attitude towards them.

Charles Kikuchi, *The Kikuchi Diary: Chronicle from an American Concentration Camp; The Tanforan Journals of Charles Kikuchi,* ed. John Modell (Urbana, IL, 1973), 51–52, 66, 73, 170, 229. (Copyright © 1973 the Board of Trustees of the University of Illinois. Reprinted with permission.)

I'm supposed to see my family at Tanforan as Jack told me to give the same family number. I wonder how it is going to be living with them as I haven't done this for years and years? I should have gone over to San Francisco and evacuated with them, but I had a last final to take. I understand that we are going to live in the horse stalls. I hope that the army has the courtesy to remove the manure first.

This morning I went over to the bank to close my account and the bank teller whom I have never seen before solemnly shook my hand and said, "Goodbye, have a nice time." I wonder if that isn't the attitude of the American people? They don't seem to be bitter against us, and I certainly don't think I am any different from them. . . .

May 3, 1942, Sunday

. . .A lot of Nisei kids come in and mix their Japanese in with their English. Now that we are cut off from the Caucasian contacts, there will be a greater tendency to speak more and more Japanese unless we carefully guard against it. Someday these Nisei will once again go out into the greater American society and it is so important that they be able to speak English well—that's why education is so important. I still think it is a big mistake to evacuate *all* the Japanese. Segregation is the least desirable thing that could happen and it certainly is going to increase the problem of future social adjustments. How can we expect to develop Americanization when they are all put together with the stigma of disloyalty pointed at them? I am convinced that the Nisei could become good Americans, and will be, if they are not treated with much suspicion. The presence here of all those pro-Japan Issei certainly will not help things out any. . . .

There was a terrific rainstorm last night and we have had to wade through the "slush alleys" again. Everyone sinks up to the ankles in mud. Some trucks came in today with lumber to build new barracks, but the earth was so soft that the truck sank over the hubs and they had a hell of a time pulling it out. The Army certainly is rushing things. About half of the Japanese have already been evacuated from the restricted areas in this state. Manzanar, Santa Anita, and Tanforan will be the three biggest centers. Now that S.F. has been almost cleared, the American legion, the Native Sons of the Golden West, and the California Joint Immigration Committee are filing charges that the Nisei should be disfranchised because we have obtained citizenship under false pretenses and that "we are loyal subjects of Japan" and therefore should never have been allowed to obtain citizenship. This sort of thing will gain momentum and we are not in a very advantageous position to combat it. I get fearful sometimes because this sort of hysteria will gain momentum. . . . I think that they are stabbing us in the back and that there should be a separate concentration camp for these so-called Americans. They are a lot more dangerous than the Japanese in the U.S. ever will or have been. . . .

July 8, 1942

. . . I keep saying to myself that I must view everything intellectually and rationally, but sometimes I feel sentiments compounded of blind feelings and irrationality. Here all of my life I have identified my every act with America but when the war broke out I suddenly find that I won't be allowed to become an integral part of the whole in these times of national danger. I find I am put aside and viewed suspiciously. My set of values gets twisted; I don't know what to think. Yes, an American certainly is a queer thing. I know what I want, I think, yet it looks beyond my reach at times, but I won't accept defeat. Americanism is my only solution and I may even get frantic about it if thwarted. To retain my loyalty to my country, I must also retain my family loyalty or what else do I have to build upon? So I can't be selfish and individualistic to such a strong degree. I must view it from either angle and abide by the majority decision. If I am to be in a camp for the duration, I may as well have the stabilizing influence of the family. . . .

. . . There are so many interesting people in camp. They are Americans! Sometimes they may say things that arise out of their bewildered feelings, but they can't throw off the environmental effects of the American way of life which is ingrained in them. The injustices of evacuation will some day come to light. It is a blot upon our national life—like the Negro problem, the way labor gets kicked around, the unequal distribution of wealth, the sad plight of the farmers, the slums of our large cities, and a multitude of things. It would make me dizzy just to think about them now.

68

WOMEN IN THE HOMEFRONT WAR EFFORT (1942)

World War II altered the economic status for many American women. As millions of men entered military service and the demand for labor increased dramatically, old stereotypes and barriers preventing women from entering the industrial workplace and the military were relaxed. Several hundred thousand women enlisted in the female versions of the military (Army's WACS, Navy's WAVES, Women Marines, Coast Guard's SPARS), but the most significant change came when over six million women joined the work force. Most women found work in the defense industries, mainly building ships and airplanes, but some accepted employment in arduous occupations—toolmaker, blacksmith, machinist, lumberjack—often reserved for men. A government campaign to encourage hiring women made "Rosie the Riveter" a symbol for those in war work. By 1945, over 50 percent of all employed workers in America were women. Excerpted next is a 1942 *Ladies' Home Journal* article describing the new world of work for four women.

Questions to Consider: According to the article, are the work opportunities for women limited because of gender? What is the attitude of the women toward their work? In what ways does the article suggest that the women retain their femininity even though they work on the assembly line? What happens to the women workers when the war is over?

Ruth Matthews and Betty Hannah, "This Changing World for Women," *Ladies' Home Journal* 59 (August 1942): 27–30. (Copyright 1942, Meredith Corporation. Used with permission of *Ladies' Home Journal* magazine.)

M ajory Kurtz, just 20, was a $15-a-week secretary in Absecon, N.J. Now she works in the Martin plant stock rooms.

Virginia Drummond, 30, ran a beauty shop in Punxsutawney, Pa. Today she wields an electric drill on the bomber assembly line.

Tommy Joseph, 24, of Clanton, Ala., wife of a young Army lieutenant in the Pacific, now drills bulkhead webs for Army planes.

Margaret Kennedy, 22, a Lancaster, Pa., schoolteacher till January, now works the midnight shift at the Glenn Martin plant.

When brisk Ginny Drummond and her covergirl roommate of the silky black hair and gentian-blue eyes, Tommy Joseph, sink dog-tired into bed these evenings, often as not a lively jive party is just starting in the adjoining room. Getting eight hours' sleep a night to bolster aching arms and feet for another eight hours' stand on the Glenn Martin aircraft-assembly line is practically impossible when four girls, sharing the same cramped one-bedroom apartment on Baltimore's sweltering Mt. Royal Avenue, keep working hours that stretch right around the clock.

Ginny and Tommy work six days in seven from 8:45 A.M. to 4:15 P.M. Their two other roommates, twenty-year-old Marge, daughter of a small-town mayor, and ex-schoolteacher Margaret Kennedy, are on the midnight shift, from 12:30 to 8:15 A.M. While waiting until it's time to leave for the plant, they try to subdue their chatter for the benefit of the two-day shift girls sharing the same lumpy bed in the next room. But long before the doorbell starts its nerve-shattering jangle over the bedroom door, and friends crash upstairs to drive Marge and Kennedy to work, the two sleepers are thoroughly awake.

"Daylight" nights pose even a greater problem for Marge and Kennedy. By the time these two are back, at 9:30 the following morning, the double bed is invitingly made up again, albeit with the same sheets. But by then the sun is warm and bright, and dawdling on the white front stoop is an irresistible temptation. All too often it's late afternoon before Marge and Kennedy drop into bed. By seven the apartment is filled with the rich odors of Ginny's cooking, and by the time everyone has eaten and the dishes are washed, a hoard of swains has arrived to keep them chattering and jiving way past the day shift's ten-o'clock bedtime. . . .

"You'll do a man's job and you'll get a man's paycheck," Glenn L. Martin tells his 4000 women employees, "but you'll be treated as the men are treated."

This means a full six-day week, taking the night shift when so assigned and, in the case of Tommy and Ginny, spending the forthcoming Thanksgiving, Christmas and New Year's holidays amid the terrific hubbub of hammers, cranes and electric drills.

Eighty per cent of the women at Martin are on the "small parts" assembly line, with a handful skilled enough to do the highly paid final installation jobs. From 3 to 5 per cent are engineers and inspectors. In aircraft manufacture for the United States as a whole, fewer than 2 per cent of the workers are women, compared with 40 to 80 per cent in some aircraft plants in Great Britain. But as more and more men are being taken into the armed forces, opportunities for women are booming. At least 2,000,000 women who have never drawn any kind of pay check in their lives—schoolgirls and housewives—will be in factories within the next year or two. They must be, if the war of production is to go forward.

Most Martin workers are between eighteen and twenty-four, although a few are over forty. Tommy, Ginny, Marge and Kennedy started off at the usual beginner's pay of 60 cents an hour with a guarantee of 75 cents an hour within three months. Already the older girls are doing skilled work such as drilling on bulkhead webs—part of the frame of a plane—and, with two raises, now net $32.67 a week. Marge and Kennedy are in the stock rooms. Although they both proudly wear bright nail polish, their hands are red and sore from handing out countless nuts, screws and bolts. (A Martin bomber has nearly 50,000 small parts, and each is nearly as important as a wing or propeller when a bomber goes into action.) They are now earning around $28 a week: "when we think what we used to make, that sure isn't hay."

An assembly-line worker has to buy her own tools, including electric hand drills, an investment that runs to about $30 cash if she's properly equipped. Tommy and Ginny say there are tools in their work kit they still don't know how to use—but they will before they're through at Martin: "There's no chance to get fed up with any particular job. The minute you've mastered one, they switch you to something harder."

Nobody at Martin has any doubt about the outcome of this war. When they watch those sleek-winged bombers line up, row on row, they feel they're helping to win it right now. . . .

And when the war is over? Some of the girls, and certainly the men they work beside, wonder just what all these women are going to do when the boys come home. Some, of course, will quit to get married. But not all of them will have husbands, because some of these boys aren't coming back. Tommy has faced that stark possibility with grim and self-searching courage. She, like many other of the women workers, may go on to a big supervisory job in aircraft production. As for the younger girls, "When the war's over we'll probably go home again and wash dishes."

"We'd better," Ginny advises with a wry smile. "It's the only way we'll ever get our hands clean again."

--- --- --- --- --- --- --- --- --- --- --- --- ---

69

"A SURGE OF DOOMLIKE SOUND" (1944)

A number of newspaper and magazine reporters covered actions in World War II. Perhaps the most famous was "Ernie" Pyle, who wrote a daily column for the Scripps-Howard news syndicate. Pyle traveled extensively with American troops, lived with them, ate their food, saw combat with them, and mourned the loss of each soldier. In short, Pyle became one of the "GIs." His columns gave the massive war a personal touch—that individuals with emotions, fears, and hopes

"In France—Ernie Pyle: Mass Air Attack Precedes Break Through German Line," *Cleveland Press,* 8 August 1944, 11. (Reprinted by permission of the Scripps-Howard Foundation.)

were doing the fighting. He gave American readers a sense of the war from the perspective of the common soldier. Excerpted below is Pyle's column on the ground soldiers' fascination with the air war above as the Allies prepared to break out of the beachhead that had been established with the earlier Normandy invasion. In 1944, Ernie Pyle was awarded the Pulitzer Prize, the highest award for journalism, for distinguished correspondence. He was killed the next year covering the war in the Pacific.

——

Questions to Consider: Why is Ernie Pyle fascinated with the air war? What mental picture is Pyle painting for his readers? Is there symbolism in his article? How did the air war affect the outcome of the war?

——

IN NORMANDY—(By Wireless): Our front lines were marked by long strips of colored cloth laid on the ground, and with colored smoke to guide our airmen during the mass bombing that preceded our breakout from the German ring that held us to the Normandy beachhead.

Dive bombers hit it just right. We stood in the barnyard of a French farm and watched them barrel nearly straight down out of the sky. They were bombing about half a mile ahead of where we stood.

They came in groups, diving from every direction, perfectly timed, one right after another. Everywhere you looked separate groups of planes were on their way down, or on their way back up, or slanting over for a dive, or circling, circling, circling over our heads, waiting for their turn.

The air was full of sharp and distinct sounds of cracking bombs and the heavy rip of the planes' machine guns and the splitting screams of diving wings. It was fast and furious, but yet distinct, as in a musical show in which you could distinguish throaty tunes and words.

And then a new sound gradually droned into our ears, a sound deep and all-encompassing with no notes in it—just a gigantic faraway surge of doomlike sound. It was the heavies. They came from directly behind us. At first they were the merest dots in the sky. You could see clots of them against the far heavens, too tiny to count individually. They came on with a terrible slowness. They came in flights of twelve, three flights to a group and in groups stretched out across the sky. They came in "families" of about seventy planes each.

Maybe these gigantic waves were two miles apart; maybe they were ten miles apart, I don't know. But I do know they came in a constant procession and I thought it would never end. What the Germans must have thought is beyond comprehension.

Their march across the sky was slow and studied. I've never known a storm, or a machine, or any resolve of man that had about it the aura of such a ghastly relentlessness. You had the feeling that even had God appeared beseechingly before them in the sky with palms outward to persuade them to turn back they would not have had within them the power to turn from their irresistible course.

I stood with a little group of men, ranging from colonels to privates, back of the stone farmhouse. Slit trenches were all around the edges of the farmyard and a dugout with a tin roof was nearby. But we were so fascinated with the spectacle overhead that it never occurred to us that we might need the foxholes.

The first huge flight passed directly over our farmyards and others followed. We spread our feet and leaned far back trying to look straight up, until our steel helmets fell off. We'd cup our fingers around our eyes like field glasses for a clearer view.

And then the bombs came. They began up ahead as the crackle of popcorn and almost instantly swelled into a monstrous fury of noise that seemed surely to destroy all the world ahead of us.

From then on for an hour and a half that had in it the agonies of centuries, the bombs came down. A wall of smoke and dust erected by them grew high in the sky. It filtered along the ground back through our own orchards. It sifted around us and into our noses. The bright day grew slowly dark from it.

By now everything was as indescribable cauldron of sounds. Individual noises did not exist. The thundering of the motors in the sky and the roar of bombs ahead filled all the space for noise on earth. Our own heavy artillery was crashing all around us, yet we could hardly hear it.

The Germans began to shoot heavy, high ack-ack. Great black puffs of it by the score speckled the sky until it was hard to distinguish smoke puffs from planes.

And then someone shouted that one of the planes was smoking. Yes, we could all see it. A long faint line of black smoke stretched straight for a mile behind one of them.

As we watched there was a gigantic sweep of flame over the plane. From nose to tail it disappeared in flame, and it slanted slowly down and banked around the sky in great wide curves, this way and that way, as rhythmically and gracefully as in a slow-motion waltz.

Then suddenly it seemed to change its mind and it swept upward, steeper and steeper and ever slower until finally it seemed poised motionless on its own black pillar of smoke. And then just as slowly it turned over and dived for the earth—a golden spearhead on the straight black shaft of its own creation—and it disappeared behind the treetops.

But before it was done there were more cries of "There's another one smoking and there's a third one now."

Chutes came out of some of the planes. Out of some came no chutes at all. One of white silk caught on the tail of a plane. Men with binoculars could see him fighting to get loose until the flames swept over him, and then a tiny black dot fell through space, all alone.

And all that time the great flat ceiling of the sky was roofed by all the others that didn't go down, plowing their way forward as if there were no turmoil in the world.

Nothing deviated them by the slightest. They stalked on, slowly and with a dreadful pall of sound, as though they were seeing only some thing at a great distance and nothing existed in between. God, how you admired those men up there and were sickened for the ones who fell.

70

TRUMAN'S DECISION TO DROP THE BOMB (1945)

At the behest of several refugee physicists from Europe who feared Germany might develop an atomic bomb, President Franklin Roosevelt established the ultra-secret Manhattan Project to build a nuclear weapon for the United States. Racing against time, a team of physicists under the direction of J. Robert Oppenheimer produced a working bomb in the summer of 1945. But Germany had already surrendered, and Roosevelt had died three months earlier. The new inexperienced president, Harry S Truman, completely uninformed about the bomb until he entered the White House, faced the decision of its use against Japan to both end the war and arrange the peace. Excerpted below is Truman's account of how he determined to use the atomic weapon.

Questions to Consider: What did the advisory committee recommend? What were Harry S Truman's alternatives to dropping the atomic bomb? Was dropping the bomb needed to end the war? How did the bomb affect foreign relations after the war?

Stimson was one of the very few men responsible for the setting up of the atomic bomb project. He had taken a keen and active interest in every stage of its development. He said he wanted specifically to talk to me today about the effect the atomic bomb might likely have on our future foreign relations.

He explained that he thought it necessary for him to share his thoughts with me about the revolutionary changes in warfare that might result from the atomic bomb and the possible effects of such a weapon on our civilization.

I listened with absorbed interest, for Stimson was a man of great wisdom and foresight. He went into considerable detail in describing the nature and the power of the projected weapon. If expectations were to be realized, he told me, the atomic bomb would be certain to have a decisive influence on our relations with other countries. And if it worked, the bomb, in all probability, would shorten the war. . . .

My own knowledge of these developments had come about only after I became president, when Secretary Stimson had given me the full story. He had told me at that time that the project was nearing completion and that a bomb could be expected within another four months. It was at his suggestion, too, that I had then set up a committee of top men and had asked them to study with great care the implications the new weapon might have for us. . . .

It was their recommendation that the bomb be used against the enemy as soon as it could be done. They recommended further that it should be used without specific warning and against a target that would clearly show its devastating strength. I had

---

Harry S Truman, *Memoirs: Year of Decisions* (Garden City, NY, 1955), 87, 419–421. (Reprinted by permission of Margaret Truman Daniel.)

realized, of course, that an atomic bomb explosion would inflict damage and casualties beyond imagination. On the other hand, the scientific advisers of the committee reported, "We can propose no technical demonstration likely to bring an end to the war; we see no acceptable alternative to direct military use." It was their conclusion that no technical demonstration they might propose, such as over a deserted island, would be likely to bring the war to an end. It had to be used against an enemy target

The final decision of where and when to use the atomic bomb was up to me. Let there be no mistake about it. I regarded the bomb as a military weapon and never had any doubt that it should be used. The top military advisers to the President recommended its use, and when I talked to Churchill he unhesitatingly told me that he favored the use of the atomic bomb if it might aid to end the war. . . .

In deciding to use this bomb I wanted to make sure that it would be used as a weapon of war in the manner prescribed by the laws of war. That meant that I wanted it dropped on a military target. I had told Stimson that the bomb should be dropped as nearly as possibly upon a war production center of prime military importance. . . .

Four cities were finally recommended as targets; Hiroshima, Kokura, Nigata, and Nagasaki. They were listed in that order as targets for the importance of these cities, but allowance would be given for weather conditions at the time of the bombing. . . .

On August 6, the fourth day of the journey home from Potsdam, came the historic news that shook the world. I was eating lunch with members of the *Augusta's* crew when Captain Frank Graham, White House Map Room watch officer, handed me the following message:

TO THE PRESIDENT

FROM THE SECRETARY OF WAR

Big bomb dropped on Hiroshima August 5 at 7:15 P.M. Washington time. First reports indicate complete success which was even more conspicuous than earlier test.

I was greatly moved. I telephoned Byrnes aboard ship to give him the news and then said to the group of sailors around me, "This is the greatest thing in history. It's time for us to get home."

71

REMEMBERING THE HIROSHIMA ATOMIC BLAST
(1945)

On August 6, 1945, a B-29 Superfortress, the *Enola Gay*, dropped a single atomic bomb on Hiroshima, Japan. The bomb emitted a sudden flash that demolished four square miles of the city, immediately killing nearly 80,000 people and setting

Hiroko Nakamoto, as told to Mildred Mastin Pace, *My Japan, 1930–1951* (New York, 1970), 56–61, 64–66. (Copyright held by the Estate of Mildred Mastin Pace. Reprinted by permission.)

fire to remaining structures. One of the survivors of this blast was Hiroko Nakamoto, a young, happy girl who came from a privileged family. Her powerful recollection of that day is excerpted below.

———

⌐ **Questions to Consider:** What was most shocking to Hiroko Nakamoto about the atomic blast? Nakamoto suggests the bombing was racially motivated. Was it? Did American officials realize the destructiveness of the bomb? Was it necessary? Compare Nakamoto's experience with Truman's justification to drop the bomb (Document 70).

———

Whenever I see strong sunshine, I remember the day very clearly, the day I will never forget as long as I live. That day, in one quick second, my world was destroyed. The day was August 6, 1945.

It was 8:15 in the morning, and I was on my way to work. I was walking. The night before, as usual, there had been alerts all night. I was groggy from lack of sleep. The all clear had sounded just as I left home. Now all seemed calm and quiet. I did not hear any sounds of airplanes overhead.

Suddenly, from nowhere, came a blinding flash. It was as if someone had taken a flashbulb picture a few inches from my eyes. There was no pain then. Only a stinging sensation, as if I had been slapped hard in the face.

I tried to open my eyes. But I could not. Then I lost consciousness.

I do not know how I got there or how long it was before I awoke. But when I opened my eyes, I was lying inside a shattered house. I was dazed and in shock, and all I knew was that I wanted to go home. I pulled myself up and started stumbling down the street. The air was heavy with a sickening odor. It was a smell different from anything I had ever known before.

Now I saw dead bodies all about me. The buildings were in ruins, and from the ruins I could hear people crying for help. But I could not help them. Some people were trying, as I was, to walk, to get away, to find their homes. I passed a streetcar that was stalled. It was filled with dead people.

I stumbled on. But now a great fire came rolling toward us, and I knew it was impossible to get home.

I passed a woman on the street. She looked at me, then turned away with a gasp of horror. I wondered why. I felt as if one side of my face was detached, did not belong to me. I was afraid to touch it with my hand.

There was a river nearby, and the people who could walk began walking toward the river—burned people with clothes in shreds or no clothes at all, men and women covered with blood, crying children. I followed them. . . .

When I reached the river, I saw that the wooden bridge which I had crossed each day on my way to the factory was on fire. I stopped. And for the first time I looked at my body. My arms, legs and ankles were burned. And I realized that the left side of my face must be burned, too. There were strange burns. Not pink, but yellow. The flesh was hanging loose. I went down to the water's edge and tried to pat the skin back with salt water from the river, as I saw others doing.

But we could not stay by the river. The fire was coming closer, and the heat was more intense. Everyone started moving again, away from the fire, moving silently, painfully. . . .

I found myself on a wide street. I saw a number of burned people standing around a policeman. He had a small bottle of iodine, and some cotton he was dabbing it on the badly burned back of a man. I stared too dazed to realize how futile and pathetic it was. . . .

When I awoke again, I asked a man sitting next to me what had happened.

He said a bomb had destroyed almost the entire city. For the first time, my heart was filled with hate, bitter hate, for a people who could do this. I remembered a propaganda picture we had been shown of Americans laughing as they looked at corpses of Japanese soldiers. At the time I did not believe it. But I believed it now. . . .

By the time we reached the doctor's, his house, his office, even his yard were filled with people lying waiting for help. I lay in the yard and waited a long time. When at last he saw me, he did not even know what to do. These were burns such as no man had ever seen before. A nurse hastily put some oil on my burns, then hurried on to the next person. People were screaming; many were begging for water. And so few hands to help!

Some people were burned so black you could not tell whether they were lying face down or on their backs. It was hard to tell they were human beings.

But they were still alive.

More and more burned and injured kept arriving. . . .

Hiroshima was burning. The sky was red. Pine Street, its trees where I spent my childhood hours, the rice warehouse, the hotel, all were destroyed.

Friends and neighbors were dead. Everything we owned was gone. The rivers where we had enjoyed boating on summer evenings were filled with dead bodies floating in the water. People were screaming as they lay along the banks of the rivers. The dead and the half dead were lying among the wreckage in the streets.

The sky was red. Hiroshima was burning. My aunt, Teruko, and all the Kaitaichi relatives sat that night, in the darkened room, watching my face in silence.

The Second World War transformed the United States as few events in its history. The war years had boosted the economy, leaving the United States the world's most prosperous and powerful nation. Unlike the 1920s, the nation did not withdraw from the world, but instead confronted its former wartime ally and new adversary, the Soviet Union, in the Cold War. Ideological differences (capitalism versus communism), a tradition of suspicion and mistrust, and the perceived threat from this rival contributed to political maneuverings and initiated a massive arms and technology race. The Second World War also helped bring about important social changes; the most significant of which was the expansion of civil rights for African Americans. The following excerpts examine differing aspects of these major issues.

72

"CONTAINMENT" (1946)

The conclusion of World War II left the United States and the Soviet Union as the two predominant world powers. But the former allies had ideological differences over political, economic, and social systems, as well as conflicting views of the postwar world. These differences made them adversaries in the Cold War, a conflict conducted on various levels though short of direct military clashes. Based in part on Soviet words and actions early in the Cold War, American leaders determined that the Soviet Union was bent on destroying capitalism and conquering the world. In 1946, George F. Kennan, a Soviet scholar and official in the American Embassy in Moscow, sent a "long telegram" to the State Department explaining the historic basis of Soviet foreign policy and warning of the Soviet threat to the United States. He also suggested how the United States could counter Soviet actions. Kennan's "long telegram" — and an article he published in *Foreign Affairs* in 1947 under the pseudonym "X" — became the foundation of America's new foreign policy of "containment," and Kennan, best known as "the father of containment," took a leading role in shaping many of the early Cold War policies. Excerpted below is his "long telegram" of February 1946.

———

Questions to Consider: According to George Kennan, what is the political ideology of the Soviet leaders and how does this affect postwar relations with the United States? What does Kennan believe are the purposes of Soviet foreign activities? How should the United States respond to the Soviet Union? Why does Kennan advocate that particular course of action? Does the United States follow his proposal? Can the United States take credit for the breakup of communism in the Soviet Union in the late 1980s?

———

A t bottom of Kremlin's neurotic view of world affairs is traditional and instinctive Russian sense of insecurity. Originally, this was insecurity of a peaceful agricultural people trying to live on vast exposed plain in neighborhood of fierce nomadic peoples. To this was added, as Russia came into contact with economically advanced West, fear of more competent, more powerful, more highly organized societies in that area. But this latter type of insecurity was one which afflicted rather Russian rulers than Russian people; for Russian rulers have invariably sensed that their rule was relatively archaic in form, fragile and artificial in its psychological foundation, unable to stand comparison on contact with political system of Western countries. For this reason they have always feared foreign penetration, feared direct contact between Western world and their own, feared what would happen if Russians learned truth about world without or if foreigners learned truth about world within. And they have learned to seek security only in

———

Department of State, *Foreign Relations of the United States, 1946*, vol. 6 (Washington, 1969), 696-709.

patient but deadly struggle for total destruction of rival power, never in compacts and compromises with it.

It was no coincidence that Marxism, which had smouldered ineffectively for half a century in Western Europe, caught hold and blazed for first time in Russia. Only in this land which had never known a friendly neighbor or indeed any tolerant equilibrium of separate powers, either internal or international, could a doctrine thrive which viewed economic conflicts of society as insoluble by peaceful means. After establishment of Bolshevist regime, Marxist dogma, rendered even more truculent and intolerant by Lenin's interpretation, became a perfect vehicle for sense of insecurity with which Bolsheviks, even more than previous Russian rulers, were afflicted. In this dogma, with its basic altruism of purpose, they found justification for their instinctive fear of outside world, for the dictatorship without which they did not know how to rule, for cruelties they did not dare not to inflict, for sacrifices they felt bound to demand. . . . This thesis provides justification for that increase of military and police power of Russian state, for that isolation of Russian population from outside world, and for that fluid and constant pressure to extend limits of Russian police power which are together the natural and instinctive urges of Russian rulers. Basically this is only the steady advance of uneasy Russian nationalism, a centuries old movement in which conceptions of offense and defense are inextricably confused. But in new guise of international Marxism, with its honeyed promises to a desperate and war torn outside world, it is more dangerous and insidious than ever before. . .

On official plane we must look for following:

(a) Internal policy devoted to increasing in every way strength and prestige of Soviet state: intensive military-industrialization; maximum development of armed forces; great displays to impress outsiders; continued secretiveness about internal matters, designed to conceal weaknesses and to keep opponents in dark.

(b) Wherever it is considered timely and promising efforts will be made to advance official limits of Soviet power. For the moment, these efforts are restricted to certain neighboring points conceived of here as being of immediate strategic necessity, such as Northern Iran, Turkey, possibly Bornholm. However, other points may at any time come into question, if and as concealed Soviet political power is extended to new areas. . . .

(c) Russians will participate officially in international organizations where they see opportunity of extending Soviet power or of inhibiting or diluting power of others. Moscow sees in UNO not the mechanism for a permanent and stable world society founded on mutual interest and aims of all nations, but an arena in which aims just mentioned can be favorably pursued. . . .

(d) Toward colonial areas and backward or dependent peoples, Soviet policy, even on official plane, will be directed toward weakening of power and influence and contacts of advanced Western nations, on theory that in so far as this policy is successful, there will be created a vacuum which will favor Communist-Soviet penetration. Soviet pressure for participation in trusteeship arrangements thus represents, in my opinion, a desire to be in a position to complicate and inhibit exertion of Western influence at such points rather than to provide major channel for exerting of Soviet power. . . .

(e) Russians will strive energetically to develop Soviet representation in, and official ties with, countries in which they sense strong possibilities of opposition to Western centers of power. This applies to such widely separated points as Germany, Argentina, Middle Eastern countries, etc.

(f) In international economic matters, Soviet policy will really be dominated by pursuit of autarchy for Soviet Union and Soviet-dominated adjacent areas taken together. . . . Soviet foreign trade may be restricted largely to Soviet's own security sphere, including occupied areas in Germany, and that a cold official shoulder may be turned to principle of general economic collaboration among nations.

(g) With respect to cultural collaboration, lip service will likewise be rendered to desirability of deepening cultural contacts between peoples, but this will not in practice be interpreted in any way which could weaken security position of Soviet peoples. . . .

(h) Beyond this, Soviet official relations will take what might be called "correct" course with individual foreign governments, with great stress being laid on prestige of Soviet Union and its representatives and with punctilious attention to protocol, as distinct from good manners. . . .

In summary, we have here a political force committed fanatically to the belief that with US there can be no permanent *modus vivendi,* that it is desirable and necessary that the internal harmony of our society be disrupted, our traditional way of life be destroyed, the international authority of our state be broken, if Soviet power is to be secure. This political force has complete power of disposition over energies of one of world's greatest people and resources of world's richest national territory, and is borne along by deep and powerful currents of Russian nationalism. In addition, it has an elaborate and far flung apparatus for exertion of its influence in other countries, an apparatus of amazing flexibility and versatility, managed by people whose experience and skill in underground methods are presumably without parallel in history. Finally, it is seemingly inaccessible to considerations of reality in its basic reactions. For it, the vast fund of objective fact about human society is not, as with us, the measure against which outlook is constantly being tested and re-formed, but a grab bag from which individual items are selected arbitrarily and tendentiously to bolster an outlook already preconceived. This is admittedly not a pleasant picture. Problem of how to cope with this force in [is] undoubtedly greatest task our diplomacy has ever faced and probably greatest it will ever have to face. It should be point of departure from which our political general staff work at present juncture should proceed. It should be approached with same thoroughness and care as solution of major strategic problem in war and if necessary, with no smaller outlay in planning effort. I cannot attempt to suggest all answers here. But I would like to record my conviction there are certain observations of a more encouraging nature I should like to make:

(1) Soviet power, unlike that of Hitlerite Germany, is neither schematic nor adventuristic. It does not work by fixed plans. It does not take unnecessary risks. Impervious to logic of reason, and it is highly sensitive to logic of force. For this reason it can easily withdraw — and usually does — when strong resistance is encountered at any point. Thus, if the adversary has sufficient force and makes

clear his readiness to use it, he rarely has to do so. If situations are properly handled there need be no prestige-engaging showdowns.

(2) Gauged against Western World as a whole, Soviets are still by far the weaker force. Thus, their success will really depend on degree of cohesion, firmness and vigor which Western World can muster. And this is factor which it is within our power to influence.

(3) Success of Soviet system, as form of internal power, is not yet finally proven. It has yet to be demonstrated that it can survive supreme test of successive transfer of power from one individual or group to another. . . . In Russia, party has now become a great and — for the moment — highly successful apparatus of dictatorial administration, but it has ceased to be a source of emotional inspiration. Thus, internal soundness and permanence of movement need not yet be regarded as assured.

(4) All Soviet propaganda beyond Soviet security sphere is basically negative and destructive. It should therefore be relatively easy to combat it by any intelligent and really constructive program. For these reasons I think we may approach calmly and with good heart problem of how to deal with Russia. As to how this approach should be made, I only wish to advance, by way of conclusion, following comments:

(1) Our first step must be to apprehend, and recognize for what it is, the nature of the movement with which we are dealing. We must study it with same courage, detachment, objectivity, and same determination not to be emotionally provoked or unseated by it, with which doctor studies unruly and unreasonable individual.

(2) We must see that our public is educated to realities of Russian situation. I cannot over-emphasize importance of this. Press cannot do this alone. It must be done mainly by Government, which is necessarily more experienced and better informed on practical problems involved. . . .

(3) Much depends on health and vigor of our own society. World communism is like malignant parasite which feeds only on diseased tissue. This is point at which domestic and foreign policies meet. Every courageous and incisive measure to solve internal problems of our own society, to improve self-confidence, discipline, morale, and community spirit of our own people, is a diplomatic victory over Moscow worth a thousand diplomatic notes and joint communiques. . . .

(4) We must formulate and put forward for other nations a much more positive and constructive picture of sort of world we would like to see than we have put forward in past. It is not enough to urge people to develop political processes similar to our own. Many foreign peoples, in Europe at least, are tired and frightened by experiences of past, and are less interested in abstract freedom than in security. They are seeking guidance rather than responsibilities. We should be better able than Russians to give them this. And unless we do, Russians certainly will.

(5) Finally we must have courage and self-confidence to cling to our own methods and conceptions of human society. After all, the greatest danger that can befall us in coping with this problem of Soviet communism, is that we shall allow ourselves to become like those with whom we are coping.

73

COMMUNISTS IN THE GOVERNMENT (1950)

The fight against communism in the Cold War abroad spread to domestic affairs in the second Red Scare. Losing Eastern Europe and China to communism and witnessing the Soviets develop an atomic bomb with alarming quickness, convinced many Americans that secret information had been leaked. Adding to this situation were the relentless accusations from the House Committee on Un-American Activities that subversives were in the government, as well as several sensational "spy trials" involving secret documents allegedly sent to the Soviets. Early in 1950, an obscure Republican senator from Wisconsin, Joseph McCarthy, exploited this growing public fear. He launched an anticommunism campaign with a speech in Wheeling, West Virginia, excerpted below, which he later repeated in Congress because there was some discrepancy over the exact number of names of communists McCarthy possessed. The speech launched a four-year witch-hunt where outrageous accusations and fear of communist subversives in the government obscured evidence and substance.

Questions to Consider: To what does Joseph McCarthy attribute America's postwar problems? Does McCarthy make a convincing argument that John S. Service should not work in the government? Was the State Department "infested with Communists"? What effect would such charges have? How did America react?

Five years after a world war has been won, men's hearts should anticipate a long peace and men's minds should be free from the heavy weight that comes with war. But this is not such a period—for this is not a period of peace. This is a time of the "cold war." This is a time when all the world is split into two vast, increasingly hostile armed camps—a time of great armaments race.

Today we can almost physically hear the mutterings and rumblings of an invigorated god of war. You can see it, feel it, and hear it all the way from the hills of Indochina, from the shores of Formosa, right over into the very heart of Europe itself.

The one encouraging thing is that the "mad moment" has not yet arrived for the firing of the gun or the exploding of the bomb which will set civilization about the final task of destroying itself. There is still a hope for peace if we finally decide that no longer can we safely blind our eyes and close our ears to those facts which are shaping up more and more clearly. And that is that we are now engaged in a show-down fight—not the usual war between nations for land areas or other material gains, but a war between two diametrically opposed ideologies. . . .

"Communists in Government Service," *Congressional Record*, 81st Congress, 2nd Session, part 2 (20 February 1950): 1952–1954.

At war's end we were physically the strongest nation on earth and, at least potentially, the most powerfully intellectually and morally. Ours could have been the honor of being a beacon in the desert of destruction, a shining living proof that civilization was not yet ready to destroy itself. Unfortunately, we have failed miserably and tragically to arise to the opportunity.

The reason why we find ourselves in a position of impotency is not because our only powerful potential enemy has sent men to invade our shores, but rather because of the traitorous actions of those who have been treated so well by this Nation. It has not been the less fortunate or members of minority groups who have been selling this Nation out, but rather those who have had all the benefits that the wealthiest nation on earth has had to offer—the finest homes, the finest college education, and the finest jobs in Government we can give.

This is glaringly true in the State Department. There the bright young men who are born with silver spoons in their mouths are the ones who have been the worst.

Now I know it is very easy for anyone to condemn a particular bureau or department in general terms. Therefore, I would like to cite one rather unusual case—the case of a man who has done much to shape our foreign policy.

When Chiang Kai-shek was fighting our war, the State Department had in China a young man named John S. Service. His task, obviously, was not to work for the communization of China. Strangely, however, he sent official reports back to the State Department urging that we torpedo our ally Chiang Kai-shek and stating, in effect, that communism was the best hope of China.

Later, this man—John Service—was picked up by the Federal Bureau of Investigation for turning over to the Communists secret State Department information. Strangely, however, he was never prosecuted. However, Joseph Grew, the Under Secretary of State, who insisted on his prosecution, was forced to resign. Two days after Grew's successor, Dean Acheson, took over as Under Secretary of State, this man—John Service—who had been picked up by the FBI and who had previously urged that communism was the best hope of China, was not only reinstated in the State Department but promoted. And finally, under Acheson, placed in charge of all placements and promotions.

Today, ladies and gentlemen, this man Service is on his way to represent the State Department and Acheson in Calcutta—by far and away the most important listening post in the Far East.

Now, let's see what happens when individuals with Communist connections are forced out of the State Department. Gustave Duran, who was labeled as (I quote) "a notorious international Communist" was made assistant to the Assistant Secretary of State in charge of Latin American affairs. He was taken into the State Department from his job as lieutenant colonel in the Communist International Brigade. Finally, after intense congressional pressure and criticism, he resigned in 1946 from the State Department—and, ladies and gentlemen, where do you think he is now? He took over a high-salaried job as Chief of Cultural Activities Section in the office of the Assistant Secretary General of the United Nations. . . .

This, ladies and gentlemen, gives you somewhat of a picture of the type of individuals who have been helping to shape our foreign policy. In my opinion the

State Department, which is one of the most important government departments, is thoroughly infested with Communists.

I have in my hand 57 cases of individuals who would appear to be either card carrying members or certainly loyal to the Communist Party, but who nevertheless are still helping to shape our foreign policy. . . .

As you hear this story of high treason, I know what you are saying to yourself, "Well, why doesn't the Congress do something about it?" Actually, ladies and gentlemen, one of the most important reasons for the graft, the corruption, the dishonesty, the disloyalty, the treason in high Government positions—one of the most important reasons why this continues is a lack of moral uprising on the part of the 140,000,000 American people. In the light of history, however, this is not hard to explain.

It is the result of an emotional hang-over and a temporary moral lapse which follows every war. It is the apathy to evil which people who have been subjected to the tremendous evils of war feel. As the people of the world see mass murder, the destruction of defenseless and innocent people, and all of the crime and lack of morals which go with war, they become numb and apathetic. It has always been thus after war.

However, the morals of our people have not been destroyed. They still exist. This cloak of numbness and apathy has only needed a spark to rekindle them. Happily, this spark has finally been supplied. . . .

74

GOVERNOR HERMAN TALMADGE'S STATEMENT ON THE *BROWN* DECISION (1954)

Beginning in the mid-1930s, the National Association for the Advancement of Colored People (NAACP) began to challenge school segregation in the hopes of ending the Jim Crow laws of the South. Its efforts culminated in the unanimous Supreme Court decision, *Brown v. Board of Education of Topeka, Kansas* (1954), which ended the "separate but equal" doctrine of racial segregation in public schools. Positive and negative responses to this decision were immediate. Georgia Governor Herman E. Talmadge, Jr., was among the first Southern politicians to issue a public statement, which came the day after the *Brown* decision. Talmadge had deep political roots in Georgia: His father was elected governor three times, and Talmadge filled the remainder of his father's last term and then was elected governor. Talmadge was proud that he spent more on public education for blacks and whites in his six years as governor than in all previous administrations combined. In 1956, he was elected to the Senate and became a prominent opponent of the Civil Rights Act of 1957. His *Brown* decision statement, offered next, reflected the sentiments of many whites in the Deep South.

"Talmadge Text," *The Atlanta Constitution*, 18 May 1954, 3.

Questions to Consider: Herman Talmadge attacked the Court's decision on what grounds? What is Georgia's "accepted pattern of life"? Why did the NAACP choose public education to challenge existing segregation laws? How did the South respond to the *Brown* decision? Compare Talmadge's statement with the editorial in the *Pittsburgh Courier* (Document 75).

The U.S. Supreme Court by its decision today has reduced our Constitution to a mere scrap of paper. It has blatantly ignored all law and precedent and usurped from the Congress and the people the power to amend the Constitution and from the Congress the authority to make the laws of the land. Its action confirms the worst fears of the motives of the men who sit on its bench and raises a grave question as to the future course of the nation.

There is no constitutional provision, statute or precedent to support the position the court has taken. It has swept aside 88 years of sound judicial precedent, repudiated the greatest legal minds of our age and lowered itself to the level of common politics.

It has attempted in one stroke to strike the 10th Amendment from the Constitution and to set the stage for the development of an all-powerful federal bureaucracy in Washington which can regulate the lives of all the citizens in the minutest detail.

The people of Georgia believe in, adhere to and will fight for their rights under the United States and Georgia Constitutions to manage their own affairs. They cannot and they will not accept a bald political decree without basis in law or practicality which overturns their accepted pattern of life.

The court has thrown down the gauntlet before those who believe the Constitution means what it says when it reserves to the individual states the right to regulate their own internal affairs. Georgians accept the challenge and will not tolerate the mixing of the races in the public schools or any of its public tax-supported institutions. The fact that the high tribunal has seen fit to proclaim its views on sociology as law will not make any difference.

If adjustments in our laws and procedures are necessary, they will be made. In the meantime all Georgians will follow their pursuits by separate paths and in accepted fashion. The U.S. and Georgia Constitutions have not been changed. The Georgia Constitution provides for separation of the races. It will be upheld.

As governor and chairman of the State Commission on Education I am summoning that body into immediate session to map a program to insure continued and permanent segregation of the races. . . .

I urge all Georgians to remain calm and resist any attempt to arouse fear or hysteria. The full powers of my office are ready to see that the laws of our state are enforced impartially and without violence.

I was elected governor of Georgia on the solemn promise to maintain our accepted way of life. So long as I hold this office it shall be done.

75

AN AFRICAN-AMERICAN NEWSPAPER EDITORIAL ON THE *BROWN* DECISION (1954)

Many of the African-American newspapers reacted joyously, yet with caution, to the *Brown* decision. The *Pittsburgh Courier,* under founding editor Robert L. Vann's leadership, had become one of the most widely respected and circulated African-American weeklies. Until his death in 1940, Vann used the *Courier* to crusade against segregation, discrimination, and, in particular, the white press's refusal to recognize significant African-American leaders or issues. Subsequent editors, Percival L. Prattis and William G. Nunn, Sr., continued Vann's editorial posture. In 1953, they began the "Double E" campaign for educational equality and to raise funds for the NAACP's legal battle to end segregation in public schools. In June 1954, the *Courier* issued the editorial below on the *Brown* decision.

Questions to Consider: How does the *Pittsburgh Courier* view the decision? Why does it want immediate integration? What does it see as the implications of this decision? Will the *Pittsburgh Courier* get its wishes? Compare the *Pittsburgh Courier's* editorial position with Herman Talmadge's statement (Document 74).

The South is in ferment over the recent Supreme Court decision outlawing racial segregation in public education, and this state of mind has been heightened by the Court's action last week in sending back three racial segregation cases in light of the historical ruling.

The cases not only covered three Universities but, significantly two public parks and a low-cost housing development, and the Court's action presages a full-scale outlawing of racial segregation all down the line, not only in schools.

If, as in the case of James Muir, a Louisville Negro, who must be admitted to a tax-supported, publicly operated park hitherto reserved for whites, what legal legs have the numerous other such parks in Dixie and elsewhere to stand on?

If, as in the case brought against the San Francisco Housing Authority, Negroes must be admitted to a housing project from which they had been barred under a "neighborhood pattern policy," then what happens to the scores and scores of such projects in the South and elsewhere from which Negroes have been barred?

If, as in Houston, Texas, A. W. Beal who was refused permission to play golf on a municipal course reserved for whites must now be accommodated, what happens on all other city-owned golf courses, tennis courts and amusement parks all over the South?

If, now, Negro Citizens must be admitted to public schools, colleges, golf courses, swimming pools, tennis courts, housing projects, and so forth, how much longer can jim crow exist in airline depots, railroad passenger stations, hotels, restaurants and bars, especially with the negro vote growing yearly throughout the South?

This is what has the South in ferment, for it was quickly realized by everybody who has given the matter any thought (which all Southern whites and Negroes have) that the Supreme Court decision was revolutionary and its effects could not be confined to public education alone.

This ferment is a mixture of fear, joy, antagonism, jubilation, opposition and acceptance ranging from the bitterly expressed antagonism of Governor Talmadge of Georgia to immediate implementation in North Carolina and the District of Columbia.

When such a state of mind prevails it is the time for drastic and forthright action, so we believe a drive should be launched to INTEGRATE NOW!

We look with favor upon the local level strategy, announced by the NAACP at its Atlanta conference, of going directly to local school boards with appeals to end school segregation NOW, thus by-passing the state politicians, with their eyes on re-election rather than law obedience.

In this connection it is unfortunate that these school boards and local officials have not previously been wooed by the NAACP for the purpose of establishing good will and understanding instead of beings subjected to blanket denunciation as Kluxers, reactionaries and apologists for terror.

In the last analysis it is these officials who will obey or evade and circumvent the Supreme Court decision or any other reform.

However, this is by no means a cause of ferment in the South alone, but must be giving most of the West considerable concern, since color discrimination is rife in that area despite the absence of legal sanction.

We must press for complete destruction of the bi-racial system NOW before the opposition to this reform becomes solidified and before the counsel of calmness and "going slow" mobilize to corrupt public opinion into glacier-like inaction.

76

SUBURBANIZATION: LEVITTOWN, NEW YORK (1950)

Following World War II, many young couples, having saved "a nest egg" to buy a home, found few houses to purchase in the cities. Responding to this growing demand for new housing, William Levitt and his sons began construction of entirely new neighborhoods away from the cities. Levitt, a self-confident and wealthy New York developer who amassed a fortune building houses during the

---

"Up From the Potato Fields," *Time* 56 (3 July 1950): 67–72. (Copyright 1950 Time Inc. Reprinted by permission.)

Great Depression and the war, introduced mass production techniques to the housing industry, transforming what was once a cottage industry into a major manufacturing enterprise. In 1947, Levitt began work on his crowning achievement, Levittown, New York, whose construction and appearance is described in the 1950 *Time* magazine article excerpted below. Home builders nationwide adopted Levitt's construction methods, producing numerous inexpensive houses and helping promote a white, middle-class suburban revolution in the 1950s.

Questions to Consider: Who was attracted to live in Levittown? Why this group? How was a suburban mentality shaped in this community? What enabled suburban communities like Levittown to develop? According to the article, what were some of the criticisms of Levittown? What impact would the suburbs have on America?

On 1,200 flat acres of potato farmland near Hicksville, Long Island, an army of trucks sped over new-laid roads. Every 100 feet, the trucks stopped and dumped identical bundles of lumber, pipes, bricks, shingles and copper tubing—all as neatly packaged as loaves from a bakery. Near the bundles, giant machines with an endless chain of buckets ate into the earth, taking just 13 minutes to dig a narrow, four-foot trench around a 25-by-32 ft. rectangle. Then came more trucks, loaded with cement, and laid a four-inch foundation for a house in the rectangle.

After the machines came the men. On nearby slabs already dry, they worked in crews of two and three, laying bricks, raising studs, nailing lath, painting, sheathing, shingling. Each crew did its special job, then hurried on to the next site. Under the skilled combination of men and machines, new houses rose faster than Jack ever built them; a new one was finished every 15 minutes. . . .

Levittown is known largely for one reason: it epitomizes the revolution which has brought mass production to the housing industry. Its creator, Long Island's Levitt & Sons, Inc., has become the biggest builder of houses in the U.S.

The houses in Levittown, which sell for a uniform price of $7,990, cannot be mistaken for castles. Each has a sharp-angled roof and a picture window, radiant heating in the floor, 12-by-16 ft. living room, bath, kitchen, two bedrooms on the first floor, and an "expansion attic" which can be converted into two more bedrooms and bath. The kitchen has a refrigerator, stove and Bendix washer; the living room a fireplace and a built-in Admiral television set. . . .

The influence of Levitt & Sons on housing goes much further than the thresholds of its own houses. Its methods of mass production are being copied by many of the merchant builders in the U.S., who are putting up four of every five houses built today. It is such mass production on one huge site which is enabling U.S. builders to meet the post-war demand and to create the biggest housing boom in U.S. history. . . .

At war's end, when the U.S. desperately needed 5,000,000 houses, the nation had two choices: the Federal Government could try to build the houses itself, or it could pave the way for private industry to do the job, by making available billions in credit. The U.S. wisely handed the job to private industry, got 4,000,000 new units built since the war, probably faster and cheaper than could have been done any other way.

The Government has actually spent little cash itself. By insuring loans up to 95% of the value of a house, the Federal Housing Administration made it easy for a builder to borrow the money with which to build low-cost houses. The Government made it just as easy for the buyer by liberally insuring his mortgage. Under a new housing act signed three months ago, the purchase terms on low-cost houses with Government-guaranteed mortgages were so liberalized that in many cases buying a house is now as easy as renting it. The new terms: 5% down (nothing down for veterans) and 30 years to pay. Thus an ex-G.I. could buy a Levitt house with no down payment and installments of only $56 a month.

The countless new housing projects made possible by this financial easy street are changing the way of life of millions of U.S. citizens, who are realizing for the first time the great American dream of owning their own home. No longer must young married couples plan to start living in an apartment, saving for the distant day when they can buy a house. Now they can do it more easily than they can buy a $2,000 car on the installment plan.

Like its counterparts across the land, Levittown is an entirely new kind of community. Despite its size, it is not incorporated, thus has no mayor, no police force, nor any of the other traditional city officers of its own. It has no movies, no nightclubs and only three bars (all in the community shopping centers).

And Levittown has very few old people. Few of its more than 40,000 residents are past 35; of some 8,000 children, scarcely 900 are more than seven years old. In front of almost every house along Levittown's 100 miles of winding streets sits a tricycle or a baby carriage. In Levittown, all activity stops from 12 to 2 in the afternoon; that is nap time. Said one Levittowner last week, "Everyone is so young that sometimes it's hard to remember how to get along with older people."

The community has an almost antiseptic air. Levittown streets, which have such fanciful names as Satellite, Horizon, Haymaker, are bare and flat as hospital corridors. Like a hospital, Levittown has rules all its own. Fences are not allowed (though here and there a home-owner has broken the rule). The plot of grass around each home must be cut at least once a week; if not, Bill Levitt's men mow the grass and send the bill. Wash cannot be hung out to dry on an ordinary clothesline; it must be arranged on rotary, removable drying racks and then not on weekends or holidays. . . .

Actually, Levittown's uniformity is more apparent than real. Though most of their incomes are about the same (average: about $3,800), Levittowners come from all classes, all walks of life. Eighty percent of the men commute to their jobs in Manhattan, many sharing their transportation costs through car pools. Their jobs, as in any other big community, range from baking to banking, from teaching to preaching. Levittown has also developed its own unique way of keeping up with the Joneses. Some Levittowners buy a new house every year, as soon as the new model is on the market. . . .

The most frequent criticism of Levittown and most other projects like it, is that it is the "slum of the future." Says Bill Levitt: "Nonsense." Many city planners agree with him, because they approve of Levittown's uncluttered plan and its plentiful recreational facilities. Nevertheless, in helping to solve the housing problem, Levittown has created other problems: new schools, hospitals, and sewage facilities will soon be needed; its transportation is woefully inadequate, even by Long Island standards. . . .

77

A REACTION TO *SPUTNIK* (1957)

As the Cold War confrontations continued, both the United States and Soviet Union boasted of each's economic strength as a means to demonstrate the superiority of either communism or capitalism, as well as keep important allies faithful. At the heart of this dispute was an emphasis on technological developments. For years, Americans were self-confident about their rocket and intercontinental ballistic missile (ICBM) supremacy, believing the Soviets were inferior in both military power and space technology. This complacent attitude ended abruptly when the Soviet Union launched *Sputnik* on October 4, 1957, which was the first man-made satellite to orbit the earth. Americans were shocked that the Soviets had such technological capability. The selection below is an editorial from *Life,* a popular weekly news and picture magazine, that reveals much about American reaction to *Sputnik* in the midst of the Cold War.

Questions to Consider: According to this editorial, what is the threat of *Sputnik*? How should America react to the launching of *Sputnik*? What are the purposes of the references to Korean War veterans and the battles of Lexington and Concord? What was America's response to *Sputnik*?

A young rocketeer named G. Harry Stine who was fired last week by the Martin Company for too volubly belittling the U.S. missile program, made a sharp remark about Sputnik. "This is really and truly 'the shot heard round the world,'" said he. "I wonder what the dead veterans of Lexington and of Korea are thinking."

The Korean veteran may be reminded of those Russian MiGs of 1950, the deadliest but not the first notice we had had that the Russians are not a technologically backward people. It had taken them only four years to break our A-bomb monopoly. It took them nine months to overtake our H-bomb. Now they

---

are apparently ahead of us on intercontinental ballistic missiles. For years no knowledgeable U.S. scientist has had any reason to doubt that his Russian opposite number is at least his equal. It had been doubted only by people—some of them in the Pentagon—who confuse scientific progress with freezer and lipstick output. Sputnik should teach them what the Korean veteran learned the hard way.

The dead Korean veteran may be reminded of other hard military realities. One is that the conflict between freedom and Communism is a long, tiresome and seesaw business in which the apparent lead can change many times. Sputnik is not a weapon, but it has immense military meaning. The propulsive thrust that launched it could launch an ICBM. Right now its coded messages are probably telling Russian weaponeers more about the upper atmosphere in which ICBM must travel and more about target-finding than they knew two weeks ago or than we know yet. But Sputnik's monopoly of outer space will be brief. The U.S. moons that will challenge it are likely to be even more informative—and less secretive, as befits our strategy of alliances.

Korea was a military standoff. The balance of caution that kept that war local and nonatomic has since been frozen into a "balance of terror." The insect analogy first tested in Korea is still the key to such peace as we enjoy: two scorpions in a bottle will claw but not sting each other. Our retaliatory sting is as mortal and deterrent as ever, even when carried in the SAC bombers Khrushchev has prematurely declared obsolete. Sputnik has not broken the bottle, just clouded and swollen it.

The clawing may also not be over. The more heat we turn on our own ICBM program, the less we can afford to neglect preparedness for limited and peripheral warfare. If SAC is not obsolete, neither are the U.S. Marines—or the guerrilla and platoon tactics so heroically learned by 16 nations in Korea. Sputnik surveys a dirty planet.

So much for hard military realities. They are only part of the common sense about Sputnik. In the long run, political realities are more important.

Russia's political prestige has been enormously magnified overnight, but not everywhere and not for long. A Swiss paper credits Sputnik's timeliness with having "virtually saved the 40th anniversary of the October revolution," since the rest of the fare for that event "was so sterile and pitiful that they could hardly expect to spark any enthusiasm even in their own Communist ranks." A Paris paper reminded its readers: "The cost of this satellite is 40 years of deprivations by the Russian people." Said another: "It is easier to make a revolution in the sky than on earth."

Perhaps that is what the dead heroes of Lexington would be thinking. The revolution they began is still a tremendous though unfinished *human* success. But Sputnik will not feed Khrushchev's subjects or cement the crumbling walls of his inhuman empire and irrational economic system. Indeed the failures of Communism have made its political defeat not only a necessary but an increasingly visible goal of U.S. policy.

Instead of changing this goal, Sputnik should remind us of what we ourselves have proved many times from Lexington to the Manhattan Project: that any great human accomplishment demands a consecration of will and a concentration of effort. This is as true of the liberation of men and nations as it is of the conquest of space.

It may seem impious to summon the ghost of the "embattled farmers" of Lexington, with their quaint optimism and simple certitudes, into our complex "age of technological imperialism," as Columbia's dean of engineering calls it. What has the assertion about human liberty heard round the world of 1775 to do with Sputnik?

"Technological imperialism," which draws or forces all human knowledge into the service of the state, is a frightening reality as man's knowledge and power increase. So is the "cultural lag" that abets this imperialism. In the next 20 years our environment may be altered more radically than in the last 200. Yet most living men are still poorer, more ignorant and more alien to scientific ways of thinking in our time than those embattled farmers in theirs. Faced with subtler and more plausible tyrannies than George III ever knew, we inherit from them a revolution that has scarcely begun. And our weapons against this new "technological imperialism" are still the weapons of Lexington: courage and reason.

U.S. foreign policy has developed in a straight line from the assertion of human freedom made at Lexington. It has been generally faithful to that assertion as a universal cause. It has been generally ready to combat and limit freedom's perennial foe, which is any form of uncontrolled power. Early in our brief atomic monopoly we began seeking international methods to control the weapons that could interrupt human history. The key feature of all our plans for controlling these weapons is an inspection system that would invite the confidence, if not guarantee the security, of reasonable men. This quest has been repeatedly rebuffed by the Iron Curtain, whose menacing mysteries inspection would undermine. Last week Henry Cabot Lodge presented still another version of this plan to the U.N., proposing immediate discussions for keeping deadly weapons out of the ionosphere, so that this vast new realm will be used for the "exclusively peaceful and scientific purposes" of the human race.

Commander George Hoover, U.S.N., a veteran of Project Vanguard, remarked last week of Sputnik: "I think this is the first step toward the unification of the peoples of the world, whether they know it or not." These words may or may not be good prophecy, for obviously the common cause is yet to be found. But they surely suggest the right vision of policy for any nation which identifies its own cause, as the U.S. identified its liberty, with the cause of all mankind.

The U.S. cannot lag in weapons against Communism, indeed we must recover our lead to strengthen our hand in seeking a reasonable agreement with Russia that free nations can accept. But while doing so we must gain strength also from our older, grander mission, the one Communism can never share. The mission is to make this world more habitable even while we explore others; and to keep the light of freedom and reason accessible to all our fellow men.

78

DWIGHT D. EISENHOWER'S FAREWELL ADDRESS
(1961)

Dwight D. Eisenhower served two consecutive terms as president in the 1950s. He brought to his job a wealth of military experience, but virtually no political seasoning. Born in Denison, Texas, but raised in Abilene, Kansas, Eisenhower finished West Point in 1915 and remained a part of the military for most of his life, serving as supreme commander of Allied forces in Europe during World War II. Pressured to seek the presidency in 1952, the popular war hero won easily on the Republican ticket. Eisenhower's presidency was often nonpartisan and conservative, as he displayed the resourceful ability to stem domestic political and social forces, legitimatized many New Deal programs, and maintained many Cold War policies. Three days before he left office, Eisenhower gave his "farewell address," which was broadcast live over radio and television. Drawing upon his knowledge of the military and changes that had taken place within the country, Eisenhower warned against dangers to American values and individual rights. His speech is excerpted below.

Questions to Consider: What changes have taken place regarding the military to prompt Eisenhower's warning? What does he fear about the military-industrial complex? Or the increasing power of the federal government? What does he ask Americans to do? Are Eisenhower's fears realized?

M y fellow Americans:
   Three days from now, after half a century in the service of our country, I shall lay down the responsibilities of office as, in traditional and solemn ceremony, the authority of the Presidency is vested in my successor . . . .

   We now stand ten years past the midpoint of a century that has witnessed four major wars among great nations. Three of them involved our own country. Despite these holocausts America is today the strongest, the most influential and most productive nation in the world. Understandably proud of this pre-eminence, we yet realize that America's leadership and prestige depend, not merely upon our unmatched material progress, riches and military strength, but on how we use our power in the interests of world peace and human betterment.

   Throughout America's adventure in free government, our basic purposes have been to keep the peace; to foster progress in human achievement, and to enhance liberty, dignity and integrity among people and among nations. To strive for less would be unworthy of a free and religious people. Any failure traceable to arro-

---

"Farewell Radio and Television Address to the American People," *Public Papers of the Presidents of the United States: Dwight D. Eisenhower, 1960–61* (Washington, DC, 1961), 1035–1040.

gance, or our lack of comprehension or readiness to sacrifice would inflict upon us grievous hurt both at home and abroad.

Progress toward these noble goals is persistently threatened by the conflict now engulfing the world. It commands our whole attention, absorbs our very beings. We face a hostile ideology—global in scope, atheistic in character, ruthless in purpose, and insidious in method. Unhappily the danger it poses promises to be of indefinite duration. To meet it successfully, there is called for, not so much the emotional and transitory sacrifices of crisis, but rather those which enable us to carry forward steadily, surely, and without complaint the burdens of a prolonged and complex struggle—with liberty the stake. Only thus shall we remain, despite every provocation, on our charted course toward permanent peace and human betterment. . . .

A vital element in keeping the peace is our military establishment. Our arms must be mighty, ready for instant action, so that no potential aggressor may be tempted to risk his own destruction.

Our military organization today bears little relation to that known by any of my predecessors in peacetime, or indeed by the fighting men of World War II or Korea.

Until the latest of our world conflicts, the United States had no armaments industry. American makers of plowshares could, with time and as required, make swords as well. But now we can no longer risk emergency improvisation of national defense; we have been compelled to create a permanent armaments industry of vast proportions. Added to this, three and a half million men and women are directly engaged in the defense establishment. We annually spend on military security more than the net income of all United States corporations.

This conjunction of an immense military establishment and a large arms industry is new in the American experience. The total influence—economic, political, even spiritual—is felt in every city, every statehouse, every office of the federal government. We recognize the imperative need for this development. Yet we must not fail to comprehend its grave implications. Our toil, resources, and livelihood are all involved; so is the very structure of our society.

In the councils of government, we must guard against the acquisition of unwarranted influence, whether sought or unsought, by the military-industrial complex. The potential for the disastrous rise of misplaced power exists and will persist.

We must never let the weight of this combination endanger our liberties or democratic processes. We should take nothing for granted. Only an alert and knowledgeable citizenry can compel the proper meshing of the huge industrial and military machinery of defense with our peaceful methods and goals, so that security and liberty may prosper together.

Akin to, and largely responsible for the sweeping changes in our industrial-military posture, has been the technological revolution during recent decades.

In this revolution, research has become central; it also becomes more formalized, complex, and costly. A steadily increasing share is conducted for, by, or at the direction of, the federal government. . . .

It is the task of statesmanship to mold, to balance, and to integrate these and other forces, new and old, within the principles of our democratic system—ever aiming toward the supreme goals of our free society.

Another factor in maintaining balance involves the element of time. As we peer into society's future, we—you and I, and our government—must avoid the impulse to live only for today, plundering, for our own ease and convenience, the precious resources of tomorrow. We cannot mortgage the material assets of our grandchildren without risking the loss also of their political and spiritual heritage. We want democracy to survive for all generations to come, not to become the insolvent phantom of tomorrow.

Down the long lane of history yet to be written America knows that this world of ours, ever growing smaller, must avoid becoming a community of dreadful fear and hate, and be, instead, a proud confederation of mutual trust and respect.

Such a confederation must be one of equals. The weakest must come to the conference table with the same confidence as do we, protected as we are by our moral, economic, and military strength. That table, though scarred by many past frustrations, cannot be abandoned for the certain agony of the battlefield.

Disarmament, with mutual honor and confidence, is a continuing imperative. Together we must learn how to compose differences, not with arms, but with intellect and decent purpose. Because this need is so sharp and apparent I confess that I lay down my official responsibilities in this field with a definite sense of disappointment. As one who has witnessed the horror and the lingering sadness of war—as one who knows that another war could utterly destroy this civilization which has been so slowly and painfully built over thousands of years—I wish I could say tonight that a lasting peace is in sight.

Happily, I can say that war has been avoided. Steady progress toward our ultimate goal has been made. But, so much remains to be done. As a private citizen, I shall never cease to do what little I can to help the world advance along that road. . . .

PART IV

AMERICA IN A WORLD
OF TRANSITION

THE TURBULENT SIXTIES

1

Many Americans believed they stood at the beginning of a new era as the 1960s began. An exuberant belief that government could solve virtually any problem seemed to assure that the nation would enjoy continued peace and prosperity. The events of the decade quickly shattered these hopes. America's effort to check the spread of communism led it into Vietnam, an issue which ultimately divided the nation. On the domestic front, the fight for civil rights continued, despite an increase in violence. Many of the children who had grown up in the prosperous surroundings of the 1950s entered colleges in record numbers and soon questioned many of the most cherished beliefs of their parents' generation. The following documents illustrate the idealism, disillusion, and turmoil that characterized the period.

79

JOHN F. KENNEDY'S INAUGURAL ADDRESS (1961)

The presidential election of 1960 was a watershed. It pitted Republican Richard Nixon, vice president under Eisenhower, against Democrat John Kennedy, a Massachusetts senator, who was Harvard educated and a war hero. Kennedy effectively disarmed the religious question (he was Roman Catholic), demonstrated his breezy youthful charm and sense of humor, and appeared more poised than Nixon in four nationally televised debates that nearly 70 million people watched. Kennedy won an extremely close election (303–219 in the electoral vote, but less than 120,000 popular votes out of 68 million cast), and at age 43, he became the youngest man elected president. The day Kennedy gave his inaugural address, Washington, DC, was draped with fresh fallen snow and was bitterly cold. His eloquent speech set a tone of vigor, youthful vision and personal elegance that dazzled many Americans and began a new political era.

———

Questions to Consider: Why does Kennedy specifically refer to "a new generation" in America and their future? What does he propose for American foreign relations? What does he want the American people to do? Was Kennedy able to begin fulfilling this vision? How?

———

We observe today not a victory of party but a celebration of freedom—symbolizing an end as well as a beginning—signifying renewal as well as change. For I have sworn before you and Almighty God the same solemn oath our forbears prescribed nearly a century and three quarters ago.

The world is very different now. For man holds the power to abolish all forms of human poverty and all forms of human life. And yet the same revolutionary beliefs for which our forebears fought are still at issue around the globe—the belief that the rights of man come not from the generosity of state but from the hand of God.

We dare not forget today that we are the heirs of that first revolution. Let the word go forth from this time and place, to friend and foe alike, that the torch has been passed to a new generation of Americans—born in this century, tempered by war, disciplined by a hard and bitter peace, proud of our ancient heritage—and unwilling to witness or permit the slow undoing of those human rights to which this nation has always been committed, and to which we are committed today at home and around the world. Let every nation know, whether it wishes us well or ill, that we shall pay any price, bear any burden, meet any hardship, support any friend, oppose any foe to assure the survival and the success of liberty.

This much we pledge—and more. . . .

———

"Inaugural Address," *Public Papers of the Presidents of the United States: John F. Kennedy, 1961* (Washington, DC, 1962), 1–3.

To those peoples in the huts and villages of half the globe struggling to break the bonds of mass misery, we pledge our best efforts to help them help themselves, for whatever period is required—not because the communists may be doing it, not because we seek their votes, but because it is right. If a free society cannot help the many who are poor, it cannot save the few who are rich.

To our sister republics south of our border, we offer a special pledge—to convert our good words into good deeds—in a new alliance for progress—to assist free men and free governments in casting off the chains of poverty. But this peaceful revolution of hope cannot become the prey of hostile powers. Let all our neighbors know that we shall join with them to oppose aggression or subversion anywhere in the Americas. And let every other power know that this Hemisphere intends to remain the master of its own house. . . .

Finally, to those nations who would make themselves our adversary, we offer not a pledge but a request: that both sides begin anew the quest for peace, before the dark powers of destruction unleashed by science engulf all humanity in planned or accidental self-destruction. . . .

So let us begin anew—remembering on both sides that civility is not a sign of weakness, and sincerity is always subject to proof. Let us never negotiate out of fear. But let us never fear to negotiate.

Let both sides explore what problems unite us instead of belaboring those problems which divide us.

Let both sides, for the first time, formulate serious and precise proposals for the inspection and control of arms—and bring the absolute power to destroy other nations under the absolute power to control all nations.

Let both sides seek to invoke the wonders of science instead of its terrors. Together let us explore the stars, conquer the deserts, eradicate disease, tap the ocean depths and encourage the arts and commerce. . . .

And if a beach-head of cooperation may push back the jungle of suspicion, let both sides join in creating a new endeavor, not a new balance of power, but a world of law, where the strong are just and the weak secure and the peace preserved.

All this will not be finished in the first one hundred days. Nor will it be finished in the first one thousand days, nor in the life of this Administration, nor perhaps in our lifetime on this planet. But let us begin.

In your hands, my fellow citizens, more than mine, will rest the final success or failure of our course. Since this country was founded, each generation of Americans has been summoned to give testimony to its national loyalty. The graves of young Americans who answered the call to service surround the globe.

Now the trumpet summons us again—not as a call to bear arms, though arms we need—not as a call to battle, though embattled we are—but a call to bear the burden of a long twilight struggle, year in and year out, "rejoicing in hope, patient in tribulation"—a struggle against the common enemies of man: tyranny, poverty, disease and war itself.

Can we forge against these enemies a grand and global alliance, North and South, East and West, that can assure a more fruitful life for all mankind? Will you join in that historic effort?

In the long history of the world, only a few generations have been granted the role of defending freedom in its hour of maximum danger. I do not shrink from this responsibility—I welcome it. I do not believe that any of us would exchange places with any other people or any other generation. The energy, the faith, the devotion which we bring to this endeavor will light our country and all who serve it—and the glow from that fire can truly light the world.

And so, my fellow Americans: ask not what your country can do for you—ask what you can do for your country.

My fellow citizens of the world: ask not what America will do for you, but what together we can do for the freedom of man.

Finally, whether you are citizens of America or citizens of the world, ask of us here the same high standards of strength and sacrifice which we ask of you. With a good conscience our only sure reward, with history the final judge of our deeds, let us go forth to lead the land we love, asking His blessing and His help, but knowing that here on earth God's work must truly be our own.

80

"THE PROBLEM THAT HAS NO NAME" (1963)

The two decades following World War II marked the nadir of the feminist movement, as returning veterans and mass culture influenced women to assume domestic roles of mother and housewife and to forsake independent careers (even working mothers were criticized). Despite the prevailing attitude, significant changes were taking place: The number of women who received a college education increased rapidly, and more women, especially married women, joined the work force. The feminist movement was revived in 1963 with Betty Friedan's best-seller, *The Feminine Mystique,* which is excerpted next. Friedan, a Smith College graduate, mother of three, and a free-lance writer, based her book on a questionnaire she sent to former classmates asking about their lives after school and some further research. The book challenged the happy suburban housewife myth and found a receptive audience among many middle-class women who identified with its thesis. Friedan became an instant celebrity and spearheaded an active woman's rights campaign; in 1966, she helped found the National Organization for Women (NOW).

·⌐ **Questions to Consider:** According to Friedan, how were women pressured into accepting the role of "housewife" in the post-World War II years? What is the "problem that has no name"? What caused the problem? What solutions does Friedan suggest? What impact does this problem have on America?

Betty Friedan, *The Feminine Mystique* (New York, 1963), 15–32. (Reprinted from *The Feminine Mystique* by Betty Friedan, with the permission of W. W. Norton & Company, Inc. Copyright (c) 1963, 1973, 1974, 1983 by Betty Friedan.)

The problem lay buried, unspoken, for many years in the minds of American women. It was a strange stirring, a sense of dissatisfaction, a yearning that women suffered in the middle of the twentieth century in the United States. Each suburban wife struggled with it alone. As she made the beds, shopped for groceries, matched slipcover material, ate peanut butter sandwiches with her children, chauffeured Cub Scouts and Brownies, lay beside her husband at night—she was afraid to ask even of herself the silent question—"Is this all?"

For over fifteen years there was no word of this yearning in the millions of words written about women, for women, in all the columns, books and articles by experts telling women their role was to seek fulfillment as wives and mothers. Over and over women heard in voices of tradition and of Freudian sophistication that they could desire no greater destiny than to glory in their own femininity. Experts told them how to catch a man and keep him, how to breastfeed children and handle their toilet training, how to cope with sibling rivalry and adolescent rebellion; how to buy a dishwasher, bake bread, cook gourmet snails, and build a swimming pool with their own hands; how to dress, look, and act more feminine and make marriage more exciting; how to keep their husbands from dying young and their sons from growing into delinquents. They were taught to pity the neurotic, unfeminine, unhappy women who wanted to be poets or physicists or presidents. They learned that truly feminine women do not want careers, higher education, political rights—the independence and the opportunities that the old-fashioned feminists fought for. Some women, in their forties and fifties, still remembered painfully giving up those dreams, but most of the younger women no longer even thought about them. A thousand expert voices applauded their femininity, their adjustment, their new maturity. All they had to do was devote their lives from earliest girlhood to finding a husband and bearing children. . . .

In the fifteen years after World War II, this mystique of feminine fulfillment became the cherished and self-perpetuating core of contemporary American culture. Millions of women lived their lives in the image of those pretty pictures of the American suburban housewife, kissing their husbands goodbye in front of the picture window, depositing their stationwagonsful of children at school, and smiling as they ran the new electric waxer over the spotless kitchen floor. They baked their own bread, sewed their own and their children's clothes, kept their new washing machines and dryers running all day. They changed the sheets on the beds twice a week instead of once, took the rug-hooking class in adult education, and pitied their poor frustrated mothers, who had dreamed of having a career. Their only dream was to be perfect wives and mothers; their highest ambition to have five children and a beautiful house, their only fight to get and keep their husbands. They had no thought for the unfeminine problems of the world outside the home; they wanted the men to make the major decisions. They gloried in their role as women, and wrote proudly on the census blank: "Occupation: housewife." . . .

If a woman had a problem in the 1950's and 1960's, she knew that something must be wrong with her marriage, or with herself. Other women were satisfied with their lives, she thought. What kind of a woman was she if she did not feel this mysterious fulfillment waxing the kitchen floor? She was so ashamed to admit her dissatisfaction that she never knew how many other women shared it. If she tried to tell her husband, he didn't understand what she was talking about. She did not really understand it herself. For over fifteen years women in America found it harder to talk about this problem than about sex. Even the psychoanalysts had no name for it. When a woman did, she would say, "I'm so ashamed," or "I must be hopelessly neurotic." . . .

Gradually I came to realize that the problem that has no name was shared by countless women in America. . . . The groping words I heard from other women, on quiet afternoons when children were at school or on quiet evenings when husbands worked late, I think I understood first as a woman long before I understood their larger social and psychological implications.

Just what was this problem that has no name? What were the words women used when they tried to express it? Sometimes a woman would say "I feel empty somehow . . . incomplete." Or she would say, "I feel as if I don't exist." Sometimes she blotted out the feeling with a tranquilizer. Sometimes she thought the problem was with her husband, or her children, or that what she really needed was to redecorate her house, or move to a better neighborhood, or have an affair, or another baby. Sometimes, she went to a doctor with symptoms she could hardly describe: "A tired feeling . . . I get so angry with the children it scares me. . . . I feel like crying without any reason." (A Cleveland doctor called it "the housewife's syndrome.") . . .

It is no longer possible to ignore that voice, to dismiss the desperation of so many American women. This is not what being a woman means, no matter what the experts say. For human suffering there is a reason; perhaps the reason has not been found because the right questions have not been asked, or pressed far enough. I do not accept the answer that there is no problem because American women have luxuries that women in other times and lands never dreamed of; part of the strange newness of the problem is that it cannot be understood in terms of the age-old material problems of man: poverty, sickness, hunger, cold. . . .

It is no longer possible today to blame the problem on loss of femininity: to say that education and independence and equality with men have made American women unfeminine. I have heard so many women try to deny this dissatisfied voice within themselves because it does not fit the pretty-picture of femininity the experts have given them. I think, in fact, that this is the first clue to the mystery: the problem cannot be understood in the generally accepted terms by which scientists have studied women, doctors have treated them, counselors have advised them, and writers have written them. Women who suffer this problem in whom this voice is tiring, have lived their whole lives in the pursuit of feminine fulfillment. They are not career women (although career women may have other problems); they are women whose greatest ambition has been marriage and children. For the oldest of these women, these daughters of the American middle class, no other dream was possible. The ones in their forties and fifties who once had other dreams gave them up and threw themselves joyously into life as housewives. For the youngest, the new wives and mothers, this was the only dream. They are the ones who quit high school and college to marry, or marked time in some job in which they had no real interest until they married. These women are very "feminine" in the usual sense, and yet they still suffer the problem. . . .

If I am right, the problem that has no name stirring in the midst of so many American women today is not a matter of loss of femininity or too much education, or demands of domesticity. It is far more important than anyone recognizes. It is the key to women and their husbands and children, and puzzling their doctors and educators for years. It may well be the key to our future as a nation and a culture. We can no longer ignore that voice within women that says: "I want something more than my husband and my children and my home."

81

"I HAVE A DREAM" SPEECH (1963)

The Civil Rights movement made sporadic gains in the decade following the *Brown* decision, but not enough to please many African Americans. Civil rights activism took the form of isolated local protests, which ultimately culminated in a massive social movement. The most famous incident was Rosa Parks' refusal to abandon her bus seat to a white rider (violating a city law) and the subsequent Montgomery bus boycott. One of the boycott's leaders was Martin Luther King, Jr., an eloquent Georgian who had recently received his Ph.D. in theology from Boston University and was a Baptist minister in Montgomery. King adapted the nonviolent resistance tactics of India's Mahatma Gandhi to the Civil Rights movement with great success. He helped form and led the clergy-based Southern Christian Leadership Conference (SCLC), and he emerged as the most prominent spokesman for African Americans. Emphasizing nonviolent, direct action on the local level to achieve national goals, King and SCLC launched a civil rights campaign in Birmingham, Alabama, which triggered similar protests in other cities and led to a huge civil rights march on Washington in August 1963. At the conclusion of the march, King delivered an impassioned address that captured the idealism of the Civil Rights movement.

Questions to Consider: What does King ask African Americans to do in the Civil Rights movement? What is King's dream? When will the dream be realized? What progress has been made in the years since this speech? What remains to be done?

Now is the time to make real the promise of democracy. Now is the time to rise from the dark and desolate valley of segregation to the sunlit path of racial justice. Now is the time to lift our nation from the quicksands of racial injustice to the solid rock of brotherhood. Now is the time to make justice a reality for all of God's children.

There will be neither rest nor tranquility in America until the Negro is granted his citizenship rights. The whirlwinds of revolt will continue to shake the foundations of our nation until the bright day of justice emerges.

And that is something that I must say to my people who stand on the threshold which leads to the palace of justice. In the process of gaining our rightful place we must not be guilty of wrongful deeds.

Again and again, we must rise to the majestic heights of meeting physical force with soul force. The marvelous new militancy which has engulfed the Negro community must not lead us to a distrust of all white people, for many of our white brothers as evidenced by their presence here today have come to realize that their destiny is tied up with our destiny.

There are those who are asking the devotees of civil rights, "When will you be satisfied?" We can never be satisfied as long as the Negro is the victim of the unspeakable horrors of police brutality. We can never be satisfied as long as our bodies, heavy with the fatigue of travel, cannot gain lodging in the motels of the highways and the hotels of the cities.

We can never be satisfied as long as our children are stripped of their selfhood and robbed of their dignity by signs stating "for whites only." We cannot be satisfied as long as the Negro in Mississippi cannot vote and the Negro in New York believes he has nothing for which to vote.

No, we are not satisfied and we will not be satisfied until justice rolls down like water and righteousness like a mighty stream.

Now, I am not unmindful that some of you have come here out of great trials and tribulations. Some of you have come fresh from narrow jail cells.

Continue to work with the faith that honor in suffering is redemptive. Go back to Mississippi, go back to Alabama, go back to South Carolina, go back to Georgia, go back to Louisiana, go back to the slums and ghettos of our Northern cities, knowing that somehow this situation can and will be changed. Let us not wallow in the valley of despair.

Now, I say to you today, my friends, so even though we face the difficulties of today and tomorrow. I still have a dream. It is a dream deeply rooted in the American dream. I have a dream that one day this nation will rise up and live out the true meaning of its creed: "We hold these truths to be self-evident, that all men are created equal."

I have a dream that one day on the red hills of Georgia the sons of former slaves and the sons of former slave owners will be able to sit down together at the table of brotherhood.

I have a dream that one day even in the state of Mississippi, a state sweltering with the people's injustice, sweltering with the heat of oppression, will be transformed into an oasis of freedom and justice.

I have a dream that my four little children will one day live in a nation where they will not be judged by the color of their skin, but by the content of their character.

This is our hope. This is that faith that I go back to the South with—this faith we will be able to hew out of the mountain of despair a stone of hope.

- - - -- - -- -- - - -- - - - - -- - -- - - -- - -- - -- - - -- - -- - -- - - -- - -- - -

82

AMERICA'S COMMITMENT TO SOUTHEAST ASIA
(1965)

In the years after World War II, the United States employed the overall policy of containment to events in Southeast Asia—Vietnam especially—and slowly dragged the country into its longest and most costly war. Policymakers allowed North Vietnam's commitment to communism to overshadow Vietnamese nationalistic desires, so that any aggressions were depicted as communistic expansion. The United States initially sent military aid to the French, who tried to maintain their Indochina colony, but when France withdrew from the region and the Geneva Accords created two Vietnams (North and South), America dispatched increasing numbers of "military advisors" to South Vietnam to train troops to fight communists from North Vietnam. America's negligible involvement changed dramatically when two U.S. destroyers were reportedly attacked in the Gulf of Tonkin off the coast of North Vietnam. President Lyndon Johnson sent the excerpted message below to Congress the next day. Congress complied with the president's request and passed the Gulf of Tonkin Resolution with only two dissenting votes. It paved the way for the "escalation" of the war in Vietnam.

·⌐ **Questions to Consider:** What authority does Johnson seek from Congress? How does he justify the request? Why is the Gulf of Tonkin Resolution important? Was South Vietnam's fate in the interest of the United States? Why?

To the Congress of the United States:
Last night I announced to the American people that the North Vietnamese regime had conducted further deliberate attacks against U.S. naval vessels operating in international waters, and that I had therefore directed air action against gun boats and supporting facilities used in these hostile operations. This air action has now been carried out with substantial damage to the boats and facilities. Two U.S. aircraft were lost in the action.

After consultation with the leaders in both parties in the Congress, I further announced a decision to ask the Congress for a Resolution expressing the unity

---

"Special Message to Congress on U.S. Policy in Southeast Asia," *Public Papers of the Presidents of the United States: Lyndon B. Johnson, 1963–64* (Washington, DC, 1965), 2: 930–932.

and determination of the United States in supporting the freedom and in protecting peace in Southeast Asia.

These latest actions of the North Vietnamese regime have given a new and grave turn to the already serious situation in Southeast Asia. Our commitments in that area are well known to the Congress. They were first made in 1954 by President Eisenhower. They were further defined in the Southeast Asia Collective Defense Treaty approved by the Senate in February 1955.

This Treaty with its accompanying protocol obligates the United States and other members to act in accordance with their Constitutional processes to meet Communist aggression against any of the parties or protocol states.

Our policy in Southeast Asia has been consistent and unchanged since 1954. I summarized it on June 2 in four simple propositions:

1. *America keeps her word.* Here as elsewhere, we must keep and shall honor our commitments.
2. *The issue is the future of Southeast Asia as a whole.* A threat to any nation in that region is a threat to all, and a threat to us.
3. *Our purpose is peace.* We have no military, political or territorial ambitions in the area.
4. *This is not just a jungle war, but a struggle for freedom on every front of human activity.* Our military and economic assistance to South Vietnam and Laos in particular has the purpose of helping these countries to repel aggression and strengthen their independence.

The threat to the free nations of Southeast Asia has long been clear. The North Vietnamese regime has constantly sought to take over South Vietnam and Laos. This communist regime has violated the Geneva Accords for Vietnam. It has systematically conducted a campaign of subversion, which includes the direction, training, and supply of personnel and arms for the conduct of guerilla warfare in South Vietnamese territory. In Laos, the North Vietnamese regime has maintained military forces, used in Laotian territory for infiltration into South Vietnam, and most recently carried out combat operations—all in direct violation of the Geneva Agreements of 1962.

In recent months, the actions of the North Vietnamese regime have become steadily more threatening. In May, following new acts of Communist aggression in Laos, the United States undertook reconnaissance flights over Laotian territory, at the request of the Government of Laos. These flights had the essential mission of determining the situation in territory where Communist forces were preventing inspection by the International Control Commission. When the Communists attacked these aircraft, I responded by furnishing escort fighters with instructions to fire when fired upon. Thus, these latest North Vietnamese attacks on our naval vessels are not the first direct attack on armed forces of the United States.

As President of the United States I have concluded that I should now ask the Congress, on its part, to join in affirming the national determination that all such attacks will be met, and that the U.S. will continue in its basic policy of assisting the free nations of the area to defend their freedom.

As I have repeatedly made clear, the United States intends no rashness, and seeks to widen war. We must make it clear to all that the United States is united in its determination to bring about the end of Communist subversion and aggression in the area. We seek the full and effective restoration of the international agreements signed in Geneva in 1954, with respect to South Vietnam, and again in Geneva in 1962, with respect to Laos.

I recommend a Resolution expressing the support of the Congress for all necessary action to protect our armed forces and to assist nations covered by the SEATO Treaty. At the same time, I assure the Congress that we shall continue readily to explore any avenues of political solution that will effectively guarantee the removal of Communist subversion and the preservation of the independence of the nations of the area.

The Resolution could well be based upon similar resolutions enacted by the Congress in the past—to meet the threat to Formosa in 1955, to meet the threat to the Middle East in 1957, and to meet the threat of Cuba in 1962. It could state in the simplest terms the resolve and support of the Congress for action to deal appropriately with attacks against our armed forces and to defend freedom and preserve peace in Southeast Asia in accordance with the obligations to the United States under the Southeast Asia Treaty. I urge the Congress to enact such a Resolution promptly and thus to give convincing evidence to the aggressive Communist nations, and to the world as a whole, that our policy in Southeast Asia will be carried forward—and that the peace and security of the area will be preserved.

The events of this week would in any event have made the passage of a Congressional Resolution essential. But there is an additional reason for doing so at a time when we are entering on three months of political campaigning. Hostile nations must understand that in such a position the United States will continue to protect its national interests, and that in these matters there is no division among us.

Lyndon B. Johnson

83

AMERICAN PRESENCE IN VIETNAM (1964–1970)

The war in Vietnam frustrated American military and political leaders. South Vietnam's terrain and lush tropical forests offered excellent cover for enemy activities, and the Vietcong's guerrilla warfare tactics allowed them to strike without warning, then blend into the local population. The United States pursued a war of attrition, using its colossal military firepower and resources to inflict such heavy losses on the Vietcong that they would abandon their efforts. But the enemy proved to be increasingly elusive and more determined, so the United States

The Wasted Nations: Report of the International Commission of Inquiry into United States Crimes in Indochina, June 20–25, 1971, ed. Frank Browning and Dorothy Forman (New York, 1972), 141–150. (Copyright © 1972 by The International Commission of Inquiry into United States Crimes in Indochina. Reprinted by permission of HarperCollins Publishers, Inc.)

escalated its war effort. By 1968, over 500,000 troops were deployed and tremendous air bombardments of North Vietnam took place. The massive use of military force and the Vietcong's popular roots placed civilians in the forefront of the conflict, often with tragic results. In 1971, an international commission interviewed civilians affected by the war. Its published report, *The Wasted Nations*, revealed an anti-American bias among some Vietnamese and a war where the people were the losers. Excerpted below are two women's accounts of the war.

⤳ **Questions to Consider:** According to the eyewitnesses, what was the American role in Vietnam? What was the impact of the American high technology warfare? How did this affect the war's outcome? Could the war have been fought differently?

Mrs. Sida

[Mrs. Sida is a middle-age Laotian woman who watched American soldiers kill her husband and her children in the summer of 1969.]

On March 26, 1969, toward noon, that day there were nine people at home, one of my children being at school; since we heard the roar of a large number of airplanes, we ran towards a little shelter located about 10 meters from the house. The bombs exploded around our shelter causing some terrible shaking, earthslides were falling from above, and we saw some flashes passing through our shelter like we were in a storm. We thought that if we stayed in the little shelter we would not be safe and that is why we decided to move to a large shelter 20 meters away. The noise of the planes had become quiet, each of us took with himself the smallest children and we ran toward the large shelter: we had nearly reached it when the planes swept back and dropped bombs near us, killing my husband's sister on the spot and wounding the child whom she carried. . . . In running behind my husband I was hit in the right thigh, in the left arm, and I had a fractured tibia, without counting many other places on my body. . . .

Toward the end of the Month of September the U.S. imperialists and the commando pirates of Vang Pao had attacked and ravaged savagely our temporary commune. That is why the people of the commune had decided to evacuate toward a safer place. . . . I walked slowly behind with the old people. My husband, with his mother, walked in front with the children carrying the supplies. At each stop my husband, having set down the children and the supplies, after having told the children to wait for him, came back to help me catch up with them. Halfway there—I walked always behind with the old people and sick people—I heard gunshot, shrieks and cries, and I saw many people fall in front of me. Seeing myself in such a situation I looked for refuge on the riverbank, hiding myself in the bushes and behind a rock, and I saw from my refuge the pirate soldiers of Vang Pao and the Americans who had rounded up the people in one place. I had seen one of the soldiers snatch a small child from the hands of his mother: the mother ran forward to grab the child, but the soldier ran her through with a bayonet. The soldier knocked the child against a tree; myself, I hid all the way through in my refuge behind the brush and the rock. I looked for my husband; I saw only one of my children near my husband. As to my husband's mother and my other three children I could no longer see them near my husband. I saw the soldiers grab my child from the hands of his father, my husband jumped to take the child back, but the soldiers shot my husband and the boy. (Here Mrs. Sida had to stop for a moment, for she was crying too much to continue.) . . .

Dang Kim Phung

[Miss Dang Kim Phung, a South Vietnamese woman from Gia Dinh province . . .]

The American GIs and the puppet troops are very savage. They have massacred the members of my family and tortured me. Two of my uncles were killed. One was shot dead, and one was decapitated. This was done by the U.S. and the puppet troops and his body was thrown into a well. One of my aunts was killed by a shell splinter. One of my little brothers was killed by toxic chemicals, I myself was three times the victim of U.S. atrocities. Once I was wounded by U.S. artillery, and the splinter is still in my leg. . . .

I still remember the day I was poisoned by toxic chemicals. It was the 24th of June, 1968. It was 8 A.M. A reconnaissance plane whirled over and over my region. It fired a rocket. My friends and I immediately took refuge in an underground shelter. Then three low-flying helicopters went over. They dropped barrels of toxic chemicals. One barrel of these chemicals was dropped over the other end of the underground tunnel, and the size of this barrel was about 250 liters. When this toxic chemical . . . hit the end of the shelter, smoke began to enter the shelter, and we were stifling in the tunnel. We tried to get out of the shelter, but then we started coughing and spitting blood. Our skins became quickly covered with blisters. A few days later I felt very tired. Even a week later I lost my appetite and had diarrhea no matter what I ate. Now these evil effects are still being felt by me. My sight is blurred, and I have many digestive difficulties, often diarrhea. . . .

On the 16th of February, 1969. . . . At about 7 A.M. a reconnaissance plane circled over and over my village and fired a rocket. Then three jet planes went over. These three bombers fired exploding bombs in a large area, at high velocity for a long time—steel pellet bombs. When the bombing was almost over I went out of the shelter and I saw that everything was destroyed and the trees were torn down. Then three more jet planes came over and began to bomb. There were incendiary bombs. One of these bombs fell directly into my house. One of these incendiary products stuck to my trousers. And to my face. Then I stripped off my clothes and took refuge. Then I fainted. I knew nothing.

More than a week later I recovered consciousness and found myself in the district hospital. For the first month after that I could see nothing. My eyes were covered with liquids. I could not open my mouth. . . . Five and six months later, still my wounds could not be healed, and we had to patch the wound up with a piece of skin. . . . The days I spent in the hospital were the saddest and most dramatic days of my life because I was a young and sound girl, and it is because of the U.S.

atrocities that I became an invalid and wounded for life.

84

A REPORT ON RACIAL VIOLENCE IN THE CITIES
(1968)

In the mid-1960s, a series of race riots convulsed America. Frustrated with the slow gains of the mainstream, nonviolent Civil Rights movement and the raised hopes of President Lyndon Johnson's Great Society, urban African Americans took matters into their own hands. Beginning with the Watts riot in Los Angeles in August 1965, each of the next three summers witnessed the eruption of widespread violence, property destruction, and looting within the black neighborhoods of cities such as Detroit, Cleveland, Chicago, and Newark, New Jersey. Several hundred people died, thousands were injured, and millions of dollars worth of property was destroyed. President Johnson selected Otto Kerner, governor of Illinois and strong civil rights advocate, as chairman of a federal commission to investigate the "civil disorders." The commission's published findings, often called the *Kerner Report*, offered the following explanation for the race riots of the 1960s.

Questions to Consider: According to the *Kerner Report*, what has helped shape white racial attitudes? Why did the riots break out in the mid-1960s? According to the report, who were the rioters and why did they riot? Could the *Kerner Report* be describing conditions in the 1990s? How do the conclusions of the *Kerner Report* compare to those presented in "What is Behind the Negro Uprisings" (Document 50)?

The record before this Commission reveals that the causes of recent racial disorders are imbedded in a massive tangle of issues and circumstances—social, economic, political, and psychological—which arise out of the historical pattern of Negro-white relations in America. . . .

Despite these complexities, certain fundamental matters are clear. Of these, the most fundamental is the racial attitude and behavior of white Americans toward black Americans. Race prejudice has shaped our history decisively in the past; it now threatens to do so again. White racism is essentially accumulating in our cities since the end of World War II. At the base of this mixture are three of the most bitter fruits of white racial attitudes:

Pervasive discrimination and segregation. The first is surely the continuing exclusion of great numbers of Negroes from the benefits of economic progress through discrimination in employment and education, and their enforced confine-

National Advisory Commission on Civil Disorders, *Report of the National Advisory Commission on Civil Disorders* (New York, 1968), 203–206.

ment in segregated housing and schools. The corrosive and degrading effects of this condition and the attitudes that underlie it are the source of the deepest bitterness and at the center of the problem of racial disorder.

Black migration and white exodus. The second is the massive and growing concentration of impoverished Negroes in our major cities resulting from Negro migration from the rural South, rapid population growth and the continuing movement of the white middle-class to the suburbs. The consequence is a greatly increased burden on the already depleted resources of cities, creating a growing crisis of deteriorating facilities and services and unmet human needs.

Black ghettos. Third, in the teeming racial ghettos, segregation and poverty have intersected to destroy opportunity and hope and to enforce failure. The ghettos too often mean men and women without jobs, families without men, and schools where children are processed instead of educated, until they return to the street—to crime, to narcotics, to dependency on welfare, and to bitterness and resentment against society in general and white society in particular.

These three forces have converged on the inner city in recent years and on the people who inhabit it. At the same time, most whites and many Negroes outside the ghetto have prospered to a degree unparalleled in the history of civilization. Through television—the universal appliance in the ghetto—and the other media of mass communications, this affluence has been endlessly flaunted before the eyes of the negro poor and the jobless ghetto youth.

As Americans, most Negro citizens carry within themselves two basic aspirations of our society. They seek to share in both the material resources of our system and its intangible benefits—dignity, respect, and acceptance. . . .

Yet these facts alone—fundamental as they are—cannot be said to have caused the disorders. Other and more immediate factors help explain why these events happened now.

Recently, three powerful ingredients have begun to catalyze the mixture.

Frustrated hopes. The expectations aroused by the great judicial and legislative victories of the civil rights movement have led to frustration, hostility and cynicism in the face of the persistent gap between promise and fulfillment. The dramatic struggle for equal rights in the South has sensitized Northern Negroes to the economic inequalities reflected in the deprivations of ghetto life.

Legitimation of violence. A climate that tends toward the approval and encouragement of violence as a form of protest has been created by white terrorism directed against nonviolent protest, including instances of abuse and even murder of some civil rights workers in the South; but the open defiance of law and federal authority by state and local officials resisting desegregation; and by some protest groups engaging in civil disobedience who turn their backs on nonviolence, go beyond the Constitutionally protected rights of petition and free assembly, and resort to violence to attempt to compel alteration of laws and policies with which they disagree. . . .

Powerlessness. Finally, many negroes have come to believe that they are being exploited politically and economically by the white "power structure." Negroes, like people in poverty everywhere, in fact lack the channels of communication, influence and appeal that traditionally have been available to ethnic minorities within the city and which enabled them—unburdened by color—to scale the walls of the white ghettos in an earlier era. The frustrations of powerlessness have led some to the conviction that there is no effective alternative to violence as a means of expression and redress, as a way of "moving the system." More generally, the result is alienation and the white society which controls them. This is reflected in the reach toward racial consciousness and solidarity reflected in the slogan "Black Power."

These facts have combined to inspire a new mood among Negroes, particularly among the young. Self-esteem and enhanced racial pride are replacing apathy and submission to "the system." Moreover, Negro youth, who make up over half of the ghetto population, share the growing sense of alienation felt by many white youth in our country. Thus, their role in recent civil disorders reflects not only a shared sense of deprivation and victimization by white society but also the rising youth throughout the society.

Incitement and encouragement of violence. These conditions have created a volatile mixture of attitudes and beliefs which needs only a spark to ignite mass violence. Strident appeals to violence, first heard from white racists, were echoed and reinforced last summer in the inflammatory rhetoric of black racists and militants. Throughout the year, extremists crisscrossed the country preaching a doctrine of black power and violence. Their rhetoric was widely reported in the mass media; it was echoed by local "militants" and organizations; it became the ugly background noise of the violent summer. . . .

The Police. It is the convergence of all these factors that makes the role of the police so difficult and so significant. Almost invariably the incident that ignites disorder arises from police action. Harlem, Watts, Newark and Detroit—all the major outbursts of recent years—were precipitated by routine arrests of Negroes for minor offenses by white police.

But the police are not merely the spark. In discharge of their obligation to maintain order and insure public safety in the disruptive conditions of ghetto life, they are inevitably involved in sharper and more frequent conflicts with ghetto residents than with the residents of other areas. Thus, to many Negroes police have come to symbolize white power, white racism and white repression. And the fact is that many police do reflect and express these white attitudes. The atmosphere of hostility and cynicism is reinforced by a widespread perception among Negroes of the existence of police brutality and corruption, and of a "double standard" of justice and protection—one for Negroes and one for whites.

85

STUDENT UNREST ON COLLEGE CAMPUSES (1969)

During the 1960s, record numbers of young Americans attended colleges and

Glenn S. Dumke, "Controversy on the Campus: Need for Peace and Order," *Vital Speeches of the Day* 35 (1969): 332–335.

universities. Some found higher education to be insensitive, mystically bureaucratic, and hierarchical, much like the corporate and political world around them. For a growing number of students, a sense of alienation and resistance developed, which led to the creation of action groups, such as the Students for Democratic Society (SDS), which advocated "participatory democracy," and the Free Speech Movement (FSM), which defended student rights and criticized the modern university. Emulating the peaceful demonstrations of the Civil Rights movement, initial student protests centered on campus life but quickly spread to other larger issues, particularly the growing American commitment to the war in Vietnam. As the protest movement against the war gathered momentum (there were over 200 major campus demonstrations in 1968), some students became more militant and some demonstrations became violent. In response to these events, Glenn Dumke, chancellor of the California State Colleges who held a Ph.D. in history, offered the following observations on the protests in a speech delivered before the Town Hall of California in Los Angeles. His address is excerpted below.

_____

Questions to Consider: According to Dumke, why are the students protesting on college campuses? Are there ways to address their concerns? How does he categorize most of the students? Is that accurate? Whom does Dumke blame for the problems facing higher education? Could Dumke's comments on higher education be applied to the 1990s?

_____

First of all, I think we must place our students in perspective. What kind of people are students, anyway? They are certainly not all bearded, sandled, and bereft of decency. What kind of a population are we dealing with in our student bodies? . . .

We are educating most of the people of California who are destined to run things—businesses, engineering projects, schools, the economy in general. We leave to others most of the training of research scholars, medical doctors, and the professions which require advanced graduate work. Most of our students are working very hard and are serious minded. Many are older, some are married, many earn their living.

All of us know the expression that no one under 30 could possibly trust anyone over 30, but if those of us in the plus-30 group are to understand the youth of today we must remember that they have had to face the pressing issue of their personal relationship to a war which has divided both political leaders and large segments of our society. They have also been affected by a violent current history where three of their hero figures (the two Kennedys and Martin Luther King) were brutally assassinated. They have also been affected by a growing unwillingness to accept the traditions and values of modern society. In spite of the violent, nihilistic and at times masochistic behavior of a few, for the most part young people of this time and place are perhaps the most moralistic, socially conscious generation in modern history.

They have demonstrated against the war in Vietnam, sometimes in violation of regulations and laws, but they have also contributed their services in large numbers to the Peace Corps and VISTA. They have demanded great "relevance" in their collegiate curriculum, and a greater "piece of the action" in determining the "uses of their university." While it is true that disruptive tactics have been used by a relatively small group of activists or radicals, the issues, if not the tactics, have been supported by large masses of young people. . . .

We are now reaping the harvest of the one unique contribution made to academic institutions by the United States—*mass higher education*. No other society in history has ever had to deal with *mass* educated youth. The problem is that we have been more concerned with the numbers we enrolled than with what we taught them after they signed up. We have, for instance, engaged in self-criticism to the point of nonsense. It has become unfashionable to be patriotic to point out what is good as well as what is bad. We brought everybody to the classroom and then failed to impress upon them that the society which made their education possible was worthy of some study and respect for its plusses as well as its minuses.

As a result, what today's younger generation is telling us is that they don't like the world as it is and they are out to change it. In large numbers they reject what they characterize as the profit-motivated, competitive, bureaucratic existence of modern man. Their existential philosophy rejects all outside authority and they identify only with the common man or universal humanity. . . .

Many people do not understand why there is so much violence connected with current student activism. I believe there are several explanations. First, some of it is simply a result of anger, frustration or revenge. Student movements however, often have another sort of violence connected with them. Leaders of revolutionary factions actually seek physical confrontations with the police. It is no accident that heads are bashed or arms twisted. I am quite surprised that one or more students haven't been seriously injured or even killed in this process of provocation and reaction. It is through this process that uncommitted students are involved in the causes of their generational class and antagonisms built not only against authority, but against an entire generation which is older and is characterized as bureaucratic, insensitive, materialistic, and anti-intellectual.

The question is asked more and more often lately—why don't educators, and particularly administrators, do more to control this disruption? Why are colleges so reluctant to crack down? Why are they so slow in responding to violence? . . .

What this means is that although academe has been relatively slow to respond to its problems of violence because of the very nature of its being, it is now learning, and some of us I think are learning quite rapidly, how to be effective in this type of combat. At any rate we're working hard at it. And while we are cooperating with the police and jailing the militants and expelling the radicals and suspending or firing troublemaking faculty members, we must do so with the full knowledge that 95 per cent of our students are not radical or violent—they are only concerned young people, as worried about the situation as we are, because their futures are being directly affected by it. . . .

I am the last to be a pollyanna about this problem. I think we have sincere revolutionaries in our midst who are poking at the higher educational structure as the soft underbelly of the culture and as a proper place to start the action. But just as higher education was not altogether responsible for the broken homes, the divided church, the decay of morality and ethics, and the dry rot caused by the affluent society which lie at the root of student discontent, so it is equally unfair to expect higher education to solve the whole problem. We will have total peace on the campus when we have total peace on the streets of our cities, and we haven't quite achieved that yet.

There is much higher education can do. It can update its old-fashioned systems of academic government so as to respond more effectively to modern challenges and problems. . . . But, when all is said and done, education hasn't got the whole answer within its zone of command. We're talking about symptoms of decay in a mature society that must confront these as well as education, if the basic problem is to be finally solved.

Higher education can help, but first we must have peace and order on our campuses.

THE NATIONAL MALAISE

2

Many of the leading issues from the previous decade continued to divide the United States during the 1970s. In addition to the lingering turmoil from the 1960s, political corruption, a decline in the standard of living, and the failure of technology combined to erode the faith that many Americans had shared previously. Efforts to heal many of the divisions failed; indeed, new social issues emerged, which soon proved as divisive as the old. By the decade's end, a number of Americans had lowered their expectations for the future. The ensuing selections reveal the issues that characterized this decade of malaise.

86

ROE V. WADE (1972)

Perhaps the most controversial issue in modern America is abortion. The social role and legal status of abortion has varied throughout American history. In the first half of the 19th century, abortions were almost commonplace (abortionists advertised in newspapers) and there was frank discussion between women and their physicians about the procedure. In the late 19th century, state legislatures, pressured by the American Medical Association which sought to upgrade and regulate medical practices, began to outlaw abortion unless a doctor deemed the procedure necessary. Despite the new laws, the practice of abortion continued "underground." As part of the women's movement of the 1960s and the medical community's change of opinion on abortion, some states relaxed or repealed their antiabortion laws. In 1972, the Supreme Court issued its decision in *Roe v. Wade,* a case involving Norma McCorvey ("Roe") who was denied an abortion under Texas law and sued the state. Justice Harry Blackmun wrote for the majority in the 7–2 opinion. Excerpted below is the majority opinion in *Roe v. Wade.*

Questions to Consider: According to the Court's decision, why did states still retain laws prohibiting abortion? And why did the Court believe those reasons were no longer valid? Upon what constitutional grounds does the Court rest its decision? Why? Under what circumstances does the Court approve of abortion?

We forthwith acknowledge our awareness of the sensitive and emotional nature of the abortion controversy, of the vigorous opposing views, even among physicians, and of the deep and seemingly absolute convictions that the subject inspires. One's philosophy, one's experiences, one's exposure to the raw edges of human existence, one's religious training, one's attitudes toward life and family and their values, and the moral standards one establishes and seeks to observe, are all likely to influence and to color one's thinking and conclusions about abortion.

In addition, population growth, pollution, poverty, and racial overtones tend to complicate and not to simplify the problem.

Our task, of course, is to resolve the issue by constitutional measurement, free of emotion and of predilection. We seek earnestly to do this, and, because we do, we have inquired into, and in this opinion place some emphasis upon, medical and medical-legal history and what that history reveals about man's attitudes toward the abortion procedure over the centuries. . . .

Three reasons have been advanced to explain historically the enactment of criminal abortion laws in the 19th century and to justify their continued existence.

It has been argued occasionally that these laws were the product of a Victorian social concern to discourage illicit sexual conduct. Texas, however, does not

---

Roe v. Wade, 410 *U.S. Reports* 113 (1972).

advance this justification in the present case, and it appears that no court or commentator has taken the argument seriously. . . .

A second reason is concerned with abortion as a medical procedure. When most criminal abortion laws were enacted, the procedure was a hazardous one for the woman. . . . Thus, it has been argued that a State's real concern in enacting a criminal abortion law was to protect the pregnant woman, that is, to restrain her from submitting to a procedure that placed her life in serious jeopardy.

Modern medical techniques have altered this situation. Appellants and various amici refer to the medical data indicating that abortion in early pregnancy, this is, prior to the end of the first trimester, although not without its risk, is now relatively safe. Mortality rates for women undergoing early abortions, where the procedure is legal, appear to be as low as or lower than the rates for normal childbirth. Consequently, any interest of the State in protecting the woman from an inherently hazardous procedure, except when it would be equally dangerous for her to forgo it, has largely disappeared. Of course, important state interests in the area of health and medical standards do remain. . . .

The third reason is the State's interest—some phrase it in terms of duty—in protecting prenatal life. Some of the argument for this justification rests on the theory that a new human life is present from the moment of conception. The State's interest and general obligation to protect life then extends, it is argued, to prenatal life. Only when the life of the pregnant mother herself is at stake, balanced against the life she carries within her, should the interest in this area need not stand or fall on acceptance of the belief that life begins at conception or at some other point prior to live birth. . . .

The right of privacy, whether it be founded in the Fourteenth Amendment's concept of personal liberty and restrictions upon state action, as we feel it is, or, as the District Court determined, in the Ninth Amendment's reservation of the rights of people, is broad enough to encompass a woman's decision whether or not to terminate her pregnancy. The detriment that the State would impose upon the pregnant woman by denying this choice altogether is apparent. Specific and direct harm medically diagnosable even in early pregnancy may be involved. Maternity, or additional offspring, may force upon a woman a distressful life and future. Psychological harm may be imminent. Mental and physical health may be taxed by child care. There is also the distress, for all concerned, associated with the unwanted child, and there is the problem of bringing a child into a family already unable, psychologically and otherwise, to care for it. In other cases, as in this one, the additional difficulties and continuing stigma of unwed motherhood may be involved. All these are factors the woman and her responsible physician necessarily will consider consultation.

On the basis of elements such as these, appellant and some amici argue that the woman's right is absolute and that she is entitled to terminate her pregnancy at whatever time, in whatever way, and for whatever reason she alone chooses. With this we do not agree. . . .

We, therefore, conclude that the right of personal privacy includes the abortion decision, but that this right is not unqualified and must be considered against important state interests in regulation. . . .

Texas urges that, apart from the Fourteenth Amendment, life begins at conception and is present throughout pregnancy, and that, therefore, the State has a compelling interest in protecting that life from and after conception. We need not resolve the difficult question of when life begins. When those trained in the respective disciplines of medicine, philosophy, and theology are unable to arrive at any consensus, the judiciary, at this point in the development of man's knowledge, is not in a position to speculate as to the answer. . . .

With respect to the State's important and legitimate interest in the health of the mother, the "compelling" point, in the light of present medical knowledge, is at approximately the end of the first trimester. This is so because of the now-established medical fact that until the end of the first trimester mortality in abortion may be less than mortality in normal childbirth. It follows that, from and after this point, a State may regulate the abortion procedure to the extent that the regulation reasonably relates to the preservation and protection of maternal health. . . .

To summarize and to repeat:

1. A state criminal abortion statute of the current Texas type, that excepts from criminality only a *life-saving* procedure on behalf of the mother, without regard to pregnancy stage and without recognition of the other interests involved, is violative of the Due Process Clause of the Fourteenth Amendment.

a. For the stage prior to approximately the end of the first trimester, the abortion decision and its effectuation must be left to the medical judgment of the pregnant woman's attending physician.

b. For the stage subsequent to approximately the end of the first trimester, the State, in promoting its interest in the health of the mother, may, if it chooses, regulate the abortion procedure in ways that are reasonably related to maternal health.

c. For the stage subsequent to viability, the State in promoting its interest in the potentiality of human life may, if it chooses, regulate, and even proscribe, abortion except where it is necessary, in appropriate medical judgment, for the preservation of the life or health of the mother. . . .

87

SOARING ENERGY COSTS (1974)

Since World War II, the American standard of living rose continuously in part because of inexpensive oil. The United States had become increasingly dependent on petroleum to fuel the economy. Americans, long accustomed to plentiful abundance in most material goods, naively believed that natural resources, especially petroleum, were boundless. As domestic oil production declined in the 1960s, demand skyrocketed. The United States began importing increasingly larger and larger amounts of foreign oil, especially from the Middle East. In October 1973, this dependency was made shockingly apparent to the American public when several Arab nations imposed an oil embargo on countries that supported Israel in the "Yom Kippur War" against Egypt. After several months, the embargo was lifted, but the Organization of Petroleum Exporting Nations (OPEC) increased the price of crude oil. Excerpted below is an article from *Newsweek*, a popular news magazine, which examined the oil price increase and its impact on America.

·⌐ **Questions to Consider:** How much were prices affected initially? What was America's response to rising oil prices? What were the long-term implications of OPEC's action? How has America altered its "energy-hoggish ways"? With what success?

In two stunning strokes last week, the Mideast masters of the world's most productive oil fields dramatically altered the international energy equation for years to come—and in so doing, forced Americans one step closer to a profound change in the way they live. In the short run, the Arab coup will mean higher prices for gasoline, fuel oil and petroleum-based products ranging from plastic toys to polyester-fiber suits. But in the long term, it presages an end to what economist Walter Heller characterizes as America's "energy-hoggish ways"—a life-style exemplified by thriving gasoline stations on nearly every corner and noxious expressways crammed curb to curb with overpowered but underpopulated automobiles.

In the first of their moves, the Muslim rulers of Iran, Iraq, Kuwait, Saudi Arabia, Qatar and Abu Dhabi quite simply ended the long era of cheap energy. They raised the posted price of Persian Gulf crude oil to $11.65 a barrel—a whopping 131 per cent increase. . . .

. . . Gasoline at the pump could jump as much as 9 cents a gallon in some areas of the country, pushing prices well above 50 cents a gallon. And should the Administration's newly announced contingency plan for gas rationing actually go into effect, the price of some gas could go up another 25 cents to 75 cents per gallon. The price of heating oil could well climb by 7 cents above the average of 30 cents per gallon. Just what effect the oil-price increase will have on the price of the thousands of other consumer goods that use oil as either a raw material or as an energy source in their manufacture is difficult to measure. But there is no doubt that nearly everything will be much more expensive. . . .

In Washington, energy czar William E. Simon underscored the potential seriousness of the petroleum situation by unveiling the Administration's stand-by rationing scheme. If and when it goes into effect, the program might limit licensed drivers over 18 to between 32 and 35 gallons of gasoline per month, require a bureaucracy of 17,000 to administer and enforce, and cost at least $1.5 billion. . . .

But Simon also cautioned that the nation was "far from being out of the woods"—and he stressed the need for consumers to continue curbing their appetites for energy to trim the gap between supply and demand. . . . Beyond gestures, Simon declared that he may later recommend such fuel-saving measures as closing gas stations another day in addition to Sunday or perhaps even proposing a partial ban on driving one day a week. "If the American public continues to cooperate," Simon emphasized, "we can avoid more stringent measures."

The Administration is depending on more than mere public cooperation with voluntary conservation measures. This weekend, for instance, year-round day-light-saving time takes effect, an action energy experts estimate could conserve the equivalent of 95,000 barrels of oil daily. And for all its apparent inequities and loopholes, the government's allocation program—now scheduled to be operative on Jan. 15—appears tough in many ways. Not only will it cut airline fuel supplies, but fuel-oil dealers will be allocated oil only on the basis of reduced indoor temperatures in homes and business establishments. Crude-oil allocations for refineries will be strictly controlled. As far as gasoline is concerned, 5 per cent of 1972 production will be diverted to the production of home-heating oil—in effect, Simon says, "a moderate form of [gas] rationing." . . .

But the most devastating problem facing American consumers, at least during the first half of the year, is inflation. Invariably, the higher cost of imported oil will ripple through the entire U.S. economy, sending prices soaring. While Administration economists are understandably reluctant to predict how much, the rate seems likely to top the pace for the last six months of 9.7 per cent. . . .

. . . The higher prices they now charge for their oil will unquestionably speed the development of economically viable substitute fuels, probably somewhat sooner than would otherwise have been possible. Perhaps most important of all, the decibel level seems finally to have lowered when the Arab oil question is discussed and debated, suggesting that the Arab leaders have come to recognize their own enormous stake in fostering stable relations with the industrialized West.

"We don't want to hurt the industrialized world," the Shah of Iran promised last week, following his announcement of the higher oil prices. "We will be one of them soon. What good will it do if the present industrialized world is crushed and terminated? What will replace it?"

88

RICHARD NIXON'S RESIGNATION SPEECH (1974)

In 1972, Republican President Richard Nixon sought reelection against Democrat George McGovern. Nixon won the Presidency by the second largest margin ever (520–17 electoral count and 60.8 percent of the popular vote), but a curious incident took place during the campaign: several "burglars" were arrested breaking into the Democratic National Committee's headquarters in the Watergate apartment complex in Washington. The burglars, it turned out, were employees of Nixon's reelection committee who planned to sabotage the Democratic Party's campaign. Although no evidence indicates Nixon knew of

Richard Nixon, "Presidential Resignation: Let He Who Is Without Sin Cast the First Stone," *Vital Speeches of the Day* 40 (15 August 1974): 643–644.

plans to break into Watergate, he used presidential power to cover up the incident and thwart investigators, actions which he steadfastly denied. The heart of the Watergate investigation became secret audiotapes Nixon kept of White House meetings, which he denied having and then refused to produce. Under a Supreme Court ruling, Nixon released the tapes, which revealed that as president he had violated the law and participated in the cover-up. Faced with demands for impeachment, Nixon became the first president to resign his position. Excerpted below is Nixon's resignation speech.

—

Questions to Consider: What appears to be Nixon's attitude toward Watergate? Why does he resign? Why does he explain the highlights of his presidency? What were the significances of Watergate and its long-term impact?

—

Good evening. This is the 37th time I have spoken to you from this office in which so many decisions have been made that shape the history of this nation.

Each time I have done so to discuss with you some matters that I believe affected the national interest. And all the decisions I have made in my public life I have always tried to do what was best for the nation.

Throughout the long and difficult period of Watergate, I have felt it was my duty to persevere; to make every possible effort to complete the term of office to which you elected me.

In the past few days, however, it has become evident to me that I no longer have a strong enough political base in the Congress to justify continuing the effort. . . .

But the interests of the nation must always come before any personal considerations. From the discussions I have had with Congressional and other leaders I have concluded that because of the Watergate matter I might not have the support of the Congress that I would consider necessary to back the very difficult decisions and carry out the duties of this office in the way the interests of the nation will require.

I have never been a quitter.

To leave office before my term is completed is opposed to every instinct in my body. But as President I must put the interests of America first.

America needs a full-time President and a full-time Congress, particularly at this time with problems we face at home and abroad.

To continue to fight through the months ahead for my personal vindication would almost totally absorb the time and attention of both the President and the Congress in a period when our entire focus should be on the great issues of peace abroad and prosperity without inflation at home.

Therefore, I shall resign the Presidency effective at noon tomorrow.

Vice President Ford will be sworn in as President at that hour in this office. . . .

As he assumes that responsibility he will deserve the help and the support of all of us. As we look to the future, the first essential is to begin healing the wounds of this nation. To put the bitterness and divisions of the recent past behind us and to rediscover those shared ideas that lie at the heart of our strength and unity as a great and as a free people.

By taking this action, I hope that I will have hastened the start of that process of healing which is so desperately needed in America.

I regret deeply any injuries that may have been done in the course of the events that led to this decision. I would say only that if some of my judgments were wrong—and some were wrong—they were made in what I believed at the time to be the best interests of the nation.

To those who have stood with me during these past difficult months, to my family, my friends, the many others who've joined in supporting my cause because they believed it was right, I will be eternally grateful for your support.

And to those who have not felt able to give me your support, let me say I leave with no bitterness toward those who have opposed me, because all of us in the final analysis have been concerned with the good of the country however our judgments might differ.

So let us all now join together in affirming that common commitment and in helping our new President succeed for the benefit of all Americans. . . .

We have ended America's longest war. But in the work of securing a lasting peace in the world, the goals ahead are even more far-reaching and more difficult. We must complete a structure of peace, so that it will be said of this generation—our generation of Americans—by the people of all nations, not only that we ended one war but that we prevented future wars.

We have unlocked the doors that for a quarter of a century stood between the United States and the People's Republic of China. We must now insure that the one-quarter of the world's people who live in the People's Republic of China will be and remain, not our enemies, but our friends.

In the Middle East, 100 million people in the Arab countries, many of whom have considered us their enemies for nearly 20 years, now look on us as their friends. We must continue to build on that friendship so that peace can settle at last over the Middle East and so that the cradle of civilization will not become its grave.

Together with the Soviet Union we have made the crucial breakthroughs that have begun the process of limiting nuclear arms. But, we must set our goal, not just limiting, but reducing and finally destroying these terrible weapons so that they cannot destroy civilization.

And so that the threat of nuclear war will no longer hang over the world and the people, we have opened a new relation with the Soviet Union. We must continue to develop and expand that new relationship so that the two strongest nations of the world will live together in cooperation rather than confrontation. . . .

When I first took the oath of President five and a half years ago, I made this sacred commitment; to consecrate my office, my energies and all the wisdom I can summon to the cause of peace among nations.

As a result of these efforts, I am confident that the world is a safer place today, not only for the people of America but for the people of all nations, and that all of our children have a better chance than before of living in peace rather than dying in war.

This, more than anything, is what I hoped to achieve when I sought the Presidency. This, more than anything, is what I hope will be my legacy to you, to our country, as I leave the Presidency.

To have served in this office is to have felt a very personal sense of kinship with each and every American. In leaving it, I do so with this prayer: May God's grace be with you in all the days ahead.

89

A MIGRATION TO THE "SUNBELT" (1976)

Americans have always been a mobile people, moving to seek a better life elsewhere in the country. The steady westward migration, the gold and silver rushes of the 19th century, and the Great Migration of African Americans are but a few examples of this mobile society. Starting in the early 1970s, another significant demographic shift took place. Large numbers of people abandoned the industrial cities of the North and East and moved to the South and the Southwest, the so-called "Sunbelt." Their migration, like the earlier movements, brought notable changes to those areas they left and to those areas they inhabited. The excerpted article in *Time,* a popular news magazine, sought to explain this migration and its impact.

Questions to Consider: According to this article, why were people migrating to the "Sunbelt"? How has this migration changed the region? How has it changed the North and East? What are the long-term impacts of this migration? Does this migration still persist?

All of these people are examples of a special breed that is rapidly increasing across the U.S.: the new American migrants. They are pulling themselves up by their roots in order to pursue the good life in places that are smaller, sunnier, safer, and perhaps saner than those they left. Their desire to move onward has spawned an exodus that is causing major changes in American society. Because of the migration, many once great cities are falling into ever more serious decline; scores of little-known communities are either booming or feeling the pains of all-too-sudden growth (or both); and millions of Americans have profoundly altered their way of life.

Americans have always been a restlessly mobile people, but their new migratory habits are quite different from those of the past. There are three interrelated patterns of movement:

Out of the Big Cities. Where once Americans thronged to the big cities and their immediate suburbs in search of jobs, education and excitement, they are now

"Americans on the Move," *Time* 107 (15 March 1976): 55–64. (Copyright 1976 by Time, Inc. Reprinted by permission.)

moving to smaller cities and towns. Between 1970 and 1974, over 1.7 million more Americans left the big metropolitan areas than moved to them. Through migration, the New York Area alone lost half a million people more than it gained; similarly, Chicago lost a quarter of a million. Of the 16 metropolitan areas that have more than 2 million people each, eight have lost population since 1970. . . .

To the Countryside. After declining for most of this century, the nation's rural areas since 1970 have been growing faster that its urban areas. The Census Bureau defines metropolitan areas as those counties that have cities of 50,000 people or more; counties with no communities of that size are predominantly rural. . . .

To the South and Southwest. Americans are rapidly leaving the Northern and Eastern regions, the old industrial quadrant from St. Louis and Chicago to Philadelphia and Boston, and increasingly heading toward the South and West. Between 1970 and last year, 2,537,000 people migrated from the Northeastern and North Central states to the Southern and Western states. . . . By far the nation's fastest-developing new boom region is the Sunbelt—the lower arc of warmlands stretching from Southern California to the Carolinas.

These new migrations suggest a major change in Americans' expectations— what they want from their careers and communities and what they are willing to give up to get it. Says Pollster Louis Harris: "Most Americans don't want more quantity of anything, but more quality in what they've got."

In such impulses is a certain chastened spirit, a feeling—no doubt a residue of the manic '60s—that smaller and quieter home pleasures are more important than acquisitiveness and ambition. This is not necessarily an edifying spiritual development in America so much as a self-interested calculation that a 90-minute commute or a triple-bolted apartment door is not worth the trouble if one can escape. The ethic suggests that bigness is no longer better, that mere dollars do not mean a more satisfying life, that success is more a matter of enjoying where one is than moving ahead. Those sentiments, of course, can carry a troubling complacency. The frankly escapist note is one theme of some of the new migrations—a kind of premature retirement, a dropping-out. That is a sweet and organically grown estimate of life, but in some cases it smacks of elitism gone to the country of the cure. Many are migrating, however, for somewhat opposite reasons. They find that in the smaller cities and towns there is more scope for their ambition, more room for competition and expansion.

"In a way it is certainly a middle-class migration," says Queens College Political Scientist Andrew Hacker. "Those who are moving out are looking for a kind of middle-class subcountry, a place where it is safer, and where there is more predictable service, and where the school system is less problematic." . . .

Employees who made the move are usually happy with their new lives. Others who relocate on their own often have to take pay cuts, but in most cases they find that the dollar goes further. People in the South and West spend comparatively less for taxes, housing, fuel, clothing and most services. The Bureau of Labor Statistics estimates that the cost of maintaining a high standard of living for a family of four in New York City is 33% higher than in Houston or Nashville. Air conditioning has made the long, hot summers bearable. And for some people the way of life—a moderate climate, plenty of outdoor activity, the residual Southern graces—is an attractive alternative to the iron chill of the North. . . .

In many ways, the migrants from the North and the East are helping to alter the character of the South, which is becoming more sophisticated and more homogenized. On the whole, Yankees who move there find themselves welcomed, mostly because they bring new money, skills and opportunity with them. At the same time, the South is changing the carpetbaggers in a number of respects. Sometimes there is no Southerner more given to Southern style and sense of place than the Confederate from, say, Chicago—the Yankee Good Ole boy.

Whatever economic advantages they bring, however, the newcomers sometimes threaten to perpetuate in new territory many of the offenses of urban sprawl around the big cities. Especially in many communities of the Sunbelt, oldtimers have grown bitterly aware that the massive invasions have overloaded public services, overwhelmed police and fire departments, water supplies and sewage systems. . . .

Another and in some ways more urgent problem is what the new migrations are doing to the big industrial cities, especially those of the Northeast quadrant. They are hemorrhaging. Economist Thomas Muller of the Urban Institute in Washington lists nine "municipal danger signals." Among them: substantial long-term outmigration, loss of private employment, high debt service, high unemployment, high tax burden, increasing proportion of low-income population. . . .

It is possible to be too apocalyptic about the big cities' prospects. They still have tremendous force, and the bulk of the nation's industry and financial power. But the migratory trend is disturbing to people who have a stake in the big old cities. The automobile has in many ways rendered them obsolete. Along the highways circling them have arisen "ring cities," shopping centers, medical complexes and the rest, which provides the services that long gave the central city its *raison d'etre*. . . .

The U.S. is more than ever a nation of immigrants, and the new internal migration is a pursuit, as much psychological as geographical, of the remaining pockets of Frederick Jackson Turner's frontier. The migration is also the last march of a kind of expansionist privilege: the old American idea that all mistakes are canceled by the horizon, by more room, by moving out. Great population movements are hardly unique in a nation that was built by its restless energy. Never before, however, have so many Americans been able to change their lives quite so quickly, and to base their decisions about where to live on the amenities they desire.

90

THE QUESTION OF REVERSE DISCRIMINATION
(1978)

During the early 1970s, efforts were made to bring about a more integrated society. The Supreme Court ordered an end to segregation in public schools and ordered that students be bused out of their neighborhoods to achieve integration.

Protests, especially from Northern white families, led ultimately to a reversal on the "busing" issue. Also implemented in this period were affirmative action programs, which were designed to achieve racial equality in both the public and private sectors. Often quotas—hiring a specific number of minorities—were adopted to fulfill the mandates. In 1973 and 1974, Allan Bakke, a white in his late 20s, applied for admission to the Medical School of the University of California at Davis, but was denied both times even though his admission rating was higher than minorities who were accepted. Bakke claimed that the medical school's "special admissions program" for 16 minority students each year (out of an incoming class of 100) was illegal and he sued for admission. The Supreme Court reached a decision in *Regents of the University of California v. Bakke* in 1978. Excerpted below is the conservative *Chicago Tribune's* editorial on the verdict and its significance.

Questions to Consider: Why was the Supreme Court so divided on this issue? Did the decision affect affirmative action programs? Are quotas a valid way to enforce affirmative action? Does this case represent a backlash against gains made from the Civil Rights movement?

The Supreme Court's long awaited, delicately balanced ruling in the Bakke "reverse discrimination" case can be welcomed by the whole spectrum of public opinion except for the extremities. The ruling's impact on existing affirmative action programs is minimal. Though many university admissions offices show some discretionary favor to "disadvantaged" individuals, few use the explicit racial quotas that the medical school of the University of California at Davis has used. This Supreme Court decision, sharply focused on university admissions, means little for other "affirmative action" contexts.

Of course the ruling is disappointing both to those who hoped the court would legitimize racial quotas and to those who hoped the court would outlay any consideration of race in allocation scarce opportunities. But everyone else can welcome it.

The court was anything but united. The decision itself was 5 to 4, with six opinions written. In a sense, Justice Powell determined the court's position. He agreed with four colleagues that Mr. Bakke should be admitted and that explicit racial quotas are invalid, and with his other four colleagues that race may properly be a factor in university admissions. The first four held that the Civil Rights Act of 1964 precluded race as a legal factor in admissions. The other four found no constitutional or statutory obstacle to explicit racial quotas. Because of Justice Powell, neither bloc of four altogether prevailed or was altogether outvoted.

Justice Thurgood Marshall, the only black on the court, wrote a separate opinion eloquently reciting the history of blacks' victimization by invidious racism. His reproaches of the Supreme Court's behavior in the decades following the Civil War are well justified. But his contention that court-countenanced discrimination then justifies court-countenanced reverse discrimination now is unconvincing. Two wrongs do not make a right. The objective of the courts and of society, when most faithful to our national aspirations, is justice. It is individuals who experience justice and injustice. Explicit racial quotas for admission to a medical school with no record of discriminating against a race are rightly held unfair to individual applicants [and all applicants are individuals] who had nothing to do with past discrimination against blacks.

But the bloc of four for which Justice Paul Stevens spoke is also unconvincing in its claim that Title VI of the Civil Rights Act of 1961 provides a sufficient basis for upholding Mr. Bakke and the California Supreme Court, and that no constitutional interpretation is necessary. The implication here is that, by definition, affirmative action is illegal. This would be intolerable. Congress has found no inconsistency in both enacting the Civil Rights Act and supporting affirmative action programs. For the court to have found some pervasive flaw in affirmative action programs, as many feared it might, would have a disastrous impact on current practice.

In a rather mysterious way, which resulted in the lonely position of a single justice becoming the decision of the court, the Supreme Court has rendered a balanced, judicious decision. As Atty. Gen. Griffin P. Bell, speaking for both himself and President Carter, said, the result is "a great gain for affirmative action"—as reasonably defined. It is a great gain, too, for academic freedom to exercise discretion. As Justice Powell affirmed, "The freedom of a university to make its own judgments as to education includes the selection of its student body"—as long as that selection is itself free from deliberate injustice and arbitrary quotas.

Because the Supreme Court's decision in the Bakke case was narrow rather than sweeping, it leaves numerous questions for later decision. It does not itself, one must hope, invite multiplied litigation. Academic admissions practices that comply with the Bakke decision can be so subjective, so plainly discretionary as to offer few handles for successful lawsuits. That may be frustrating to some of the losers, but any alternative would be damaging to many an individual and to both institutions and abstract justice.

91

A "CRISIS OF CONFIDENCE" (1979)

Jimmy Carter became president at a time when the nation was disillusioned with politics in the aftershock of Watergate, was socially fragmented, and was angry from the senseless loss in Vietnam. Carter, a Georgia peanut farmer and former governor, adopted an informal style—walking down Pennsylvania Avenue on inauguration day, wearing a cardigan sweater during a nationally televised speech, attending town meetings—to appeal to the American people. He hoped to mobilize the nation toward larger purposes, but he lacked the necessary charisma

"Energy and National Goals," *Public Papers of the Presidents of the United States: Jimmy Carter, 1979* (Washington, DC, 1980), 2: 1235–1241.

and leadership skills. In 1979, as his popularity plummeted, Carter gave the following televised speech to the nation. Carter struck at the "crisis of confidence" that plagued the nation, and he hoped to revive the American spirit.

Questions to Consider: What was the national "crisis of confidence"? How does Carter propose to solve the problems? Why had America developed this attitude? Was Carter's warning of "fragmentation and self-interest" accurate or alarmist? Has America rediscovered its confidence?

I know, of course, being President, that government actions and legislation can be very important. That's why I've worked hard to put my campaign promises into law—and I have to admit, with just mixed success. But after listening to the American people I have been reminded again that all the legislation in the world can't fix what's wrong with America. So, I want to speak to you first tonight about a subject even more serious than energy or inflation. I want to talk to you right now about a fundamental threat to American democracy.

I do not mean our political and civil liberties. They will endure. And I do not refer to the outward strength of America, a nation that is at peace tonight everywhere in the world, with unmatched economic power and military might. The threat is nearly invisible in ordinary ways. It is a crisis of confidence. It is a crisis that strikes at the very heart and soul and spirit of our national will. We can see this crisis in the growing doubt about the meaning of our own lives and in the loss of a unity of purpose for our Nation.

The erosion of our confidence that we have always had as a people is not simply some romantic dream or a proverb in a dusty book that we read just on the Fourth of July. It is the idea which founded our Nation and has guided our development as a people. Confidence in the future has supported everything else—public institutions and private enterprise, our own families, and the very Constitution of the United States. Confidence has defined our course and has served as a link between generations. We've always believed in something called progress. We've always had a faith that the days of our children would be better than our own.

Our people are losing that faith, not only in government itself but in the ability as citizens to serve as the ultimate rulers and shapers of our democracy. As a people we know our past and we are proud of it. Our progress has been part of the living history of America, even the world. We always believed that we were part of a great movement of humanity itself called democracy, involved in the search for freedom, and that belief has always strengthened us in our purpose. But just as we are losing our confidence in the future, we are also beginning to close the door on our past.

In a nation that was proud of hard work, strong families, close-knit communities, and our faith in God, too many of us now tend to worship self-indulgence and consumption. Human identity is no longer defined by what one does, but by what one owns. But we've discovered that owning things and consuming things does not satisfy our longing for meaning. We've learned that piling up material goods cannot fill the emptiness of lives which have no confidence or purpose. . . .

As you know, there is a growing disrespect for government and for churches and for schools, the news media, and other institutions. This is not a message of happiness or reassurance, but it is the truth and it is a warning.

These changes did not happen overnight. They've come upon us gradually over the last generation, years that were filled with shocks and tragedy.

We were sure that ours was a nation of the ballot, not the bullet, until the murders of John Kennedy and Robert Kennedy and Martin Luther King, Jr. We were taught that our armies were always invincible and our causes were always just, only to suffer the agony of Vietnam. We respected the Presidency as a place of honor until the shock of Watergate.

We remember when the phrase "sound as a dollar" was an expression of absolute dependability, until 10 years of inflation began to shrink our dollar and our savings. We believe that our Nation's resources were limitless until 1973, when we had to face a growing dependence on foreign oil.

These wounds are still very deep. They have never been healed.

Looking for a way out of this crisis, our people have turned to the Federal Government and found it isolated from the mainstream of our Nation's life. Washington, D.C., has become an island. The gap between our citizens and our Government has never been so wide. The people are looking for honest answers, not easy answers; clear leadership, not false claims and evasiveness and politics as usual.

What you see too often in Washington and elsewhere around the country is a system of government that seems incapable of action. You see a Congress twisted and pulled in every direction by hundreds of well-financed and powerful special interests. . . .

Often you see paralysis and stagnation and drift. You don't like it, and neither do I. What can we do?

First of all, we must face the truth, and then we can change our course. We simply must have faith in each other, faith in our ability to govern ourselves, and faith in the future of this Nation. Restoring that faith and that confidence to America is now the most important task we face. It is a true challenge of this generation of Americans. . . .

We are at a turning point in our history. There are two paths to choose. One is a path I've warned about tonight, the path that leads to fragmentation and self-interest. Down that road lies a mistaken idea of freedom, the right to grasp for ourselves some advantage over others. That path would be one of constant conflict between narrow interests ending in chaos and immobility. It is a certain route to failure.

All the traditions of our past, all the lessons of our heritage, all the promises of our future point to another path, the path of common purpose and the restoration of American values. That path leads to true freedom for our Nation and ourselves. We can take the first steps down that path as we begin to solve our energy problem.

Energy will be the immediate test of our ability to unite this Nation, and it can also be the standard around which we rally. On the battlefield of energy we can win for our Nation a new confidence, and we can seize control again of our common destiny.

92

THE NUCLEAR DILEMMA: THE THREE MILE ISLAND ACCIDENT (1979)

Since the inception of the nuclear age, the splitting of the atom has been used for military purposes and for power generation. In the 1950s, nuclear physicists predicted that atomic power would provide virtually unlimited and inexpensive energy, and atomic reactors were developed to generate electricity. A nationwide construction boom of these reactors occurred in the 1960s and 1970s with the Atomic Energy Commission, which regulated the industry, both establishing safety guidelines and promoting the power source as safe. In 1979, at the Three Mile Island nuclear generating plant along the Susquehanna River near Harrisburg, Pennsylvania, a combination of faulty machinery and human error led to the partial meltdown of the reactor core and the release of radioactive gases. The accident had tremendous effects on the industry and the American people. An article in *The New Yorker* magazine indicates the public reaction to Three Mile Island and the problem with nuclear power. Many power companies cancelled plans to build more nuclear generating plants, and by the 1990s, no new orders were placed.

·— **Questions to Consider:** Why does *The New Yorker* emphasize "forever" and "human error" in this article? Why do those words have such a significant impact on nuclear energy? How were Americans convinced that nuclear energy was safe? Is it today? Compare David Wells' commentary (Document 14) on the changes technology brought to the 1880s with those presented in this article.

Arecent headline in the *Washington Post* concerning the afflicted nuclear power plant on Three Mile Island, in Pennsylvania, read, "Aides Wonder if Contamination May Close Plant Forever." The plant may have been rendered permanently inoperable, the story that followed explained, because of the release into the reactor-containment chamber of large quantities of radio-active isotopes, some of which will remain dangerous for as much as a thousand years. And within the reactor there are damaged fuel rods containing radioactive elements with half-lives of some twenty-four thousand years. That "Forever" stood out on the page; we could not remember having seen the word used in a newspaper headline before. (In human terms, twenty-four thousand years—roughly five times the span of recorded history, or the equivalent of almost a thousand generations of men—is forever.) Journalism has always dealt with what is historical and is therefore transient—even empires rise and decline—but now the papers were discussing a future of incomprehensible remoteness, as though they had given up on human affairs

---

"Notes and Comments," *The New Yorker* 55 (16 April 1979): 27–28. (Reprinted by permission; ©1979 *The New Yorker* Magazine, Inc.)

and instead interested themselves in the doings of immortal beings. The appearance in news stories of words like "forever" is one more clear signal, if we still need it, that with the discovery of nuclear energy events of a new order of magnitude, belonging to a new dimension of time, have broken into the stream of history. In unleashing nuclear chain reactions, we have brought a cosmic force, virtually never found in terrestrial nature, onto the earth—a force that, both in its visible, violent form of nuclear explosions and in its invisible, impalpable form of radiation, is alien and dangerous to earthly life, and can, through damage to life's genetic foundation, break the very frame on which generations of mankind are molded. In the midst of the ups and downs of human fortunes, decisions of everlasting consequence have presented themselves. Last week, these decisions were being made in Pennsylvania. "We all live in Pennsylvania!" West German anti-nuclear demonstrators shouted, in an inversion of President Kennedy's famous declaration *"Ich bin ein Berliner."* The danger of extinction is posed above all by nuclear war, but it was nevertheless symbolized during last week's disaster by the evacuation of children and pregnant women—who represent the future generations—from the vicinity of the plant. The lesson was plain: when atomic fission is brought in, the human future is driven out.

Another headline that caught our attention was one in the *News* which read, "Human Error Probed in Leak." The concept of "human error" has cropped up often during the Pennsylvania crisis. The alleged error referred to in the *News* story was an operator's decision to turn off a certain cooling system at an untimely moment, and this was contrasted with possible "technical" errors that could supposedly be made by machinery alone. But, even assuming that operators made mistakes, the question remains of who designed the plant in such a way that one or two untimely decisions could lead to a complete breakdown. Gods did not design the plant; human beings, each one as capable of error as any operator, did. That being so, it appears that the larger human error must lie in the decision to build plants of that design in the first place. But even this conclusion is too narrow—fails to get to the bottom of this matter of human error. The most striking aspect of the Pennsylvania disaster was not that a very unlikely (or "astronomically improbable," as the advocates of nuclear energy used to like to say) series of events occurred but that so many *entirely unpredicted* problems developed, the most important one to date being, of course, the sudden appearance inside the reactor of the explosive hydrogen bubble, which Harold Denton, the chief of reactor regulation for the Nuclear Regulatory Commission, called "a new twist." Events at the plant have turned out to be not at all like the well-ordered scenarios of the nuclear experts but, instead, to be like almost everything else in life—full of new twists. And the surprises within the plant were compounded by rumor and misinformation outside it, so that even when the scientists at the plant were in possession of reliable technical information Governor Richard Thornburgh, who had final responsibility for the lives of the people in the area, often was not. "There are a number of conflicting versions of every event that seems to occur," he observed to reporters at one point. In short, the conditions—reminiscent of New York's blackout two summers ago—that prevailed during this crisis were no different from the ones that prevail in almost every large crisis: erroneous prediction, more or less inadequate preparation, mass confusion and misunderstanding of the facts (accompanied by large amounts of cynicism and black humor), and official sleep-lessness and improvisation. The main thing that planners concerned with nuclear power left out of their scenarios was not the correct workings of some valve or control panel. It was the thing that no scenario can ever take into account: simple human fallibility per se—an ineradicable ingredient in the actions not only of power-plant operators but also of power-plant designers, of government officials, and of general public as well. What the experts know and most of the rest us will never know is how to build a nuclear power plant. What we know and they seem to have forgotten is that human imperfection is ingrained in everything that human beings undertake. In almost every enterprise—for example, in air travel—mistakes are somehow tolerated, but in this one case they cannot be, because the losses, which include not only the lives of tens of thousands of people but the habitability of our country and of the earth, are so high, and are "forever." At the deepest level, then, the human error in our nuclear program may be the old Socratic flaw of thinking that we know what we don't know and can't know. The Faustian pro-posal that the experts make to us is to let them lay their fallible human hands on eternity, and it is unacceptable.

OUR TIMES

3

The 1980s began as a reaction against the malaise and skepticism of the previous decade. The ascendence of conservatism in American life promoted a pro-business domestic stance, coupled with a strongly anticommunist foreign policy. The United States economy grew unevenly in the decade, creating pockets of great wealth and attracting growing numbers of immigrants, while simultaneously excluding large numbers of citizens from the new wealth. By the end of the decade, the Soviet threat had diminished, and America faced a greatly changed world where one of the greatest hazards would be biological. The following selections reveal various aspects of the themes that distinguished the era.

93

THE REAGAN REVOLUTION (1981)

As the decade of the 1980s began, a conservative mood pervaded the country, and Ronald Reagan both symbolized and galvanized this atmosphere. Reagan, born in Illinois and a devoted New Deal Democrat, began his career as a radio broadcaster, then became a Hollywood actor until he moved into television as an actor and program host. In the early 1960s, he switched to the Republican party and was elected to two terms as governor of California by appealing to middle-class resentments—taxes and big government. Using these issues again in 1980, Reagan won the Republican party nomination with the support of a powerful conservative coalition, and in the campaign against Democrat Jimmy Carter, he benefitted from double-digit inflation and the Iranian hostage crisis associated with Carter. He won the election easily, beginning the "Reagan Revolution." Reagan's inaugural address, excerpted below, established the initial broad themes of his administration.

·⁓ **Questions to Consider:** What does Reagan propose for the nation? Does he accomplish them? How does Reagan attack the "crisis of confidence" that Jimmy Carter noted (Document 91)? What is the impact of the "Reagan Revolution"?

To a few of us here today this is a solemn and most momentous occasion, and yet in the history of our nation it is a commonplace occurrence. The orderly transfer of authority as called for in the Constitution routinely takes place, as it has for almost two centuries, and few of us stop to think how unique we really are. In the eyes of many in the world, this every-4-year ceremony we accept as normal is nothing less than a miracle.

Mr. President, I want our fellow citizens to know how much you did to carry on this tradition. By your gracious cooperation in the transition process, you have shown a watching world that we are a united people pledged to maintaining a political system which guarantees individual liberty to a greater degree than any other, and I thank you and your people for all your help in maintaining the continuity which is the bulwark of our Republic.

The business of our nation goes forward. The United States are confronted with an economic affliction of great proportions. We suffer from the longest and one of the worst sustained inflations in our national history. It distorts our economic decisions, penalizes thrift, and crushes the struggling young and the fixed-income elderly alike. It threatens to shatter the lives of millions of our people.

Idle industries have cast workers into unemployment, human misery, and personal indignity. Those who do work are denied a fair return for their labor by a tax

---

"Inaugural Address," *Public Papers of the Presidents of the United States: Ronald Reagan, 1981* (Washington, DC, 1982), 1–4.

system which penalizes successful achievement and keeps us from maintaining full productivity.

But great as our tax burden is, it has not kept pace with public spending. For decades we have piled deficit upon deficit, mortgaging our future and our children's future for the temporary convenience of the present. To continue this long trend is to guarantee tremendous social, cultural, political, and economic upheavals.

In this present crisis, government is not the solution to our problem; government is the problem. From time to time we've been tempted to believe that society has become too complex to be managed by self-rule, that government by an elite group is superior to government for, by, and of the people. Well, if no one among us is capable of governing himself, then who among us has the capacity to govern someone else? All of us together, in and out of government, must bear the burden. The solutions we seek must be equitable, with no one group singled out to pay a higher price.

Well, this administration's objective will be a healthy, vigorous, growing economy that provides equal opportunity for all Americans, with no barriers born of bigotry or discrimination. Putting America back to work means putting all Americans back to work. Ending inflation means freeing all Americans from the terror of runaway living costs. All must share in the productive work of this "new beginning," and all must share in the bounty of a revived economy. With the idealism and fair play which are the core of our system and our strength, we can have a strong and prosperous America, at peace with itself and the world.

So, as we begin, let us take inventory. We are a nation that has a government—not the other way around. And this makes us special among the nations of the Earth. Our government has no power except that granted it by the people. It is time to check and reverse the growth of government, which shows signs of having grown beyond the consent of the governed.

It is my intention to curb the size and influence of the Federal establishment and to demand recognition of the distinction between the powers granted to the Federal Government and those reserved to the States or to the people. All of us need to be reminded that the Federal Government did not create the States; the States created the Federal Government.

Now, so there will be no misunderstanding, it's not my intention to do away with government. It is rather to make it work—work with us, not over us; to stand by our side, not ride on our back. Government can and must provide opportunity, not smother it; foster productivity, not stifle it.

It is no coincidence that our present troubles parallel and are proportionate to the intervention and intrusion in our lives that result from unnecessary and excessive growth of government. It is time for us to realize that we are too great a nation to limit ourselves to small dreams. We're not, as some would have us believe, doomed to an inevitable decline. I do not believe in a fate that will fall on us no matter what we do. I do believe in a fate that will fall on us if we do nothing. So, with all the creative energy at our command, let us begin an era of national renewal. Let us renew our determination, our courage, and our strength. And let us renew our faith and our hope.

We have every right to dream heroic dreams. Those who say that we're in a time when there are no heroes, they just don't know where to look. You can see heroes every day going in and out of factory gates. Others, a handful in number, produce enough food to feed all of us then the world beyond. You meet heroes across a counter, and they're on both sides of the counter. There are entrepreneurs with faith in themselves and faith in an idea who create new jobs, new wealth and opportunity. They're individuals and families whose taxes support the government and whose voluntary gifts support church, charity, culture, art, and education. Their patriotism is quiet, but deep. Their values sustain our national life.

To those neighbors and allies who share our freedom, we will strengthen our historic ties and assure them of our support and firm commitment. We will match loyalty with loyalty. We will strive for mutually beneficial relations. We will not use our friendship to impose on their sovereignty, for our own sovereignty is not for sale.

As for the enemies of freedom, those who are potential adversaries, they will be reminded that peace is the highest aspiration of the American people. We will negotiate for it, sacrifice for it; we will not surrender for it, now or ever.

Our forbearance should never be misunderstood. Our reluctance for conflict should not be misjudged as a failure of will. When action is required to preserve our national security, we will act. We will maintain sufficient strength to prevail if need be, knowing that if we do so we have the best chance of never having to use that strength.

Above all, we must realize that no arsenal or no weapon in the arsenals of the world is so formidable as the will and moral courage of free men and women. It is a weapon our adversaries in today's world do not have. It is a weapon that we as Americans do have. Let that be understood by those who practice terrorism and prey upon other neighbors.

94

THE IMMIGRATION QUESTION RENEWED (1981)

In the years after the passage of the Immigration Act of 1965, which abolished the old national origins quota system and switched to one based on the family, the nature of immigration changed. The number of European immigrants declined, while Latin Americans (with Mexico providing the greatest number) and Asians comprised the majority of new arrivals. There was also a significant refugee immigration, especially Cubans and Indochinese. Another element in this new wave of immigration—and one that alarmed many Americans—was the significant number of illegal immigrants who slipped into the country, mainly across the United States-Mexico border. In 1980, a federal commission—with the Reverend

Select Commission on Immigration and Refugee Policy, "Introduction to the Final Report of the Select Commission on Immigration and Refugee Policy," *U.S. Immigration Policy and the National Interest: The Final Report and Recommendations of the Select Commission on Immigration and Refugee Policy* (Washington, DC, 1981), 1–17.

Theodore Hesburgh, president of Notre Dame University, as its chair—investigated immigration and the American policy. The commission's findings and recommendations are excerpted below. In 1986, Congress passed the Immigration Reform Act, which reflected some of the commission's recommendations.

Questions to Consider: Why is there a renewal of world migration? Why is the United States a "magnet"? What is the central feature of the proposed immigration policy? What does the commission also propose? Why are undocumented/illegal aliens a particularly sensitive issue? Does the United States have an immigration problem?

Our history is largely the story of immigration. Even the Indians were immigrants. The ancestors of all other Americans—when measured in terms of world history—came here only yesterday.

As a refuge and a land of opportunity, the United States remains the world's number one magnet. This fact reaffirms the faith of our founding fathers and the central values we have adopted as a nation—freedom, equality under the law, opportunity and respect for diversity. . . .

The United States of America—no matter how powerful and idealistic—cannot by itself solve the problems of world migration. This nation must continue to have some limits on immigration. Our policy—while providing opportunity to a portion of the world's population—must be guided by the basic national interests of the people of the United States.

The emphasis in the Commission's recommendation, which are themselves complex, can be summed up quite simply: We recommend closing the back door to undocumented/illegal migration in the interests of this country, defining our immigration goals clearly and providing a structure to implement them effectively, and setting forth procedures which will lead to fair and efficient adjudication and administration of U.S. immigration laws.

In emphasizing that our recommendations must be consistent with U.S. national interests, we are aware of the fact that we live in a shrinking, interdependent world and that world economic and political forces result in the migration of peoples. We also are aware of how inadequately the world is organized to deal with the dislocations that occur as a result of such migrations. None of the great international issues of our time—arms control, energy, food or migration—can be solved entirely within the framework of a nation-state world. Certainly, there is no unilateral U.S. solution to any of these problems; we must work with a world organized along nation-state lines and with existing international organizations. As a nation responsible for the destiny of its people and its descendants, we can better deal with these problems by working with other nations to build more effective international mechanisms. That is why we begin our recommendations with a call for a new emphasis on internationalizing world migration issues. Since many, large-scale, international migrations are caused by war, poverty and persecution within sending nations, it is in the national interest of the United States to work with other nations to prevent or ameliorate those conditions.

That immigration serves humanitarian ends is unquestionable: most immigrants come to the United States seeking reunion with their families or as refugees. But in examining U.S. immigration policy and developing its recommendations, the Select Commission also asked another question: Is immigration and the acceptance of refugees in the U.S. national interest? That question was asked by many in this country when Fidel Castro pushed his own citizens out of Cuba knowing their main destination would be the United States. Nothing about immigration— even widespread visa abuse and illegal border crossings—seems to have upset the American people more than the Cuban push-out of 1980. But these new entrants were neither immigrants nor refugees, having entered the United States without qualifying for either. Their presence brought home to most Americans the fact that U.S. immigration policy was out of control. It also brought many letters to the Select Commission calling for restrictions on U.S. immigration. . . .

To the question: Is immigration in the U.S. national interest?, the Select Commission gives a strong but qualified yes. A strong yes because we believe there are many benefits which immigrants bring to U.S. society; a qualified yes because we believe there are limits on the ability of this country to absorb large numbers of immigrants effectively. Our work during the past 19 months has confirmed the continuing value of accepting immigrants and refugees to the United States, in addition to the humanitarian purpose served. The research findings are clear: Immigrants, refugees and their children work hard and contribute to the economic well-being of our society; strengthen our social security system and manpower capability; strengthen our ties with other nations; increase our language and cultural resources and powerfully demonstrate to the world that the United States is an open and free society. . . .

But even though immigration is good for this country, the Commission has rejected the arguments of many economists, ethnic groups and religious leaders for a great expansion in the number of immigrants and refugees to be accepted by the United States. Many of those in favor of expanded immigration have argued that the United States is capable of absorbing far greater numbers of immigrants than are now admitted. . . .

The Select Commission is, however, recommending a more cautious approach. This is not the time for large-scale expansion in legal immigration—for resident aliens or temporary workers—because the first order of priority is bringing undocumented/illegal immigration under control, while setting up a rational system for legal immigration.

The Commission is, therefore, recommending a modest increase in legal immigration sufficient to expedite the clearance of backlogs—mainly to reunify families—which have developed under the current immigration system and to introduce a new system, which we believe will be more equitable and more clearly reflect our interests as a nation. . . .

The strong desire to regain control over U.S. immigration policy is one of the several reasons for the Commission's unanimous vote to legalize a substantial portion of the undocumented/illegal aliens now in our country. Another is its acknowledgement that, in a sense, our society has participated in the creation of the problem. Many undocumented/illegal migrants were induced to come to the

United States by offers of work from U.S. employers who recruited and hired them under protection of present U.S. law. A significant minority of undocumented/illegal aliens have been part of a chain of family migrants to the United States for at least two generations.

95

BUSINESS IN THE 1980S: A VIEW OF DONALD TRUMP (1985)

The Reagan administration followed a laissez-faire approach to business in the 1980s. It reduced income taxes, especially to the wealthy in the belief they would invest in business; cut corporate taxes; and accelerated the policies of deregulation (eliminating governmental control) begun in the Carter Presidency, removing any restraints to free enterprise and an expanding economy. These efforts brought business—especially some businessmen who made huge fortunes with modest investments—to the forefront again. Among those individuals who became noticed was multimillionaire Donald J. Trump, a publicity-craving developer from New York whose ostentatious living standard and notorious business deals captured the attention as well as the scorn of many. In many ways, Trump epitomized the greed of the era, a period some have called "the new Gilded Age." Excerpted below is an article from *Business Week* that examines Trump's meteoric career.

·᠆ **Questions to Consider:** How was Trump able to assemble a real estate empire? Is he a self-made multimillionaire? What are the liabilities of his enterprise? Some have argued that Trump's operation mirrored the American economy in the 1980s. What are the positive and negative consequences? Compare this article with the life-styles described in "The Plight of the Homeless" (Document 96).

Donald J. Trump turned 39 last month, but he missed the birthday party at his office in midtown Manhattan's lavish Trump Tower. Instead, the impetuous real estate promoter was in Atlantic City sealing the biggest deal of his life. In one of his few all-cash purchases, Trump bought Hilton Hotels Corp.'s casino for $320 million. He immediately renamed it Trump's Castle Casino & Hotel and strutted around the glittery gaming room, making sure the opening came off without a hitch. "I got the castle for my birthday," Trump beams.

A revealing comment: Trump is that rare man who can afford to give himself the kind of present he thinks he deserves. If he is not the most successful real estate

Terri Thompson and Marc Frons, "The World of Donald Trump: Giant Buildings and an Ego to Match," *Business Week* (22 July 1985): 121–122. (Reprinted from July 22, 1985, issue of *Business Week* by special permission; copyright 1985 by McGraw-Hill, Inc.)

developer of his generation, Trump is certainly the most visible—a master of self-promotion with a reputation for attaching his name to every building he has a hand in. (Every building, that is, except for some subsidized housing projects he once built for his father. "That," says Trump, "wouldn't be appropriate.")

This virtual obsession seem designed to create the appearance of great wealth and vast real estate holding. But with Donald Trump, appearances are deceiving. While he is wealthy, he is not nearly as wealthy as he would like people to believe. And while he has been successful, he sometimes fails to acknowledge those who have helped him. . . .

Trump's admirers tend to forgive his exaggerations, because, they say, he has so much to exaggerate about. While his father Fred, a savvy real estate developer in his own right, built a $40 million family fortune by developing modest apartment complexes, it was Donald who turned those holdings into an empire worth an estimated $1.3 billion. During his 17-year career at the Trump Organization, he has succeeded through a unique combination of luck, charm, financial acumen, and sheer nerve.

Trump had friends in high places to help him on his way: He traded off his father's vast New York political connections to win the generous tax abatements that made some of his earlier projects possible, and he has attracted some of the country's most canny and well-heeled financial backers. Equitable Life Assurance Society, for example, financed the $200 million construction of the 68-story Trump Tower on Manhattan's Fifth Avenue. With a 10-year tax abatement and no debt on the property, Trump and Equitable take in about $14 million a year each by renting retail and office space at some of the highest rates in New York.

That deal was vintage Trump: He rarely puts up much money when taking on a new project, and when there is cash involved, it's usually someone else's. There are other risks to doing business with Trump—among them, the possibility of a lawsuit. "He sues almost everybody," says David Rosenholc, an attorney for the tenants of 100 Central Park South, who are fighting a plan by Trump to demolish the building. "There's not a deal that everybody's happy with. He's either crying that somebody's trying to cheat him, or somebody else is saying that he's trying to cheat them."

The barrage of legal actions often seems to be a business tactic, a way to wear down Trump's opponents. But some of his lawsuits may have more to do with personal vanity than business. In one case that Trump is appealing, he is suing Eddie and Julius Trump of Trump Group because, he says, they are trying to cash in on "my name." Never mind that it also happens to be their name and that they've been using it in their business for about 20 years. Says the defiant Donald: "I would like them to change their name." Explaining his penchant for lawsuits, Trump says: "You can't let people push you around." . . .

Much of Trump's success is the result of good timing. His first major coup, the renovation and conversion of the old Commodore Hotel into the 1,407-room Grand Hyatt Hotel, was started amid New York's fiscal crisis in 1975. Trump's negotiations with local government officials, including his father's politically influential friends, resulted in a generous 40-year tax abatement for the Grand Hyatt—the first awarded in Manhattan for a commercial property. The city started making its comeback while construction was under way, and when the hotel opened in 1982, "you couldn't get a room in New York," recalls Trump. Today the hotel is a financial success. . . .

Sometimes the legal actions concern more than just a name. In one particularly long and heated battle, the tenants of a rent-controlled and rent-stabilized apartment building overlooking Manhattan's Central Park are suing Trump for harassment.

The tenants say he has allowed building services to deteriorate and hired a management company to force tenants out so that he can demolish the building and erect another luxury apartment tower. In his defense, Trump rails against New York City's "ridiculous system" of rent controls that allows "multimillionaires to live in park-view apartments and pay $300 a month." But in the same breath, Trump admits that if it were not for such controls, he would not have been able to buy the building and the adjoining Barbizon-Plaza Hotel for a mere $13 million in 1981.

This is one case where Trump's notoriety has probably worked against him. The city and state also have sued him for harassment, and the building is operating under a temporary court order restraining him from harassing his tenants. The dispute has become acrimonious. "He is a deceitful, vicious liar," says John C. Moore III, head of the 100 Central Park South Tenants Assn. "Behind the scenes, he is an awful man." Trump responds by saying. "This is a comment made by an unsuccessful man who nobody ever heard of except that he's a tenant fighting Donald Trump." . . .

. . . The Trump empire produces income of approximately $110 million a year. "And it will only get better," he declares.

Such boasting is par for the Trump course. It gets him the kind of attention that has made his name practically a household word—which is possibly his single, most significant success to date. Where does he go from here? In a rare moment of tentativeness, Trump responds: "I don't know. With a fertile, creative mind, hopefully there will be lots of things to do." After all, there are still several buildings around without his name on them.

96

THE PLIGHT OF THE HOMELESS (1984)

The economic expansion and federal government cuts in social programs during the 1980s helped polarize American society into the wealthy, whose money was concentrated in fewer and fewer hands, and the poor, whose numbers increased. While some of the new poor were former mental patients removed from institutions and abandoned to the streets, many were once self-supporting families

U.S. Congress, House, "The Federal Response to the Homeless Crisis," *Hearings before a Subcommittee of the Committee on Government Operations,* 98th Congress, 2nd session (October, December 1984), 306-308; 1243-1245.

who had fallen on difficult times. Children — comprising 40 percent of the poor — and households headed by single women were the hardest hit. This growing underclass huddled in shelters or existed in "welfare hotels" awaiting a chance to turn their lives around. The nation's best-known advocate for the homeless was Mitch Snyder, whose hunger strike in 1984 helped to obtain an abandoned Federal building as a homeless shelter, although the promise of several million dollars for renovation was never fulfilled. Using various publicity tactics — hunger strikes, protest marches, and Hollywood celebrities — to alert the American public, Snyder was able to attract attention to homelessness. Excerpted below are the statements of Mitch Snyder and Laurel, a "homeless citizen," before the House Subcommittee of the Committee on Government Operations as it investigated the "homeless crisis" in 1984.

Questions to Consider: What does Mitch Snyder hope to change? According to Laurel, what obstacles do the homeless encounter? What faults does Laurel find in the existing system for the homeless? What changes does she want? How do homeless conditions compare to those described in "Life in the Tenements of New York City" (Document 23)? What should or can be done to help the poor?

Nothing is moving now. No money is moving. No buildings are moving. All that is moving are people, from day to day, from bath-room to shower room to soup kitchen to shelter, who are suffering and dying in numbers beyond our comprehension, and with a depth of pain that none of us sitting in a room like this can even begin to comprehend no matter where we were 10 minutes ago, because unless you are out there, freezing, getting rained on, having people look at you like you don't exist, and living in a building like the one we are running that is fit for trash and vermin, when 8 million bucks was sitting there waiting to fix that building up, that does something to you that makes you less than human.

The administration's position has been, as far as we are concerned, un-American. Americans do not let human beings languish on the streets, tell people they are this by choice, and then rip away from them what little they might have. . . .

There are people behind me who are fasting, including myself. There are now 12 of us in the 19th day of a fast, and we are fasting for a change of prayer, a change of heart, and a change of position, and we are praying for both on the part of the administration, because . . . we cannot live with . . . a Federal Government policy in our name as well as everybody else's, that says of homeless people:

> We wash our hands. Go to the city to get your building picked up. It is the mayor's responsibility. Go to the churches to get the food. Go to the private sector and the corporations.

Why should any of them be expected to do anything in a land that is built on nothing but rampant individualism and competition, where people are trained from birth to be at each other's throat to get ahead and if you see somebody on the street, you step over their body as gently as possible, but you just keep on walking?

. . . If people only had a chance to know what was going on, really going on, their response would be loud and quick, except there is a lot of confusion, there is a lot of double talk, there is a lot of bureaucracies at work, and people are growing in numbers on the streets and they are freezing and dying, and so I suppose that is the message that we bring here.

It is the same as the message we bring to the administration every day in front of their building; that is that the men and women and children on the streets are our sisters and brothers, that our religion no matter what it is, tells us that we must love and respect and care for, and it is not loving or respectful to allow them to crawl along the streets like vermin, eating out of trash bins, being abused in the most abominable ways, and being denied their very basic rights and humanity. That situation is coming to a screaming halt now. It must. . . .

Statement of Laurel, Homeless Citizen

Ms. Laurel. Turning Point is a privately run organized shelter. It runs in the basement section of the church. The only thing we lack there is a house where the same treatment we get now would be extended to at least for the person or persons staying there the hope, the joy of knowing that OK, I'm getting 6 months here, I can work nights, I can work days and I can get out.

We don't pay for anything there. We get everything. Like I said, what we're lacking is an extended rest period because like for the ones of us who work like from 3 to 2 in the morning, you have to be up at 6. It's not the organization's building. It's just the basement of a church. They need that place for their own thing, and so we have to get out by 8 o'clock. If you don't have a job, you hit the streets, do whatever, and be back at 5.

Even if you work till 2. These same people would extend that sleeping period to the people who work nights. I think they would enable those people to sleep days, get some sleep because they have to go to work at night, but they can't do it because they don't have the facilities. . . .

As to the voucher hotel, some of them are frauds. They are ripoffs and this is where the Federal Government put its money. I tried to get shelter through one. I was asked short of well, what's your great-great-great-grandmother's maiden name. . . .

Then I was told okay, one night. After that one night, forget it. It was rat infested, roach infested and every other kind of infestation was there. I also went to another shelter that was OK to stay there for a week or a month, but you pay $1.50 the first week. They say that's for cleaning the linen, and then if you stay 2 weeks, you have to pay $5 a week. You get no hot food.

There are donations of food coming in, and I myself have had to unload some food, but it goes upstairs to the families. We're downstairs. You can't work nights because you have to be back at 9 and if you're not there by 9, then don't come in, you won't be let in. And, on the other side of that same coin, you couldn't take a job that had you work past 6 o'clock on Wednesdays because you have to go and pray. Who wants to pray for misery anyway? . . .

So, even if you stay there, you build up enough courage to stay there, it's hard to work. There is a lot of us who find comfort in working because at least we have the assurance that tomorrow or the day after, I will have made enough money to get out of there. But, if somebody says I give you shelter but you have to pray first and not only that, you can't — you are restricted to working here to fit their prayer time, that's unfair. . . .

To me, it's embarrassing and I don't see myself as sick and all I want is a little bit to get a job, support myself. In the area of job training, we skip a lot of training programs. In America, the trucking industry is on the rise. It's a Federal thing, once you get into driving 18 wheelers, but the Federal Government, as I understand it, especially here in Los Angeles, has no training program going. . . .

Training programs like that, telling a man with a family or a woman with a family here is an opportunity to get out, and look ahead. Federal Government want to do something for us. What they are to do is like provide shelter, 6 months, period. . . .

So, that don't mean this month you get out and the month after, you're right back in the shelter again. Or, you get out this morning and you walk around and you're not able to find a shelter — home because you have kids. This is another thing. You have one child, forget it. Go drown him and come back and we will rent you a place. As long as you keep the kid, we shan't rent you a place.

But if you try to keep the kid living in a car, they take the kid from you. What then? So, it's either hit the bottle, or prostitution. When you turn to prostitution, you're not only hurting yourself but you could be destroying your entire community, depending on God help you, what you pick up. . . .

97

A PERSPECTIVE ON AIDS (1987)

The AIDS (acquired immune deficiency syndrome) epidemic brought significant change to accepted social and medical norms. First detected in 1981, the HIV virus that leads to AIDS breaks down the body's immune system with fatal results. Initially, the disease was associated with male homosexuals and drug addicts who used "dirty" needles. It intensified animosity toward the homosexual community (Patrick Buchanan, White House director of communications, said homosexuals had "declared war on nature, and now nature is extracting an awful retribution"), but as the HIV virus spread through blood or sexual contact to infect alarming numbers of heterosexual individuals, this attitude softened. To help limit the spread of the virus and calm popular fear of AIDS, the federal government launched an education campaign about the disease and to encourage "safe sex" through the use of condoms. Sexual experimentation and promiscuity declined. With escalating medical costs to treat the disease and few advances toward a cure, AIDS remains a frightening dilemma. Excerpted next is David C. Jones' 1987 speech to medical students at Duke University about AIDS. Jones is from the North Carolina AIDS Service Coalition.

David C. Jones, "Perspective on AIDS," *Vital Speeches of the Day* 54 (1987): 176–179. (Reprinted with permission of David C. Jones.)

‸ **Questions to Consider:** Why does Jones argue that AIDS will alter existing health insurance and health care? Why does he believe that HIV antibody testing could lead to blatant discrimination? What six-point proposal does Jones make to change attitudes about AIDS? Have attitudes about AIDS changed? Why?

Too many of my friends have died and far too many more are ill or living in fear. You are being pulled into a maelstrom of controversy about the disease that is killing them. In fact, I believe that Society is setting you up to have to deal with its own doubt, fear and anger. I believe that you are going to have to be the arbiters of some very profound and even radical questions that will shake the very foundations of the delivery of health care as we know it. . . .

First, who will get what care? Some of the ethical dilemmas you will face will be generated by the creeping obsolescence of insurance as we know it. Health insurance as we know it today will not exist twenty years from now. AIDS is not the first but it is the most startling example of a confluence of forces that will change dramatically how we will decide who is going to get what medical care. Let me explain.

We believe that society should share the burden of injury or loss. So we have insurance. . . .

Now comes AIDS. It seems universally fatal, there is not much we can do and care costs a great deal. The financial impact on an insurance company can be great.

The first response of some companies fell somewhere between silly and sinister. My favorite is the letter that one company sent to agents telling them to be suspicious of single men ". . . in such occupations that do not require physical exertion . . . such as antique dealers, interior decorators or florists."

Then there came a blood test to detect antibodies to the virus that causes AIDS also with epidemiological data indicating that large numbers of people with antibodies are infected, and that a growing portion of them are going to die very expensive deaths.

Insurance companies fought for the right to use the antibody test to deny new coverage. Their position is simple and traditional: it identifies a new potential risk. . . .

We are standing on the brink of an explosion of diagnostic capability. This will be possible as a result of breakthroughs in our ability to read and understand our genetic program, and the technological elegance of rapidly evolving new generations of precise, affordable diagnostic systems. . . .

We will be able to run a series of tests and print out the probable health events of an individual. We will have a good picture of what diseases this person is likely to experience naturally, and others that will probably be experienced should certain environmental conditions be encountered.

What it means, based on the structure and management of private insurance today, is that a staggering number of people will be uninsurable and many will be unemployable. We face the very real possibility of creating an entire caste of nonpersons, people for whom there is no work, no promise, no place. . . .

I will go so far as to say that society will not tolerate it. The only question in my mind is how soon people will react. It may be soon as thoughtful people begin to recognize the implications of financing care the way we have always done it when this information is available. Or it may be after millions of people are forced into poverty and we face a cataclysmic reaction from society. How we respond to AIDS now and the problem of a growing number of terminally ill Americans without insurance will tell us a lot about what our future holds.

We will finally be forced to resolve a debate that has been simmering in this country for years. Is good health care a right or a privilege? We were going to have to face up to this sooner or later. AIDS has just made it sooner. . . .

The HIV antibody test represents the first time that medical information has been used widely as the basis for social and political discrimination of an unpopular minority. Society's reaction to homosexuality as a lifestyle ranges from acceptance to scorn. AIDS has even brought forth again the condemnation of those with the astonishing arrogance to claim God's proxy to judge. . . .

But we have to look at the real world in which this disease is spreading. AIDS is not like any other disease. Punitive discrimination does occur, regularly. And now we hear threats of prison. Now we have added fear upon fear. And it is fear that will assure that this system, in this environment, in this state, simply will not work. Fewer people will seek testing, fewer people will know that they are infected, and more people will die from the complications of an acquired immune deficiency.

The members of the AIDS Service Coalition have been dealing with AIDS for a long time. We know how terrible it is and we want to do everything we can to see that no one is ever consumed by it again. We would like to make a specific six-point proposal that should be part of public health policy. We believe it will cause the largest number of people to change the behavior that places them at risk and to seek information, counseling and medical care.

First, a statewide AIDS education program should be the state's first priority. Education is the only hope we have of preventing people from being infected in the first place. Further, people are more likely to seek counseling or testing when they are told that they may have been exposed if they have already received some education about AIDS.

Second, adequate counseling must be available, both before and after testing. . . .

Third, anonymous testing for HIV should continue to be available to all who seek it. It should be the policy of the state to require informed consent before any person is tested, and that every person tested in any setting should be notified of the result.

Fourth, a system of contact notification should be developed that emphasizes voluntary self-referral, with the option of notification by trained AIDS counseling specialists at the state level. Counseling should include both the necessity of informing sexual and needle contacts, and effective and sensitive techniques for notifying others. . . .

Fifth, we must dispel the fear of losing one's apartment or job by making it clear that North Carolina prohibits discrimination based on a positive HIV test or a diagnosis of AIDS.

Sixth, we should reduce the financial burden of AIDS by making alternatives to extended hospitalization available, and thereby make more resources available for controlling AIDS. . . .

The forces that have been unleashed by AIDS are so powerful that if we do not find a way to harness them productively, and with dignity, we shall all be consumed by them.

All I can really ask you to do is to ask the questions now, over and over, in good faith, within a framework that recognizes a respect for people and a commitment to do no harm, a framework that causes us to act in the interests of others and share the benefits and the burdens of what we do. Please deal with them now, while you may still have time.

98

AN EDITORIAL ON THE REMOVAL OF THE BERLIN WALL (1989)

For over 40 years, the Cold War had divided much of the world into two opposing camps. In Europe, the division was along the "iron curtain" boundary separating the communist East, under Soviet influence, from the capitalistic West, under American influence. Even Germany and its old capital of Berlin were divided along these lines. In 1985, Soviet leader Mikhail Gorbachev began policies called "perestroika" (economic restructuring) and "glasnost" (openness) to revitalize the Soviet Union's sagging economy and to achieve better relations—especially trade—with the West. These policies triggered dissent, then growing demands for more rapid reforms both within the Soviet Union and in Eastern Europe. When Gorbachev agreed not to intervene in the affairs of East-bloc countries in 1989, popular uprisings ended Communist party rule and new governments were formed. Perhaps the most sensational incident of this collapse came in November 1989, when the Berlin Wall—the symbol of the Cold War since its erection in 1961—was removed and the borders between the two Germanies opened. Excerpted next is *The New York Times* editorial which places the removal of the Berlin Wall in an historical perspective.

·⌐ **Questions to Consider:** *The New York Times* editorial argues that the destruction of the Berlin Wall ended 75 years of European catastrophes. Is this true? What else did destruction of the Berlin Wall signify? What resulted in the aftermath of this event? How did the United States react to creation of "a European house"?

"The End of the War to End Wars," *The New York Times*, 11 November 1989, 26. (Copyright 1989 by The New York Times Company. Reprinted by permission.)

Crowds of young Germans danced on top of the hated Berlin wall Thursday night. They danced for joy, they danced for history. They danced because the tragic cycle of catastrophes that first convulsed Europe 75 years ago, embracing two world wars, a Holocaust and a cold war, seems at long last to be nearing an end.

November 11, now named Veterans Day, is the day of the armistice that ended World War I. But that war to end wars was lost when the victors bungled the peace. They exacted heavy reparations from Germany, paving the way to chaos and the rise of National Socialism. The years between the two wars turned out to be merely a truce. Hitler in 1940 received the surrender of the French forces in the same railroad car in which Germany's delegates surrendered in 1918, and Europe was again plunged into strife.

Some 20 million people died in World War I, perhaps 50 million in World War II, but even these two appalling acts of miscalculation and bloodletting did not bring Europe's torments to an end. The tragedy had a third act: the cold war divided a Europe freed from Hitler's tyranny from a Europe bowed under Stalin's. The Berlin wall, erected by Erich Honecker in 1961, stood as the foremost symbol of that division and the Continent's continuing stasis.

The reveling crowds of Berliners mingling from East and West could scarcely believe that the hated wall had at last been breached. Those watching them around the world could only share their delight—and their wonder at the meaning of it all.

If the horrifying cycle that began in 1914 is at last completed, what new wheels have begun to turn? Instability in Eastern Europe has seldom brought good news. But this dissolution may lead to settlement, even if the settlement's shape remains unclear.

Armistice is only the laying down of arms, not peace. And for as long as it has stood, the Berlin wall has symbolized a Europe not at peace, and a world polarized by Soviet-American rivalry.

Mikhail Gorbachev has spoken of a European house. No one, not even he, can yet be sure how the rooms might fit together. Still, no house has a wall through its middle, and for the first time in a generation, neither does Europe.

—— · —— · —— · —— · —— · —— · —— · —— · —— · —— · —— · —— · —— · ——

99

"A NEW WORLD ORDER" (1991)

The dramatic and rapid breakdown of communist rule in Europe in 1989–1990 indicated that the Cold War was concluding and that neither the Soviet Union nor the United States could control world events. The new Eastern European governments, the remarkable reunification of Germany, and the disintegration of the Soviet Union into 15 republics revealed an increasingly fractured and unpredictable Europe that asserted newfound autonomy. An abortive democratic

George Bush, "The Challenge of Building Peace: A Renewal of History," *Vital Speeches of the Day* 58 (1991): 2–4.

reform movement in China, however, and communist control of Cuba, Angola, and North Korea demonstrated that communism still persisted. And African, Middle Eastern, and Latin American countries, freed from the Cold War tensions, became more self-reliant. Clearly a new era of international relations had begun, and world inclination viewed the United States as the model for modern society. In the context of these turbulent times, President George Bush addressed the United Nations General Assembly on his vision of "a new world order" as what he called the "renewal of history" changed global relationships. Excerpted below is his speech.

Questions to Consider: Why does Bush believe history has resumed? According to Bush, what opportunities and perils exist in the post-Cold War era? What role should the United Nations play in the "new world order"? In what instances should the United States become involved in maintaining the new order? Compare the ideas in Bush's speech to those in Theodore Roosevelt's Corollary to the Monroe Doctrine (Document 39).

My speech today will not sound like any you've heard from a President of the United States. I'm not going to dwell on the superpower competition that defined international politics for half a century. Instead, I will discuss the challenges of building peace and prosperity in a world leavened by the Cold War's end and the resumption of history.

Communism held history captive for years. It suspended ancient disputes; and it suppressed ethnic rivalries, nationalistic aspirations, and old prejudices. As it has dissolved, suspended hatreds have sprung to life. People who for years have been denied their pasts have begun searching for their own identities—often through peaceful and constructive means, occasionally through factionalism and bloodshed.

This revival of history ushers in a new era, teeming with opportunities and perils. And let's begin by discussing the opportunities.

First, history's renewal enables people to pursue their natural instincts for enterprise. Communism froze that progress until its failures became too much for even its defenders to bear.

And now citizens throughout the world have chosen enterprise over envy; personal responsibility over the enticements of the state; prosperity over the poverty of central planning. . . .

Frankly, ideas and goods will travel around the globe with or without our help. The information revolution has destroyed the weapons of enforced isolation and ignorance. In many parts of the world technology has overwhelmed tyranny, proving that the age of information can become the age of liberation if we limit state power wisely and free our people to make the best use of new ideas, inventions and insights.

By the same token, the world has learned that free markets prove levels of prosperity, growth and happiness that centrally planned economies can never offer.

Even the most charitable estimates indicate that in recent years the free world's economies have grown at twice the rate of the former communist world. . . .

I cannot stress this enough: Economic progress will play a vital role in the new world. It supplies the soil in which democracy grows best.

People everywhere seek government of and by the people. And they want to enjoy their inalienable rights to freedom and property and person. . . .

The challenge facing the Soviet peoples now—that of building political systems based upon individual liberty, minority rights, democracy and free markets—mirrors every nation's responsibility for encouraging peaceful, democratic reform. But it also testifies to the extraordinary power of the democratic ideal.

As democracy flourishes, so does the opportunity for a third historical breakthrough: international cooperation. A year ago, the Soviet Union joined the United States and a host of other nations in defending a tiny country against aggression—and opposing Saddam Hussein. For the very first time on the matter of major importance, superpower competition was replaced with international cooperation.

The United Nations, in one of its finest moments, constructed a measured, principled, deliberate and courageous response to Saddam Hussein. It stood up to an outlaw who invaded Kuwait, who threatened many states within the region, who sought to set a menacing precedent for the post-Cold War World. . . .

We will not revive these ideals if we fail to acknowledge the challenge that the renewal of history presents.

In Europe and Asia, nationalist passions have flared anew, challenging borders, straining the fabric of international society. At the same time, around the world, many age-old conflicts still fester. You see signs of this tumult right here. The United Nations has mounted more peacekeeping missions in the last 36 months than during its first 43 years. And although we now seem mercifully liberated from the fear of nuclear holocaust, these smaller, virulent conflicts should trouble us all.

We must face this challenge squarely: first, by pursuing the peaceful resolution of disputes now in progress; second, and more importantly, by trying to prevent others from erupting.

No one here can promise that today's borders will remain fixed for all time. But we must strive to ensure the peaceful, negotiated settlement of border disputes.

We also must promote the cause of international harmony by addressing old feuds. . . .

Government has failed if citizens cannot speak their minds; if they can't form political parties freely and elect governments without coercion; if they can't practice their religion freely; if they can't raise their families in peace; if they can't enjoy a just return from their labor; if they can't live fruitful lives and, at the end of their days, look upon their achievements and their society's progress with pride.

The renewal of history also imposes an obligation to remain vigilant about new threats and old. We must expand our efforts to control nuclear proliferation. We must work to prevent the spread of chemical and biological weapons and the missiles to deliver them.

We can never say with confidence where the next conflict may arise. And we cannot promise eternal peace—not while demagogues peddle false promises to people hungry with hope; not while terrorists use our citizens as pawns, and drug dealers destroy our peoples. We, as a result—we must band together to overwhelm affronts to basic human dignity.

It is no longer acceptable to shrug and say that one man's terrorist is another man's freedom fighter. Let's put the law above the crude and cowardly practice of hostage-holding.

The United Nations can encourage free-market development through its international lending and aid institutions. However, the United Nations should not dictate the particular forms of government that nations should adopt. But it can and should encourage the values upon which this organization was founded. Together, we should insist that nations seeking our acceptance meet standards of human decency.

Where institutions of freedom have lain dormant, the United Nations can offer them new life. These institutions play a crucial role in our quest for a new world order, an order in which no nation must surrender one iota of its own sovereignty; an order characterized by the rule of law rather than the resort to force; the cooperative settlement of disputes, rather than anarchy and bloodshed; and an unstinting belief in human rights.

Finally, you may wonder about America's role in the new world that I have described. Let me assure you, the United States has no intention of striving for a Pax Americana. However, we will remain engaged. We will not retreat and pull back into isolationism. We will offer friendship and leadership. And in short, we seek a Pax Universalis built upon shared responsibilities and aspirations.

To all assembled, we have an opportunity to spare our sons and daughters the sins and errors of the past. We can build a future more satisfying than any our world has ever known. The future lies undefined before us, full of promise; littered with peril. We can choose the kind of world we want; one blistered by the fires of war and subjected to the whims of coercion and chance, or one made more peaceful by reflection and choice. Take this challenge seriously. Inspire future generations to praise and venerate you, to say: On the ruins of conflict, these brave men and women built an era of peace and understanding. They inaugurated a new world order, an order worth preserving for the ages.